SUPPORT VECTOR MACHINES: DATA ANALYSIS, MACHINE LEARNING AND APPLICATIONS

COMPUTER SCIENCE, TECHNOLOGY AND APPLICATIONS

Additional books in this series can be found on Nova's website under the Series tab.

Additional E-books in this series can be found on Nova's website under the E-books tab.

COMPUTER SCIENCE, TECHNOLOGY AND APPLICATIONS

SUPPORT VECTOR MACHINES: DATA ANALYSIS, MACHINE LEARNING AND APPLICATIONS

BRANDON H. BOYLE
EDITOR

Nova Science Publishers, Inc.
New York

Library of Congress Cataloging-in-Publication Data

Support vector machines : data analysis, machine learning, and applications / editor, Brandon H. Boyle.
   p. cm. -- (Computer science, technology, and applications)
 Includes bibliographical references and index.
 ISBN 978-1-61209-342-0 (hardcover : alk. paper)
 1. Support vector machines. I. Boyle, Brandon H.
 Q325.5.S867 2011
 006.4--dc22
                     2011003595

Published by Nova Science Publishers, Inc. † New York

CONTENTS

Preface   vii

Chapter 1   The Support Vector Machine in Medical Imaging   1
                  Jacob E. D. Levman

Chapter 2   A SVM-Based Regression Model to Study the Air Quality
                  in the Urban Area of the City of Oviedo (Spain)   27
                  *P. J. García Nieto, E. F. Combarro, J. J. del Coz Díaz,
                  F. P. Álvarez Rabanal and E. Montañés*

Chapter 3   Image Interpolation Using Support Vector Machines   51
                  Liyong Ma, Yi Shen and Jiachen Ma

Chapter 4   Utilization of Support Vector Machine (SVM) for Prediction
                  of Ultimate Capacity of Driven Piles in Cohesionless Soils   67
                  Pijush Samui and S. K. Sekar

Chapter 5   Support Vector Machines in Medical Classification Tasks   81
                  David Gil and Magnus Johnsson

Chapter 6   Kernel Latent Semantic Analysis using Term Fusion Kernels   103
                  Alberto Munoz, Javier Gonzalez and Javier Arriero

Chapter 7   SVR for Time Series Prediction   117
                  M. Serdar Yumlu and Fikret S. Gurgen

Chapter 8   Application of Neural Networks and Support Vector Machines
                  in Coding Theory and Practice   131
                  Stevan M. Berber and Johnny Kao

Chapter 9   Pattern Recognition for Machine Fault Diagnosis Using
                  Support Vector Machine   153
                  Bo-Suk Yang and Achmad Widodo

Index   197

PREFACE

Chapter 1 - This chapter outline the various ways that the support vector machine is used in medical imaging research and related applications. The chapter presents examples of the use of the support vector machine for classification (supervised learning) as well as texture analysis. A major focus of the chapter is a series of examples of recent research into using the support vector machine for a wide array of medical imaging problems. A specific focus is placed on using the support vector machine to detect breast cancer from magnetic resonance imaging (MRI) examinations. Furthermore, the chapter includes alternative vector machine formulations which are an extension of the established support vector machine and demonstrates these techniques for the classification / prediction problem. Novel perspectives on the use of the support vector machine are presented.

Chapter 2 - This work presents a method of monthly air pollution modelling by using support vector machine (SVM) technique in the city of Oviedo (Spain). Hazardous air pollutants or toxic air contaminants refer to any substances that may cause or contribute to an increase in mortality or in serious illness, or that may pose a present or potential hazard to human health. In this research work, based on the observed data of NO, NO_2, CO, SO_2, O_3 and dust (PM_{10}) for the years 2006, 2007 and 2008, the support vector regression (SVR) technique is used to build the nonlinear dynamic model of the air quality in the urban area of the city of Oviedo (Spain). One aim of this model was to make an initial preliminary estimate of the dependence between primary and secondary pollutants in the city of Oviedo. A second aim was to determine the factors with the greatest bearing on air quality with a view to proposing health and lifestyle improvements. The United States National Ambient Air Quality Standards (NAAQS) establishes the limit values of the main pollutants in the atmosphere in order to ensure the health of healthy people. They are known as the *criteria pollutants*. This SVR model captures the main insight of statistical learning theory in order to obtain a good prediction of the dependence among the main pollutants in the city of Oviedo. Finally, on the basis of these numerical calculations using SVR, from the experimental data, conclusions of this work are exposed.

Chapter 3 - Image interpolation has a wide range of applications in remote sense, medical diagnoses, multimedia communication, and other image processing fields. Support vector machines (SVMs) have been used successfully for various supervised classification tasks, regression tasks, and novelty detection tasks. In this chapter, support vector machines based image interpolation schemes for image zooming and color filter array interpolation are discussed.

Firstly, a local spatial properties based image interpolation scheme using SVMs is introduced. After the proper neighbor pixels region is selected, SVMs are trained with local spatial properties that include the mean and the variations of gray value of the neighbor pixels in the selected region. The support vector regression machines are employed to estimate the gray value of unknown pixels with the neighbor pixels and local spatial properties information. Some interpolation experiments show that the proposed scheme is superior to the linear, cubic, neural network and other SVMs based interpolation approaches.

Secondly, a SVMs based color filter array interpolation scheme is proposed to effectively reduce color artifacts and blurring of the CFA interpolation. Support vector regression (SVR) is used to estimate the color difference between two color channels with applying spectral correlation of the R, G, B channels.

The neighbor training sample models are selected on the color difference plane with considering spatial correlation, and the unknown color difference between two color channels is estimated by the trained SVR to get the missing color value at each pixel. Simulation studies indicate that the proposed scheme produces visually pleasing full-color images and obtains higher PSNR results than other conventional CFA interpolation algorithms.

Chapter 4 - This chapter examines the capability of Support Vector Machine (SVM) for prediction of ultimate capacity (Q) of driven piles in cohesionless soils. SVM that is firmly based on the theory of statistical learning theory, uses regression technique by introducing ε-insensitive loss function has been adopted. SVM achieves good generalization ability by adopting a structural risk minimization (SRM) induction principle that aims at minimizing a bound on the generalization error of a model rather than the minimizing the error on the training data only. SVM is trained with optimization of a convex, quadratic cost function, which guarantees the uniqueness of the SVM solution. In this chapter, the developed SVM model outperforms the artificial neural network (ANN) model based on root-mean-square-error (RMSE) and mean-absolute-error (MAE) performance criteria. An equation has been developed for the prediction of Q of driven piles based on the developed SVM model. A sensitivity analysis has been also done to determine the effect of each input parameter on Q. This chapter shows that the developed SVM model is a robust model for prediction of Q of driven piles in cohesionless soils.

Chapter 5 - This chapter explores Support Vector Machines (SVMs)in medical classification tasks, which could be used for decision support. The authors present some experiments with Breast Cancer, Parkinson's and Urological data. The Breast Cancer and Parkinson's data are well-known and widely used, whereas the Urological data are proprietary and have been obtained after several years of cooperation with the urology team at the Alicante University Hospital. Breast cancer comprises 10.4% of all cancer incidences among women, making it the most common type of non-skin cancer in women and the fifth most common cause of cancer death. Parkinson's disease is the second most common neurodegenerative affliction only surpassed by Alzheimer's disease. Further- more, urinary incontinence is an increasing problem affecting between 10 and 30% of the adult population with rising treatment costs expected in the next decade. Due to the importance of these afflictions and their implications it would be very interesting to create Decision Support Systems (DSSs) to aid experts in their decisions. Moreover, these general DSSs could be adapted for other kinds of data as well since they offer a good general vision. The results of the authors' experiments are very encouraging with high accuracy. The parameters used to validate the system are classification accuracy, sen- sitivity, specificity, positive predictive value and negative predictive value confusion matrices ROC curves.

Chapter 6 - Text mining is an interesting field in which complex data mining problems arise, such as document or term classification, topic extraction, web page recommendation and others. In recent years relevant research has focused on probabilistic models, such as Latent Dirichlet Allocation or Probabilistic Latent Semantic Analysis. The output of such models are probabilities that allow to solve classification problems, but these models do not provide explicit geometric representations of documents, terms or top- ics. In this work the authors follow a Regularization Theory approach to propose appropriate kernels for diverse Text Mining tasks that can be used to solve representation, regres- sion and classification problems (via Support Vector Machines). One advantage of this proposal is the ability to combine different sources of information (for instance, the term by document matrix and the co-citation matrix) and to provide explicit term or document maps that incorporate all this information. In addition, the system provides explicit conditional probabilities, as the Latent Dirichlet Allocation model does, but avoiding the computational burden usually involved in the iterative step of probabilis- tic models. Finally the authors perform several experiments involving real data bases, showing the advantages of the new approach.

Chapter 7 - This chapter makes a comparison of support vector machines and neural prediction models for the financial time series prediction problem. Support Vector Machines (SVMs) are very successful at classification and regression tasks and provide a good alternative to neural network architectures. Unlike neural networks training which requires nonlinear optimization with the danger of getting stuck at local minima, the SVM solution is always unique and globally optimal. By considering this unique and globally optimal property, the authors have used SVM as a regression approach to financial time series forecasting. This chapter discusses the advantages and disadvantages of each model by using a real-world data: 22 years Istanbul Stock Exchange ISE 100 index data from 1988 to 2010. Several performance metrics are used to compare these models including regression metrics, prediction trend accuracy metrics and special metrics such as Spearman's and Kendall's rank correlation coefficients Finally, it is observed that the support vector predictors becomes advantageous in capturing volatility in index return series when it is compared to global and feedback neural models.

Chapter 8 - In this chapter a mathematical model of a K'/n rate conventional convolutional encoder/decoder system was developed to be applied for decoding based on the gradient descent algorithm. For the system a general expression for the noise energy function, which is required for the recurrent neural networks decoding, is derived. The derivative is based on the representation of the encoding procedure as a mapping of a K'-dimensional message into n-dimensional Euclidean encoded bit set vector. The universal nature of derivative is demonstrated through its application for particular cases of a general 1/n rate code, a 1/2 encoder, and a 2/3 rate encoder. In order to eliminate the local minimum problem presented in the recurrent neural network, another global optimisation technique called support vector machine is investigated. Preliminary simulation results have been carried out, showing its potential to be applied as an alternative method to decode convolutional codes.

Chapter 9 - Recently, pattern recognition became a famous method in the area of artificial intelligent and machine learning. Various kinds of majors using this method is for detecting and recognizing the objects such as face detection, character recognition, speech recognition, information and image retrieval, cancer detection and so on. In this chapter, the complete study of pattern recognition for machine fault diagnosis is presented. In this study, fault occurrence in the machine is considered as the object of recognition. The complete study consists of basic theory of feature representation in time and frequency domain, feature extraction method and classification process using support vector machine (SVM). The case study is also presented using data acquired from induction motor to clearly describe fault diagnosis procedure. Moreover, a new classification method using wavelet support vector machine (W-SVM) is introduced to enrich the understanding of classification method. W-SVM is used to induction motor for fault diagnosis based on vibration signal. The results show that W-SVM has potential to serve fault diagnosis routine.

In: Support Vector Machines
Editor: Brandon H. Boyle

ISBN: 978-1-61209-342-0
© 2011 Nova Science Publishers, Inc.

Chapter 1

THE SUPPORT VECTOR MACHINE IN MEDICAL IMAGING

*Jacob E. D. Levman**

Department of Medical Biophysics, Sunnybrook Research Institute,
University of Toronto, ON, Canada

ABSTRACT

This chapter outline the various ways that the support vector machine is used in medical imaging research and related applications. The chapter presents examples of the use of the support vector machine for classification (supervised learning) as well as texture analysis. A major focus of the chapter is a series of examples of recent research into using the support vector machine for a wide array of medical imaging problems. A specific focus is placed on using the support vector machine to detect breast cancer from magnetic resonance imaging (MRI) examinations. Furthermore, the chapter includes alternative vector machine formulations which are an extension of the established support vector machine and demonstrates these techniques for the classification / prediction problem. Novel perspectives on the use of the support vector machine are presented.

1. INTRODUCTION

The support vector machine is a high performing pattern recognition technology used in many fields of research. This chapter focuses on highlighting how the support vector machine has been applied within the context of medical imaging. The chapter will begin with a description of the support vector machine (subsection 2) followed by an overview of its applications in medical imaging which involves a wide range of imaging modalities and tissues of interest. As can be seen in subsection 3 of this chapter, the support vector machine has been heavily compared with many existing pattern recognition technologies and regularly

---

* 2075 Bayview Avenue, Room S605, Toronto, ON, Canada, M4N 3M5, 416-480-6100 x3390, fax: 416-480-5714.
jacob.levman@sri.utoronto.ca

is the best performing technique avialable. Researchers in the pattern recognition community should make note of the support vector machine's many promising results if they have not already done so. This chapter will further illustrate the use of the support vector machine (SVM) with a case study addressing the use of the SVM in the context of breast cancer diagnosis from magnetic resonance imaging (MRI) examinations (subsection 4). The chapter concludes in subsection 5.

2. THE SUPPORT VECTOR MACHINE

The support vector machine (SVM) is an established supervised learning technique that creates a boundary separating two groups based on a set of provided training data [1]. Despite their strengths, support vector machines include one or more parameters that the researcher needs to fully explore in order to produce an optimal classifier. Support vector machines (SVMs) operate by locating a decision function that attempts to split the training data into two categories. The decision function is selected such that its distance to the nearest training data on either side of the surface is maximized. If no decision function is capable of linearly separating the data, a kernel transformation function is used to map the data into a different dimensional space (called a feature space) so that it can be linearly separated using standard support vector machine decision function techniques. Multiple types of kernels have been developed to map data into differing dimensions. If the kernel transformation function does not fully separate our data, a slack error variable is used to create a soft margin decision function for data separation. Figure 1 illustrates an example SVM decision function and displays the margin.

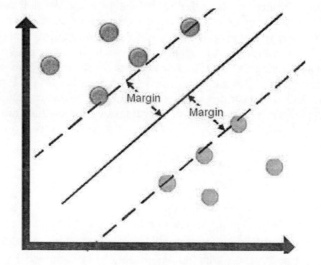

Figure 1. A support vector machine decision function (solid line) demonstrating the margin separating it from neighbouring training samples.

3. THE SUPPORT VECTOR MACHINE'S USE IN MEDICAL IMAGING

The most common medical imaging use of supervised learning techniques such as the support vector machine (which require a set of training data) is found in computer-aided detection and diagnosis of medical conditions. The support vector machine is typically provided with a set of measurements representing both abnormal and normal conditions and the SVM will be responsible for classifying new unknown samples as either normal tissue or some abnormal pathological condition. This section will overview the main uses of the support vector machine within the context of medical imaging.

3.1. Breast Cancer Imaging

The support vector machine has been used extensively in a research setting towards the detection of breast cancer. El-Naqa et al. showed that the support vector machine could be used as a texture analysis method towards the detection of microcalcifications from x-ray mammograms [2]. It was later shown by Papadopoulis et al. that the support vector machine outperforms the popular artificial neural network when applied to microcalcification detection from x-ray mammogramms [3] with the SVMs producing robustness improvements in the receiver operating characteristic curve area [4] of up to a substantial 0.09. Liyang Wei et al. also showed that the support vector machine outperforms a variety of alternative pattern recognition techniques in microcalcification detection from x-ray mammograms, including a ROC area robustness improvement of 0.05 over a clinically proven neural network based system [5]. Liyang Wei et al. have also shown that the relevance vector machine, a more recent technology inspired by the support vector machine can produce faster solutions (made of sparser sets of training vectors) while producing equal classification performance to that of the support vector machine when applied to microcalcification detection from x-ray mammograms [6].

Mavroforakis et al. also showed that when analyzing x-ray mammograms using fractal analysis, the support vector machine outperforms a variety of alternative technologies (linear discriminant analysis, least-squares minimum distance, K-nearest-neighbors and multi-layer perceptron artificial neural network) [7]. Cao et al. have proposed the vicinal support vector machine for use in breast cancer detection from x-ray mammogram examinations [8]. Campanini et al. have also used support vector machines for the classification of malignancies from x-ray mammograms [9]. Similarly, Xu et al. also showed that the support vector machine can be used for cancer detection from x-ray mammograms [10].

The support vector machine has been shown to be effective as a method for texture analysis of breast tumours imaged by Ultrasound [11]. It was shown that the support vector machine outperforms the artificial neural network in this task. Another study by Huang and Chen demonstrates that the support vector machine is much faster than the artificial neural network on this application [12]. Piliouras et al. demonstrated that the support vector machine could be used to build a computer-aided detection algorithm operating on Ultrasound examinations that achieves a 98.7% classification accuracy [13]. Chang et al. also showed that the support vector machine in conjunction with speckle-emphasis texture analysis can improve breast tumour discrimination from Ultrasound images [14].

The support vector machine has also been used in the research of computer-aided diagnosis systems for breast cancer detection from state-of-the-art magnetic resonance imaging examinations, however, that topic is addressed in more detail in the case study presented in subsection 4 of this chapter.

3.2. Brain Imaging

The support vector machine has been used for the detection of abnormal MR brain images by Chaplot et al. [15]. The study showed that the support vector machine achieved an impressive 98% classification accuracy, even outperforming the highly popular artificial neural network (which achieved a 94% classification accuracy). Zhang et al. also showed that the support vector machine has a lower error rate and faster computation time that the artificial neural network in the classification of brain tissues [16]. The support vector machine has also been applied to the atlas guided identification of brain structures from magnetic resonance images [17]. Quddus et al. have also used the support vector machine for white matter lesion segmentation in MR images [18].

The support vector machine has also been applied to the segmentation of brain tumours with conditional random fields [19]. Lao et al. also showed that the support vector machine could be used to assist in the segmentation of white matter lesions from three dimensional magnetic resonance images of the brain [20]. Li et al. also showed that the support vector machine could be used to predict the degree of malignancy in brain gliomas [21]. Lao et al. also showed that the support vector machine could be used to determine the gender of a subject from their MRI based brain image with a 97% classification accuracy [22].

Fung and Stoeckel showed that the support vector machine could be used for the classification of Alzheimer's disease from the spatial information acquired in SPECT imaging [23]. Results indicated that the support vector machine outperformed the Fisher linear discriminant classifier, statistical parametric mapping and outperformed human experts. Gorriz et al. also used the support vector machine for the computer aided diagnosis of Alzheimer's from functional SPECT data [24]. Alvarez et al. also showed that the support vector machine could be used in the diagnosis of Alzheimer's from SPECT data [25].

The support vector machine has also been applied to the classification of schizophrenia patients and performed well (91.8% accuracy) [26].

Mourão-Miranda et al. have shown that the support vector machine can be used to discriminate between activation patterns in functional magnetic resonance imaging (fMRI) of the brain [27] (a type of imaging method that acquires data representative of brain function as opposed to a more standard image of brain structure). It was also demonstrated that the support vector machine is capable of classifying brain states from fMRI data. LaConte et al. have also shown that support vector machines can be used for the temporal classification of functional MRI data [28]. Wang et al. also used the support vector machine for the analysis of functional magnetic resonance imaging data [29, 30].

3.3. Skin and Oral Imaging

The support vector machine has been applied to the detection of malignant lesions from digital images of the skin by Maglogiannis and Zafiropoulos [31]. The support vector machine was compared with the statistical discriminant analysis and the popular neural network based classifier. The support vector machine was the best performing classifier achieving a 94.1% accuracy compared to an 88% accuracy for either of the other techniques. Ubeyli has also shown that the support vector machine can be used to assist in the diagnosis of erythemato-squamous diseases [32].

Majumder et al. have also shown that the support vector machine can be used for the detection of oral cancer using spectral data acquired in a clinical *in vivo* laser-induced fluorescence (LIF) spectroscopic study [33]. Lin et al. showed that the support vector machine can be used to classify light-induced autofluorescence data for the detection of nasopharyngeal carcinoma with a diagnostic accuracy of 98% [34].

3.4. Liver Imaging

The support vector machine has been used for the classification of hepatic tissues from CT images [35]. The support vector machine has also been applied to the visualization of CT images [36]. Huang et al. used support vector machines for the diagnosis of hepatic tumours in non-enhanced computed tomography images [37]. Wen-Chun Yeh et al. demonstated that the support vector machine could be used for liver fibrosis grade classification from B-mode ultrasound images [38].

3.5. Lung Imaging

The support vector machine has been used for lung nodule classification and was shown to outperform the neural network [39]. Zhao et al. showed that the support vector machine can be used to reduce false positives in lung nodule computer-aided detection [40]. Boroczky et al. also used support vector machines in the detection of lung nodules [41].

3.6. Reproductive System Imaging

The support vector machine has been applied to the classification of prostate cancer from MRI examinations [42]. Zhan and Shen have also used the support vector machine towards segmentation of 3D ultrasound prostate images [43]. Mohamed et al. have used the support vector machine for the detection of prostate cancer from trans-rectal ultrasound images [44]. Hambrock et al. used the support vector machine for the computerized analysis of prostate lesions from dynamic contrast enhanced MRI examinations [45]. The support vector machine has also been applied to the preoperative prediction of malignancy of ovarian tumours [46].

3.7. Eye Imaging

The support vector machine has been applied to the segmentation and visualization of retinal structures in volumetric optical coherence tomography [47]. Ricci and Perfetti showed that support vector machines could also be employed using line operators for the segmentation of retinal blood vessels [48]. Bowd et al. also investigated the use of the support vector machine and the generally faster (and sparser solution producing) relevance vector machine in scanning laser polarimetry retinal nerve fiber layer measurements [49]. It was shown that the support vector machine marginally outperformed the relevance vector machine by a ROC area of 0.01 in the diagnosis of glaucoma.

3.8. Other Imaging Applications

A wide variety of additional applications have been found for the support vector machine in medical imaging. Li et al. showed that the support vector machine can be used for clinical image segmentation of dental x-ray images [50]. The support vector machine has also been applied for assessing the malignancy risk for thyroid cancer based on ultrasound imaging [51]. The support vector machine has been applied to Doppler signals for the detection of heart valve disease [52]. Polat et al. showed that the support vector machine could be used for the detection of atherosclerosis from Carotid Artery Doppler signals [53]. The support vector machine has also been applied to assess the severity of idiopathic scoliosis from surface topographic images of human backs [54]. Guo et al. showed that the support vector machine can be used for the segmentation of white blood cells from multispectral images of bone marrow [55]. The support vector machine has also been coupled with level-set functions for autonomous volumetric image segmentation [56]. Jerebko et al. showed that the support vector machine can be used to help detect polyps from CT colonography [57]. The support vector machine has also been used for content based image retrieval by Rahman et al. [58].

4. CASE STUDY: THE SUPPORT VECTOR MACHINE IN BREAST CANCER DETECTION FROM MAGNETIC RESONANCE IMAGING

In this subsection I am presenting a case study on the use of the support vector machine (and some extensions thereof) for the detection and diagnosis of breast cancer from magnetic resonance imaging examinations. After highlighting the literature that indicates that the support vector machine is the top performing pattern recognition algorithm for breast cancer detection from MRI examinations (subsection 3), this case study will proceed to present some alternative vector machine formulations that reformulate the approaches taken in support vector machines into a single mathematical equation.

4.1. Case Study - Introduction

Support vector machines (SVMs) have been shown to perform well as a computer-aided diagnostic classification mechanism for breast cancer screening in ultrasound [11-14] and mammography [2-10]. More recently it has been shown that support vector machines outperform a variety of other machine learning and computer-aided diagnosis techniques when applied to the separation of malignant and benign dynamic contrast-enhanced magnetic resonance breast lesions, including the k-nn density classifier, Fisher Discriminant Analysis [59], Linear Discriminant Analysis [60] and the commercially used signal enhancement ratio [61]. The support vector machine has also been shown to outperform the use of the c-means unsupervised learning technique applied to the classification problem [62]. Twellmann et al. also used the support vector machine and compared the technique with c-means based unsupervised learning [63]. Bathen et al. have also showed that the support vector machine can be used to classify spectra from MR metabolomics data [64] where it was shown that the techniques can be used to predict long term breast cancer survival. It has also been shown that acquiring breast MR volume images at short time intervals does not improve the diagnostic accuracy of support vector machine based breast cancer detection from the temporal data of an MRI examination [65].

In this case study I will focus on demonstrating that some alternative vector machine formulations can perform equally to (or even outperform) the traditional support vector machine formulation when applied to a magnetic resonance imaging (MRI) breast cancer screening dataset. This case study will present two new vector machine formulations that act as an alternative to the traditional support vector machine. This case study also presents evaluations of the proposed vector machine techniques and the established SVM technique using the established statistical robustness test known as receiver operating characteristic (ROC) curve analysis [4].

Screening trials have compared the performance of dynamic contrast enhanced magnetic resonance imaging (DCE-MRI), ultrasound, mammography and clinical breast examination as diagnostic screening methodologies for high risk women [66-69]. Results have indicated that magnetic resonance imaging is the most sensitive modality evaluated. These studies suggest that breast cancer screening by MRI is likely to play an increasingly significant clinical role in the future.

4.2. Case Study - Methods

Support Vector Machine Classification

In order to evaluate our proposed classification method, we elected to compare our technique with the established support vector machine which has been shown to be the best performing classification technique for breast MRI when compared with the signal enhancement ratio, k-nn, and others [59, 61]. Support vector machine based classification has been implemented using the libsvm open source library [70].

The linear kernel based support vector machine is a single parameter classification function where the parameter biases the test along the regression output values of the support vector machine. The radial basis function kernel has two relevant parameters. One parameter is the same as in the linear kernel: a biasing parameter applied along the regression output values of the SVM.

The second parameter is directly applied to the RBF kernel as the γ parameter which is referred to as the support vector radius, which affects the curvature or tightness of the support vector machine decision function. For the purpose of this case study, we are evaluating the linear kernel, K_L (equation 1) and the radial basis function (RBF) kernel, K_R (equation 2) which has been previously shown to be the best performing kernel function in many applications including CAD for breast MRI [59,61].

$$K_L(x_i, x_j) = x_i \bullet x_j \tag{1}$$

$$K_R(x_i, x_j) = e^{-\gamma * |x_i - x_j|^2} \tag{2}$$

where x_i and x_j are input vectors comprised of the lesion measurements described in the Methods, $\bullet$ is the dot product operation, and γ is a kernel parameter. Non-linear kernel functions such as the radial basis function (equation 2) provide flexibility to the SVM hyperplane calculation. The equation allows the definition of the classification function to be non-linear in the input space (unlike the linear kernel – equation 1).

Proposed Vector Machine Formulations

This first proposed vector machine has been published [71]. A classification technique operates by inputting a set of training data with known labels/classes. A classification technique will then be able to predict an unknown test sample as belonging to one of the provided labeled groups by evaluating it with respect to the provided training data. Our first proposed supervised learning / classification technique takes only a single input parameter that biases the test towards one of the two groups. Unlike the established SVM, the proposed technique consists of no training phase responsible for down-sampling the provided training data.

Instead, the supervised learning approach uses all the training samples and thus consists of only a single equation responsible for classification. For our proposed vector machine's kernel function we selected the parameter-free inverse of the mean distance between our test sample and all of our training samples. Instead of applying our biasing parameter as a threshold on regression results (as in the support vector machine described above), we have applied our input biasing parameter to define the weights on the training samples themselves. The proposed technique will predict the class of a given sample as defined in equation 3 as follows:

$$sign\left(\alpha \left(\frac{n_p}{\sum_{i=1}^{n_p} \sqrt{\sum_{j=1}^{d} (t_p(i,j) - t_s(j))^2}} \right) - (1 - \alpha) \left(\frac{n_n}{\sum_{i=1}^{n_n} \sqrt{\sum_{j=1}^{d} (t_n(i,j) - t_s(j))^2}} \right) \right) \tag{3}$$

where, n_p is the number of positive training data samples
n_n is the number of negative training data samples
d is the number of measurements per sample
t_p is the positively labeled training data
t_n is the negatively labeled training data
t_s is the input sample vector to be tested
$sign(x)=1, x>=0; sign(x)=-1, x<0$
α is the input bias parameter, range from 0 to 1

This is a vector machine formulation with every training sample used as a support vector with an associated weight value equal to the bias term (α and $-(1- \alpha)$ for the two classes respectively) which influences the classification results towards one of the two groups. A plot of how the α parameter affects the overall decision function is provided in the results section in figure 5 (upper pane). This figure demonstrates how the curvature of the decision boundary changes with respect to the bias parameter setting and the underlying data distribution. The similarity measure (the inverse of the mean of the distances between the test sample and the training data) is analogous to a kernel transformation function (as is used in support vector machines).

The above formulation adjusts for situations when we have a differing number of samples in each of our two groups by normalizing the inverse of the sum of the distances (the similarity measure) by the number of positive and negative samples respectively.

The input bias term (α) can account for this effect on its own, however, the appropriate setting of the bias term will be related to the relative number of samples in either group. By scaling the similarity measure by the number of samples in each group we can ensure that sensible settings for the α parameter are found around the setting 0.5 as is demonstrated in figure 5 upper pane (note that our data set has about 4 benign lesions for every cancer).

This similarity kernel measure was selected as it can provide curved decision functions like the radial basis function support vector machine without the need for a kernel parameter.

This proposed formulation (equation 3) involves a classification function that divides two classes/groups. For instances when a problem has more than two classes the equation can still be used but will have to be repeated for each class to be tested with the positive label assigned to the class currently being tested and a negative label assigned to all other samples. The breast magnetic resonance imaging computer-aided detection example used in this study consists of only two classes (malignant and benign lesions).

It is recommended that when using the proposed supervised learning technique each feature measurement should be scaled to a fixed range (in this paper scaling was performed from 0 to 1). This will ensure that a single measurement does not dominate the prediction process due to an inherently larger scale.

A recent publication at the conference of the IEEE's Engineering in Medicine and Biology Society in Buenos Aires, Argentina, September 2010 revealed a new development, a two-parameter vector machine that outperformed the established support vector machine in randomized robustness analyses [72]. The equation is re-expressed here, note the use of the radial basis function (equation 2) within the same biasing framework recommended in equation (3) to form equation 4:

$$Class = sign\left(\alpha e^{\overline{-\gamma * |x_{pos} - x_{test}|^2}} + (1-\alpha)e^{\overline{-\gamma * |x_{neg} - x_{test}|^2}} \right) \qquad (4)$$

where, x_{pos} is the positively labeled training data

x_{neg} is the negatively labeled training data

x_{test} is the test sample with an unknown label

γ is the tightness parameter

$sign(x)=1, x>=0; sign(x)=-1, x<0$

α is the input bias parameter, range from 0 to 1

Breast MRI Database for Case Study

Image Acquisition and Data Preprocessing

The screening protocol used is as follows. Simultaneous bilateral magnetic resonance imaging was performed using a 1.5T magnet (GE Signa, version 11.4). Sagittal images were obtained with a phased-array coil arrangement using a dual slab interleaved bilateral imaging method [73]. This provided 3D volume data over each breast obtained with an RF spoiled gradient recalled sequence (SPGR, scan parameters: TR/TE/angle=18.4/4.3/30°, 256x256x32 voxels, FOV: 18x18x6-8cm). Imaging is performed before and after a bolus injection of 0.1 mmol/kg of contrast agent (Gd-DTPA). Each bilateral acquisition was obtained in 2 minutes and 48 seconds. Slice thickness was 2 to 3 mm.

Dynamic contrast-enhanced magnetic resonance breast examinations from high risk patients were obtained with pathologically proven malignancies (44 examinations) or benign lesions (173 examinations). Ground truth is based on the diagnosis of the histopathologist, who analyzes the tissue biopsies. Surgical biopsy of lesions was performed under MR guidance [74]. In cases where a patient with a suspicious lesion did not receive a biopsy but returned to screening for greater than one year without observed changes to the lesion, a benign diagnosis is accepted.

Image registration is the process of aligning images that vary in position over time. This is performed in order to compensate for any patient motion that takes place during the examination. For this study we have used a three dimensional non-rigid registration technique for magnetic resonance breast images [75].

Breast MR Lesion Measurements

For each of the lesions addressed in this study, 4 features were measured (lesion slope, lesion washout, lesion irregularity and lesion diffuseness/sharpness) from regions of interest (ROIs) on lesions identified by radiological analysis. This yields a four dimensional data space within which malignancies will be predicted by a multidimensional classification (or supervised learning) technique. Each of these features has been scaled to the range 0 to 1. The features are described below and defined in the literature:

Feature Measurement #1: Average Slope

The technique computes the enhancement as specified for each voxel in our suspect lesion and normalizes by the time to peak in seconds. The average of these slope values form the final lesion measurement. This measurement was selected as malignant lesions are often fed by characteristically leaky blood vessels that allow our contrast agent to pool in lesion tissue. The measured enhancement and time to peak enhancement are directly linked to the permeability of the vasculature in the lesion. This measurement has been defined in the literature [71].

Feature Measurement #2: Average Washout

A breast MR examination involves the injection of a contrast agent which will pool in lesion tissue. Over the course of a breast MR examination the concentration of contrast agent in the blood plasma will typically diminish and contrast agents that have leaked into a lesion may begin to diffuse out of the lesion and back into the blood plasma – a process known as washout. Washout measurements are an alternative measure of lesion vascularity. This measurement has been defined in the literature [71].

Feature Measurement #3: Sphericity / Irregularity

It is known that irregularly shaped lesions are more likely to be malignant by virtue of consisting of tissues that grow irregularly and often invasively. Benign lesions are more likely to be encapsulated and thus exhibit spherical shapes. We have elected to measure the irregularity of a lesion by sphericity. This measurement has been defined in the literature [71].

Feature Measurement #4: Average Edge Diffuseness

The motivation behind this measurement is that malignancies tend to grow into neighbouring tissues thus they tend to exhibit diffuse edges on breast MR images. Benign lesions tend to be encapsulated and as such tend to exhibit sharp edges on breast MR images. The measurement is made by exhaustively selecting two neighbouring voxels, one of which is in our region-of-interest and one of which is not. This measurement has been defined in the literature [71].

Each of these four feature measurements addressed in this study are scaled to the range 0 to 1. The two-parameter vector machine results presented involve a different feature set for testing: the simple signal-intensity time-series data of the most enhancing voxel within the radiologically identified lesions.

Receiver Operating Characteristic Curve Analysis and Validation

Overall classification accuracy is one of the most common metrics for evaluating a classification function. Unfortunately, overall accuracy does not provide enough information in order to robustly evaluate a test's performance. In order to perform a robust evaluative analysis we have elected to compare classification performance with the receiver operating characteristic (ROC) curve area [4]. The receiver operating characteristic (ROC) curve area is computed by examining the tradeoff between sensitivity and specificity values obtained for a given test. This is accomplished by varying a threshold which divides our dataset into two groups (see figure 2 left), for each value of the threshold a sensitivity and specificity value is computed and plotted (figure 2 right). This creates a curve that extends from 0% sensitivity, 100% specificity to 100% sensitivity, 0% specificity. The area under this curve is used as our robustness metric for comparing classification approaches.

ROC curve analysis is typically performed unidimensionally (on samples with only a single measurement per sample). The analyses presented in this paper are multi-dimensional (with multiple measurements per sample). ROC analysis on the established SVM technique is performed by a standard method, i.e. by varying the threshold along the regression results of the SVM classifier. This has the result of biasing the decision function along its own normal axis, thus the SVM classification function does not change its shape but only its position as the ROC biasing term is varied (illustrated in figure 1 bottom pane). The proposed approach functions differently by varying the alpha parameter in order to yield a range of sensitivity and specificity values which can be used for receiver operating characteristic curve analysis. Thus no unidimensional threshold is applied (figure 2 left), instead, varying the alpha parameter directly yields sensitivity and specificity points along the ROC curve (figure 2 right). This results in a decision function whose curvature changes based on the setting of the bias parameter and underlying data distribution (illustrated in figure 5 upper pane).

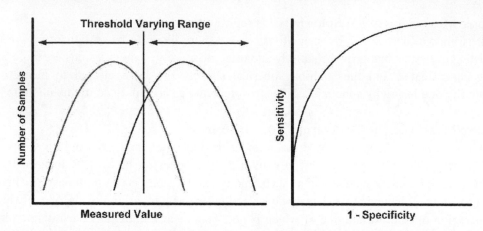

Figure 2. Illustration of how the ROC curve (left) is obtained by varying a threshold value which separates our two groups (right).

We perform leave-one-out cross-validation for both the proposed technique and for the SVMs as applied to the breast MRI dataset. The radial basis function support vector machine has its input parameter varied by the following equation: $\gamma = e^{GammaExponent}$, where $GammaExponent \in \{-7.0, 4.5\}$ in steps of 0.1. For each setting of the input parameter γ, the area under the receiver operating characteristic (ROC) curve [4] is computed. For the two SVM approaches, the ROC area is computed by varying the biasing threshold parameter along the regression results of the classifier (3000 evenly sized steps were used). For the proposed technique a single ROC curve is computed by varying the input parameter α from 0 to 1 in steps of 0.0005.

Randomized trials were also used to quantify the variability in classification performance. 50% of the samples in our data set were randomly selected and assigned for use in training while the remaining 50% of the samples were used for testing. This random selection process was repeated 100 times and both the proposed classification technique and support vector machines were compared in terms of the mean ROC values for the set of 100 randomized trials. Finally, bar plots with confidence intervals were computed comparing the proposed technique with the two support vector machine techniques.

4.3. Case Study - Results

For the combined set of breast MRI measurements addressed in the Methods, the separation obtained between malignant and benign lesions is measured by receiver-operating characteristic (ROC) curve analysis. Changes in the ROC area for leave-one-out validation on the breast MRI dataset are tracked with variations in the input parameter for the RBF support vector machine technique and the single ROC areas for the proposed technique and the linear SVM are also provided in figure 3. These ROC area calculations were repeated for the randomized trial experiments and also provided in figure 3. We have also provided a bar plot with confidence intervals summarizing the best ROC area performances for each of the techniques addressed on the breast MRI data in figure 4. We have also provided a classifier visualization plot [61] to assist in qualitative understanding of the effects of the input parameters on the classifying hyperplane and to assist with a general understanding of the two techniques being compared (see figure 5).

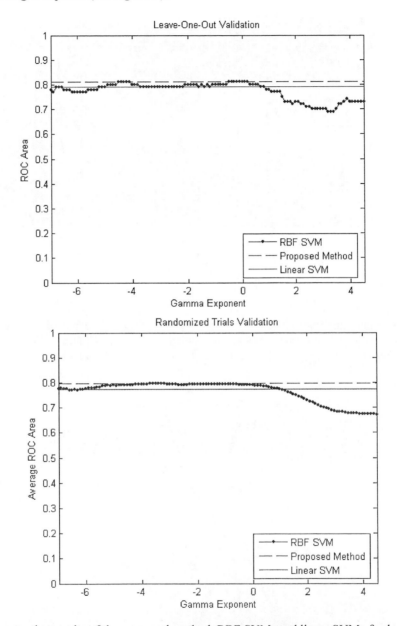

Figure 3. Comparative results of the proposed method, RBF SVMs and linear SVMs for leave-one-out (top) and randomized trials (bottom) based validation on the breast MRI dataset.

We also provide a variant of a recently published figure at a conference of the IEEE Engineering in Medicine and Biology Society, which demonstrates that the two parameter vector machine equation presented (equation 4) [72] outperforms the support vector machine

on an expanded breast MRI dataset (259 total lesions - see figure 6). I have also provided a
principal component plot with a projection of the two parameter vector machine formulation
in order to demonstrate its behaviour with respect to variations in its biasing parameter (see
figure 7).

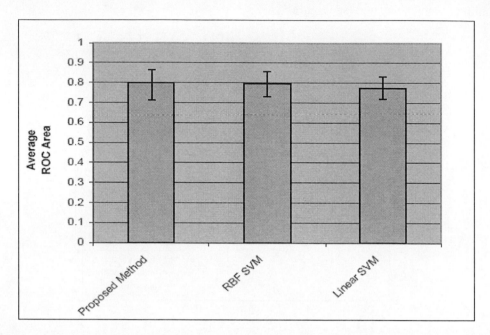

Figure 4. A bar plot with 95% confidence intervals for the ROC area distributions obtained from the
randomized trials for each of the techniques addressed on the breast MRI dataset. The RBF SVM bar
was generated at γ exponent = -3.4 (γ =0.0334) where the highest average ROC area was obtained.

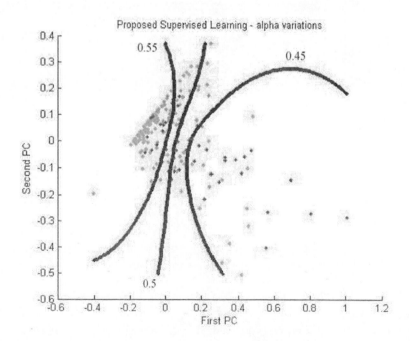

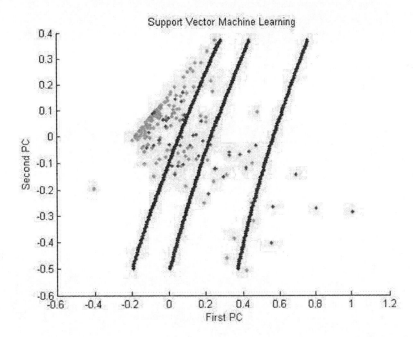

Figure 5. Principal component space projection plots with classifier boundaries (blue) for the single parameter proposed method (above, alpha values provided) and the RBF SVM method (below, γ = 0.12, three bias threshold boundaries provided (left to right): -0.89, -0.87, -0.82).

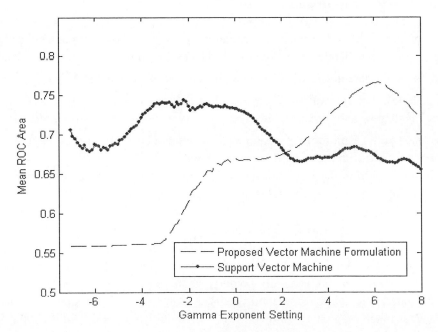

Figure 6. Variations in the mean ROC area from bootstrap validated trials comparing the proposed two-parameter vector machine and the established support vector machine.

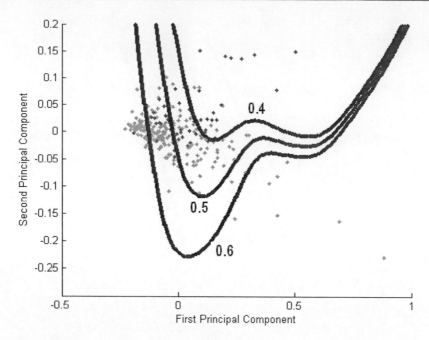

Figure 7. Principal component space projection plot with classifier boundaries (blue) for the two parameter proposed method (alpha values provided).

4.4. Case Study - Discussion

The first proposed vector machine formulation presented above was developed in order to create a flexible classification approach that produces non-linear decision boundaries without the need for a γ parameter (which is used in the established radial basis function support vector machine). The motivation for removing the γ parameter was that a researcher does not know in advance appropriate settings for the curvature of their resultant decision function and thus must fully explore the γ parameter in order to be certain they have achieved the best results possible with the support vector machine.

It can be seen from the results provided in figure 3 that when tested on the breast MRI dataset, the proposed technique yields ROC areas around 0.80 to 0.81 depending on the validation technique selected. A two-sample t-test reveals that the p-value obtained from comparing the ROC area distributions from the randomized trials is 0.897, indicating that there is no statistically significant difference between the proposed single parameter technique and the established radial basis function support vector machine. Solutions that involve fewer parameters are generally favoured as more parameters lead to more values that need to be tuned. The proposed method was also compared with the single parameter linear support vector machine with a 2 sample t-test which yielded a p-value of 0.00003, indicating a statistically significant difference between the two single parameter techniques.

It should be noted that the proposed technique is entirely data-driven and as such should also perform well in applications outside of breast MRI. One of the strengths of the proposed technique is its robustness and ease-of-use. Another advantage of the proposed technique is how it simplifies ROC curve area calculations [4]. ROC areas can be easily computed by simply varying the α parameter across its bounded range (0 to 1) to achieve a series of sensitivity and specificity values that form the ROC curve itself. ROC area calculations are extremely common in CAD applications and in testing theory in general. The proposed method produces decision functions whose curvature is based on both the input alpha parameter setting and the underlying distribution of the data (as is illustrated in figure 1 upper pane). The established RBF SVM method produces curved decision functions as well, however, ROC analysis is typically performed unidimensionally on the regression results of the classifier. Thus, as the bias is varied, the decision function's curvature does not change, however its position changes along the decision function's normal axis (as is illustrated in figure 1 lower pane).

The radial basis function based support vector machine's γ parameter is described as the radius of each support vector which in turn affects the curvature of the separating hyperplane. This causes the radial basis function support vector machine to exhibit linear classifier behaviour (underperforming) as γ approaches 0 and produces consistently over-fitted solutions as γ gets very large. Good solutions are typically found at parameter settings somewhere in between and this unbounded parameter space needs to be thoroughly explored to ensure the generation of high quality results.

The proposed techniques are very similar in operation to support vector machines without an optimization step that down-samples and assigns weights to the training data (to establish our support vectors). Instead, the technique can be thought of as a support vector machine with every sample included as a support vector in an effort to maintain statistical precision. The weight on each support vector is simply the bias term in equation 3 (α and $-(1-\alpha)$ for the two classes respectively), thus making the weights different for the positive and negative classes. The similarity kernel function (the inverse of the mean of the sum of the distances) is analogous to a support vector machine kernel function. In the second vector machine formulation the standard radial basis function kernel was used and demonstrated to outperform the support vector machine [72]. The proposed method is also similar to the technique proposed by Mazurowski et al., which relies on a genetic algorithm for an SVM-like training phase [76].

A common use of classification functions such as support vector machines is to use them in regression mode. When predicting in regression mode a classifier will output a floating point number instead of the typical +1 or -1 to indicate which of the two groups it belongs to. Regression prediction can be used as a measure of how far the given sample is from the hyperplane decision function. The proposed technique (equation 3) can support regression by simply removing the *sign* function from the equation.

Although the first proposed vector machine bears some similarities to the k-nearest neighbour approach, there are also many differences. The main similarity is that both techniques rely on the distance between the test sample and some of the training samples. The differences are that the k-nn approach bases prediction only on the training samples that are local with respect to our test sample. At low values of k the k-nn approach can yield over-fitted solutions. The k-nn classifier has also been shown to under-perform the support vector machine in the computer-aided diagnosis of breast cancer from magnetic resonance imaging [59]. Finally, unlike the proposed vector machine, the k-nn approach was not built for providing convenient biasing abilities between our two groups in order to support ROC curve analysis.

The main disadvantage of the proposed technique is that the prediction process is slower than that of support vector machines by virtue of having every data sample contribute to the decision function. This is equivalent to having every data sample being a support vector. In support vector machines, prediction is accomplished by combining the test vector with each of the support vectors via the kernel function.

The same is true with our proposed technique, but all of the training samples are included. If a researcher wanted to speed up this formulation, the simplest way would be to take each training sample and consider them test samples and run them through the vector machine in regression mode. These regression values are then sorted and only the lowest valued samples (those closest to the decision function itself) are retained as support vectors for the final faster vector machine.

The two parameter vector machine approach presented outperforms the existing support vector machine which can yield test sensitivity improvements of up to 9.8%. It has been observed that this two-parameter formulation is sensitive to bad features. If you have a non-discriminating noise introducing feature in your feature set it has the potential to degrade the performance of this two-parameter vector machine classifier. Furthermore, both vector machine techniques do not perform down-sampling.

Speeding up the techniques can be performed by down-sampling after optimizing your classifier. This can be accomplished by testing the training data through the classifier in regression mode. The classifier will assign a floating point number to each of the training samples and that number is representative of that training vector's distance from the optimized decision function. The researcher can then select any number of samples close to the decision function in order to produce a speed improved approximation of the optimized classifier. The fewer samples kept, the faster the resultant classifier. If too many samples are removed, the classifier will no longer do a good job of approximating the optimized classifier and so classification accuracy will degrade.

4.5. Case Study - Conclusions

In this case study we presented two vector machines for classification (supervised learning) and comparatively evaluated them against the established linear and radial basis function based support vector machines as a classification mechanism for delineating malignant and benign lesions from DCE-MRI breast examinations. We demonstrated that the proposed single parameter vector machine formulation outperforms the linear SVM and performs comparably to the RBF SVM while facilitating ROC analysis and being considerably easier to use. We also presented published results indicating that the proposed two parameter vector machine can outperform the traditional radial basis function support vector machine on breast cancer data from magnetic resonance imaging.

More research is needed to fully implement the proposed techniques in a clinically acceptable manner. This needs to be followed by extensive clinical validation against known pathology across a broad range of disease entities in order to draw firm conclusions about the significance of this technique. However, results from this case study suggest that the proposed techniques may be generally useful and that they perform effectively on DCE-MRI breast data.

CONCLUSION

This chapter presented a brief introduction to the support vector machine. An overview of the use of the support vector machine in medical imaging was presented which helps demonstrate the substantial usefulness of this technique. A number of studies were highlighted which demonstrate that the support vector machine regularly outperforms existing competing technologies. Furthermore, a single parameter reformulation of the support vector machine has been presented from the literature and demonstrated to tie the established radial basis function support vector machine. A two parameter reformulation of the support vector machine has been presented from the literature and demonstrated to outperform the established radial basis function support vector machine.

ACKNOWLEDGMENTS

The author would like to thank Dr. Anne Martel for her guidance and support in my growth as a research scientist. Furthermore, my research has benefited greatly from her research in image registration which has been clinically relied upon at Sunnybrook Health Sciences Centre (Toronto, ON, Canada). I would also like to thank Dr. Elizabeth Ramsay for her assistance in image acquisition. The MRI data was provided by Dr. Ellen Warner and was acquired using funding from the Canadian Breast Cancer Research Alliance. I would also like to thank Dr. Petrina Causer for radiological analysis. Finally, I would like to acknowledge funding support received from the Canadian Breast Cancer Foundation.

REFERENCES

[1] V. N. Vapnik, *The Nature of Statistical Learning Theory*. New York, NY: Springer, 2000.

[2] El-Naqa, I.; Yongyi Yang; Wernick, M.N.; Galatsanos, N.P.; Nishikawa, R.M., "A support vector machine approach for detection of microcalcifications," *IEEE Transactions on Medical Imaging,* Vol. 21(12), December 2002, pp. 1552-1563.

[3] A. Papadopoulos, D. I. Fotiadis, A. Likas, "Characterization of clustered microcalcifications in digitized mammograms using neural networks and support vector machines," *Artificial Intelligence in Medicine*, Vol. 34(2), June 2005, pp. 141-150.

[4] J. Eng, "Receiver Operating Characteristic Analysis: A Primer," *Academic Radiology*, vol. 12(7), 2005, pp.909-916.

[5] Liyang Wei, Yongyi Yang, Nishikawa, R.M., Yulei Jiang, "A study on several Machine-learning methods for classification of Malignant and benign clustered microcalcifications," *IEEE Transactions on Medical Imaging*, Vol. 24(3), March 2005, pp. 371-380.

[6] Liyang Wei, Yongyi Yang, Nishikawa, R.M., Wernick, M.N., Edwards, A., "Relevance vector machine for automatic detection of clustered microcalcifications," *IEEE Transactions on Medical Imaging*, Vol. 24(10), October 2005, pp. 1278-1285.

[7] Michael E. Mavroforakisa, Harris V. Georgioua, Nikos Dimitropoulosb, Dionisis Cavourasc and Sergios Theodoridisa, "Mammographic masses characterization based on localized texture and dataset fractal analysis using linear, neural and support vector machine classifiers," *Artificial Intelligence in Medicine*, Vol. 37(2), June 2006, pp. 145-162.

[8] Aize Cao, Qing Song, Xulei Yang, Sheng Liu, Chengyi Guo, "Mammographic mass detection by vicinal support vector machine," *Proceedings of the IEEE International Joint Conference on Neural Networks*, Vol. 3, July 2004, pp. 1953-1958.

[9] Renato Campanini, Danilo Dongiovanni, Emiro Iampieri, Nico Lanconelli, Matteo Masotti, Giuseppe Palermo, Alessandro Riccardi and Matteo Roffilli, "A novel featureless approach to mass detection in digital mammograms based on support vector machines," *Physics in Medicine and Biology*, Vol. 49(6), 2004.

[10] R. Xu, X. Zhao, X. Li, C. Kwan, and C.-I Chang, "Target Detection with Improved Image Texture Feature Coding Method and Support Vector Machine," *International Journal of Intelligent Technology*, Vol. 1(1), 2006.

[11] Yu-Len Huang, Kao-Lun Wang and Dar-Ren Chen, "Diagnosis of breast tumors with ultrasonic texture analysis using support vector machines," *Neural Computing and Applications*, vol. 15(2), pp. 164-169.

[12] Yu-Len Huang, and Dar-Ren Chen, "Support vector machines in sonography: Application to decision making in the diagnosis of breast cancer," *Clinical Imaging*, Vol. 29(3), 2005, pp. 179-184.

[13] N. Piliouras, I. Kalatzis, N. Dimitropoulos, D. Cavouras, "Development of the cubic least squares mapping linear-kernel support vector machine classifier for improving the characterization of breast lesions on ultrasound," *Computerized Medical Imaging and Graphics*, Vol. 28, 2004, pp. 247–255.

[14] Ruey-Feng Chang, Wen-Jie Wu, Woo Kyung Moon and Dar-Ren Chen, "Improvement in Breast Tumor Discrimination by Support Vector Machine and Speckle-Emphasis Texture Analysis," *Ultrasound in Med. and Biol.*, Vol. 29(5), 2003, pp. 679–686.

[15] Sandeep Chaplot, L.M. Patnaik, and N.R. Jagannathan, "Classification of magnetic resonance brain images using wavelets as input to support vector machine and neural network," *Biomedical Signal Processing and Control*, Vol. 1(1), January 2006, pp. 86-92.

[16] X. Zhang, X. L. Xiao, J. W. Tian, J. Liu, and G. Y. Xu, "Application of support vector machines in classification of magnetic resonance images," *International Journal of Computers and Applications*, Vol. 28(2), April 2006, pp. 122 – 128.

[17] Ayelet Akselrod-Ballin, Meirav Galun, Moshe John Gomori, Ronen Basri and Achi Brandt, "Atlas Guided Identification of Brain Structures by Combining 3D Segmentation and SVM Classification," *Medical Image Computing and Computer-Assisted Intervention – MICCAI*, Volume 4191, 2006, pp. 209-216.

[18] A. Quddus, P. Fieguth, O. Basir, "Adaboost and Support Vector Machines for White Matter Lesion Segmentation in MR Images," *Annual International Conference of the IEEE Engineering in Medicine and Biology Society*, 2005, pp. 463-466.

[19] Chi-Hoon Lee, Mark Schmidt, Albert Murtha, Aalo Bistritz, Jöerg Sander and Russell Greiner, "Segmenting Brain Tumors with Conditional Random Fields and Support Vector Machines," *Lecture Notes in Computer Science Computer Vision for Biomedical Image Applications*, Vol. 3765, 2005, pp. 469-478.

[20] Zhiqiang Lao, Dinggang Shen, Dengfeng Liu, Abbas F. Jawad, Elias R. Melhem, Lenore J. Launer, R. Nick Bryan, and Christos Davatzikos, "Computer-Assisted Segmentation of White Matter Lesions in 3D MR images, Using Support Vector Machine," *Academic Radiology*, Vol. 15(3), 2008, pp. 300–313.

[21] Guo-Zheng Li, Jie Yang, Chen-Zhou Ye, and Dao-Ying Geng, "Degree prediction of malignancy in brain glioma using support vector machines," *Computers in Biology and Medicine*, Vol. 36(3), March 2006, pp. 313-325.

[22] Zhiqiang Lao, Dinggang Shen, Zhong Xue, Bilge Karacali, Susan M. Resnick and Christos Davatzikos, "Morphological classification of brains via high-dimensional shape transformations and machine learning methods," *NeuroImage*, Vol. 21(1), January 2004, pp. 46-57.

[23] Glenn Fung and Jonathan Stoeckel, "SVM feature selection for classification of SPECT images of Alzheimer's disease using spatial information," Knowledge and Information Systems, Vol. 11(2), 2007, pp. 243-258.

[24] Gorriz, J. M., Ramirez, J., Lassl, A., Salas-Gonzalez, D., Lang, E. W., Puntonet, C. G., Alvarez, I., Lopez, M., Gomez-Rio, M., "Automatic computer aided diagnosis tool using component-based SVM," *The IEEE Nuclear Science Symposium*, 2008, pp. 4392-4395.

[25] Álvarez, J. M. Górriz, J. Ramírez, D. Salas-Gonzalez, M. López, F. Segovia, C. G. Puntonet and B. Prieto, "Alzheimer's Diagnosis Using Eigenbrains and Support Vector Machines," *Lecture Notes in Computer Science Bio-Inspired Systems: Computational and Ambient Intelligence*, Vol. 5517, 2009, pp. 973-980.

[26] Yong Fan, Dinggang Shen and Christos Davatzikos, "Classification of Structural Images via High-Dimensional Image Warping, Robust Feature Extraction, and SVM," *Medical Image Computing and Computer-Assisted Intervention – MICCAI 2005*, Vol. 3749.

[27] Janaina Mourão-Mirandaa, Arun L.W. Bokdeb, Christine Bornc, Harald Hampelb and Martin Stettera, "Classifying brain states and determining the discriminating activation patterns: Support Vector Machine on functional MRI data," *NeuroImage*, Vol. 28(4), December 2005, pp. 980-995.

[28] Stephen LaConte, Stephen Strother, Vladimir Cherkassky, Jon Anderson and Xiaoping Hu, "Support vector machines for temporal classification of block design fMRI data," *NeuroImage*, Vol. 26(2), June 2005, pp. 317-329.

[29] Ze Wang, Anna R. Childress, Jiongjiong Wang, and John A. Detre, "Support vector machine learning-based fMRI data group analysis," *NeuroImage*, Vol. 36(4), July 2007, pp. 1139-1151.

[30] Yongmei Michelle Wang, Robert T. Schultz, R. Todd Constable and Lawrence H. Staib, "Nonlinear Estimation and Modeling of fMRI Data Using Spatio-temporal Support Vector Regression," Lecture Notes in Computer Science Information Processing in Medical Imaging, Vol. 2732, 2003, pp. 647-659.

[31] Ilias G Maglogiannis and Elias P Zafiropoulos, "Characterization of digital medical images utilizing support vector machines," *BMC Medical Informatics and Decision Making*, 2004, Vol. 4(4).

[32] Elif Derya Übeyli, "Multiclass support vector machines for diagnosis of erythemato-squamous diseases," *Expert Systems with Applications*, Vol. 35(4), November 2008, pp. 1733-1740.

[33] S. K. Majumder, N. Ghosh, and P. K. Gupta, "Support vector machine for optical diagnosis of cancer," *J. Biomed. Opt.*, Vol. 10, 2005.

[34] WuMei Lin, Xin Yuan, Powing Yuen, William I. Wei, Jonathan Sham, PengCheng Shi and Jianan Qu, "Classification of in vivo autofluorescence spectra using support vector machines," *J. Biomed. Opt.*, Vol. 9(1), 2004.

[35] Luyao Wang, Zhi Zhang, Jingjing Liu, Bo Jiang and Xiyao Duan, et al., "Classification of Hepatic Tissues from CT Images Based on Texture Features and Multiclass Support Vector Machines," *Lecture Notes in Computer Science Advances in Neural Networks*, Vol. 5552, 2009, pp. 374-381.

[36] Garcia, C., Moreno, J.A., "Application of support vector clustering to the visualization of medical images," IEEE International Symposium on Biomedical Imaging: Nano to Macro, Vol. 2, April 2004, pp. 1553-1556.

[37] Yu-Len Huang, Jeon-Hor Chen and Wu-Chung Shen, "Diagnosis of Hepatic Tumors With Texture Analysis in Nonenhanced Computed Tomography Images," *Academic Radiology*, Vol. 13(6), June 2006, pp. 713-720.

[38] Wen-Chun Yeh, Sheng-Wen Huang and Pai-Chi Li, "Liver fibrosis grade classification with B-mode ultrasound," *Ultrasound in Medicine and Biology*, Vol. 29(9), September 2003, pp. 1229-1235.

[39] Wail A.H. Mousa and Mohammad A. U. Khan, "Lung Nodule Classification Utilizing Support Vector Machines," Proceedings of the IEEE International Conference on Image Processing, Vol. 3, 2002, pp. 153-156.

[40] Luyin Zhao, Lilla Boroczky and K.P. Lee, "False positive reduction for lung nodule CAD using support vector machines and genetic algorithms," International Congress on Computer Assisted Radiology and Surgery, Vol. 1281, May 2005, pp. 1109-1114.

[41] Boroczky, L., Luyin Zhao, Lee, K.P., "Feature Subset Selection for Improving the Performance of False Positive Reduction in Lung Nodule CAD," *IEEE Transactions on Information Technology in Biomedicine*, Vol. 10(3), July 2006, pp. 504-511.

[42] Ian Chan, William Wells, III, Steven Haker, Jianqing Zhang, Kelly H. Zou, Clare M. C. Tempany, Robert V. Mulkern, and Stephan E. Maier, "Detection of prostate cancer by integration of line-scan diffusion, T2-mapping and T2-weighted magnetic resonance imaging; a multichannel statistical classifier," *Medical Physics*, Vol. 30(9), 2003.

[43] Yiqiang Zhan, Dinggang Shen, "Deformable segmentation of 3-D ultrasound prostate images using statistical texture matching method," *IEEE Transactions on Medical Imaging*, Vol. 25(3), March 2006, pp. 256-272.

[44] S S Mohamed, M M A Salama, M Kamel, E F El-Saadany, K Rizkalla and J Chin, "Prostate cancer multi-feature analysis using trans-rectal ultrasound images," *Physics in Medicine and Biology*, Vol. 50(15), 2005.

[45] Pieter C. Vos, Thomas Hambrock, Christina A. Hulsbergen - van de Kaa, Jurgen J. Fütterer, Jelle O. Barentsz, and Henkjan J. Huisman, "Computerized analysis of prostate lesions in the peripheral zone using dynamic contrast enhanced MRI," *Medical Physics*, Vol. 35, 2008.

[46] Lu, T. Van Gestel, J. A. K. Suykens, S. Van Huffel, I. Vergote and D. Timmerman, "Preoperative prediction of malignancy of ovarian tumors using least squares support vector machines," *Artificial Intelligence in Medicine*, Vol. 28(3), July 2003, pp. 281-306.

[47] Robert J. Zawadzki, Alfred R. Fuller, David F. Wiley, Bernd Hamann, Stacey S. Choi and John S. Werner, "Adaptation of a support vector machine algorithm for segmentation and visualization of retinal structures in volumetric optical coherence tomography data sets," *J. Biomed. Opt.*, Vol. 12, 2007.

[48] Ricci, E., Perfetti, R., "Retinal Blood Vessel Segmentation Using Line Operators and Support Vector Classification," *IEEE Transactions on Medical Imaging*, Vol. 26(10), October 2007, pp. 1357-1365.

[49] Christopher Bowd, Felipe A. Medeiros, Zuohua Zhang, Linda M. Zangwill, Jiucang Hao, Te-Won Lee, Terrence J. Sejnowski, Robert N. Weinreb, and Michael H. Goldbaum, "Relevance Vector Machine and Support Vector Machine Classifier Analysis of Scanning Laser Polarimetry Retinal Nerve Fiber Layer Measurements," *Investigative Ophthalmology and Visual Science*, 2005;46:1322-1329.

[50] Shuo Li, Thomas Fevens, Adam Krzyżak, and Song Li, "Automatic clinical image segmentation using pathological modeling, PCA and SVM," *Engineering Applications of Artificial Intelligence*, Vol. 19(4), June 2006, pp. 403-410.

[51] Stavros Tsantis, Dionisis Cavouras, Ioannis Kalatzis, Nikos Piliouras, Nikos Dimitropoulos and George Nikiforidis, "Development of a support vector machine-based image analysis system for assessing the thyroid nodule malignancy risk on ultrasound," *Ultrasound in Medicine and Biology*, Vol. 31(11), November 2005, pp. 1451-1459.

[52] Emre Çomak, Ahmet Arslan and İbrahim Türkoğlu, "A decision support system based on support vector machines for diagnosis of the heart valve diseases," *Computers in Biology and Medicine*, Vol. 37(1), January 2007, pp. 21-27.

[53] Kemal Polat, Sadık Kara, Fatma Latifoğlu and Salih Güneş, "Pattern Detection of Atherosclerosis from Carotid Artery Doppler Signals using Fuzzy Weighted Pre-Processing and Least Square Support Vector Machine (LSSVM)," *Annals of Biomedical Engineering*, Vol. 35(5), pp. 724-732.

[54] Ramirez, L., Durdle, N.G., Raso, V.J., Hill, D.L., "A support vector machines classifier to assess the severity of idiopathic scoliosis from surface topography," *IEEE Transaction on Information Technology in Biomedicine*, Vol. 10(1), January 2006, pp. 84-91.

[55] Ningning Guo, Libo Zeng and Qiongshui Wu, "A method based on multispectral imaging technique for White Blood Cell segmentation," *Computers in Biology and Medicine*, Vol. 37(1), January 2007, pp. 70-76.

[56] S. Li, T. Fevens and A. Krzyżak, "A SVM-based framework for autonomous volumetric medical image segmentation using hierarchical and coupled level sets," *Proceedings of the 18th International Congress on Computer Assisted Radiology and Surgery*, Vol. 1268, June 2004, pp. 207-212.

[57] Anna K. Jerebko, James D. Malley, Marek Franaszek and Ronald M. Summers, "Computer-aided polyp detection in CT colonography using an ensemble of support vector machines," *Proceedings of the 17th International Congress on Computer Assisted Radiology and Surgery*, Vol. 1256, June 2003, pp. 1019-1024.

[58] Md. Mahmudur Rahman, Bipin C. Desai and Prabir Bhattacharya, "Medical image retrieval with probabilistic multi-class support vector machine classifiers and adaptive similarity fusion," *Computerized Medical Imaging and Graphics*, Vol. 32(2), March 2008, pp. 95-108.

[59] T. W. Nattkemper, et al., "Evaluation of radiological features for breast tumour classification in clinical screening with machine learning methods," *Artificial Intelligence in Medicine*, vol. 34, 2005, pp. 129-139.

[60] J. Levman, D. Plewes, A. L. Martel, "Validation of SVM Based Classification of DCE-MRI Breast Lesions," *Proceedings of the Medical Image Computing and Computer Assisted Interventions (MICCAI) Workshop on the Challenges in Clinical Oncology*, 2006, pp. 8-16.

[61] J. Levman, et al., "Classification of dynamic contrast-enhanced magnetic resonance breast lesions by support vector machines," *IEEE Transactions on Medical Imaging*, vol. 27(5), 2008, pp. 688-696.

[62] Chuin-Mu Wang, *et al.*, "Classification for Breast MRI Using Support Vector Machine," *Proceedings of the IEEE International Conference on Computer and Information Technology*, July 2008, pp. 362-367.

[63] T. Twellmann, *et al.*, "Model-free Visualization of Suspicious Lesions in Breast MRI Based on Supervised and Unsupervised Learning," *Eng Appl Artif Intell.*, Vol. 21(2), 2008, pp. 129-140.

[64] T. F. Bathen, *et al.*, "Prediction of Long Term Breast Cancer Survival Using MR Metabolomics," *Proceedings of the International Symposium on Magnetic Resonance in Medicine*, May 2008, Toronto, Canada.

[65] J. Levman, P. Causer, E. Warner, D. Plewes, and A. Martel, "Evaluation of the diagnostic accuracy of computer-aided detection of breast cancer using MRI at different temporal resolutions," *Proceedings of the International Symposium on Magnetic Resonance in Medicine*, May 2008, Toronto, Canada.

[66] E. Warner, et al., "Surveillance of BRCA1 and BRCA2 mutation carriers with magnetic resonance imaging, ultrasound, mammography, and clinical breast examination," *Journal of the American Medical Association*, vol. 292, 2004, pp. 1317-1325.

[67] C. D. Lehman, et al., "MRI Evaluation of the Contralateral Breast in Women with Recently Diagnosed Breast Cancer," *New England Journal of Medicine*, vol.356(13), 2007, pp. 1295-1303.

[68] F. Pediconi, et al., "Contrast-enhanced MR Mammography for Evaluation of the Contralateral Breast in Patients with Diagnosed Unilateral Breast Cancer or High-Risk Lesions," *Radiology*, vol. 243(3), 2007, pp. 670-680.

[69] S. G. Lee, et al., "MR Imaging Screening of the Contralateral Breast in Patients with Newly Diagnosed Breast Cancer: Preliminary Results," *Radiology*, vol. 226(3), 2003, pp. 773-778.

[70] C.-C. Chang, C.-J. Lin. (Accessed Jan. 25, 2009). LIBSVM [Online]. http://www.csie.ntu.edu.tw/~cjlin/libsvm/

[71] J. Levman, "Pattern Recognition Applied to the Computer-Aided Detection and Diagnosis of Breast Cancer from Dynamic Contrast-Enhanced Magnetic Resonance Images," University of Toronto, January 2010. Available online: https://tspace.library.utoronto.ca/bitstream/1807/24361/1/Levman_Jacob_ED_201001_PhD_thesis.pdf

[72] J. Levman and A. L. Martel, "Computer-Aided Diagnosis of Breast Cancer from Magnetic Resonance Imaging Examinations by Custom Radial Basis Function Vector Machine," *Proceedings of the conference of the IEEE Engineering in Medicine and Biology Society*, September 2010.

[73] R. L. Greenman, R. E. Lenkinski, M. D. Schnall, "Bilateral imaging using separate interleaved 3D volumes and dynamically switched multiple receive coil arrays," *Magnetic Resonance in Medicine*, vol. 39, 1998, pp. 108-115.

[74] P. Causer, et al., "MR Imaging-guided Breast Localization System with Medial or Lateral Access," *Radiology*, vol.240(2), 2006, pp. 369-379.

[75] A. L. Martel, et al., "Evaluating an optical-flow based registration algorithm for contrast-enhanced magnetic resonance imaging of the breast," *Physics in Medicine and Biology,* vol. 52(13), 2007, pp. 3803-3816.

[76] M. A. Mazurowski, et al., "Decision optimization of case-based computer-aided decision systems using genetic algorithms with application to mammography," *Physics in Medicine and Biology*, vol. 53, 2008, pp. 895-908.

In: Support Vector Machines
Editor: Brandon H. Boyle

Chapter 2

A SVM-BASED REGRESSION MODEL TO STUDY THE AIR QUALITY IN THE URBAN AREA OF THE CITY OF OVIEDO (SPAIN)

P. J. García Nieto[1], E. F. Combarro[2], J. J. del Coz Díaz[3], F.P. Álvarez Rabanal[3] and E. Montañés[2]

[1]Department of Mathematics, University of Oviedo, Oviedo, Spain
[2]Department of Computer Science, University of Oviedo, Ovicdo, Spain
[3]Department of Construction, University of Oviedo, Gijón, Spain

ABSTRACT

This work presents a method of monthly air pollution modelling by using support vector machine (SVM) technique in the city of Oviedo (Spain). Hazardous air pollutants or toxic air contaminants refer to any substances that may cause or contribute to an increase in mortality or in serious illness, or that may pose a present or potential hazard to human health. In this research work, based on the observed data of NO, NO_2, CO, SO_2, O_3 and dust (PM_{10}) for the years 2006, 2007 and 2008, the support vector regression (SVR) technique is used to build the nonlinear dynamic model of the air quality in the urban area of the city of Oviedo (Spain). One aim of this model was to make an initial preliminary estimate of the dependence between primary and secondary pollutants in the city of Oviedo. A second aim was to determine the factors with the greatest bearing on air quality with a view to proposing health and lifestyle improvements. The United States National Ambient Air Quality Standards (NAAQS) establishes the limit values of the main pollutants in the atmosphere in order to ensure the health of healthy people. They are known as the *criteria pollutants*. This SVR model captures the main insight of statistical learning theory in order to obtain a good prediction of the dependence among the main pollutants in the city of Oviedo. Finally, on the basis of these numerical calculations using SVR, from the experimental data, conclusions of this work are exposed.

Keywords: Air quality; Pollutant substances; Machine learning; Support vector regression.

1. INTRODUCTION

Air pollution is one of the important environmental problems in metropolitan cities [1-4]. There are many air pollution indicators affecting human health [1,5]. The information of the meteorological pollution, such as CO, NO, NO_2, SO_2, O_3 and particulate matter (PM10) is more and more important due to their harmful effects on human health [1-2,6]. The automatic measurements of the concentration of these pollutants provide the instant registration of the harmful pollution just to inform or alarm the local inhabitants of the incoming danger. EU and many national environmental agencies have set standards and air quality guidelines for allowable levels of these pollutants in the air [7-9]. When the concentration levels of these indicators exceed the air quality guidelines, short term and chronic human health problems may occur [10]. Air is never perfectly clean [7]. Air pollution is a continuing threat to our health and welfare [9]. An average adult male requires about 13.5 kilograms of air each day compared with about 1.2 kilograms of food and 2 kilograms of water. Therefore, the cleanliness of air should certainly be as important to us as the cleanliness of our food and water. The aim of this research work is to construct a model for the averaged next month pollution that would be applicable for the use by the authority responsible for air pollution regulation in the appropriate region of the country. The use of the artificial neural networks [11] of multilayer perceptron (MLP) type as the model of pollution was exploited frequently in the last years [6, 12-18]. We propose here the system based on the support vector machine (SVM). We build the SVM networks for the prediction of each considered pollutant here: CO, NO, NO_2, SO_2, O_3 and dust. The support vector machine (SVM) [19-21] has been developing very fast in recent years. Like conventional feed-forward (FF) neural networks (NN), the SVM has been used by researchers to solve classification and regression problems [22-24]. Possessing similar universal approximation ability, SVR can also be used to model nonlinear processes, just as conventional NNs are. In this paper, the SVR is used as a new tool to build a model of the air quality in the city of Oviedo (Spain). Compared with the FF NN models, the SVR model has certain advantages. Firstly, training for the SVR results in a global optimum. This is due to the fact that SVR is formulated as a convex quadratic optimization problem for which there is a global optimum [19-21]. On the other hand, the training of FF NNs may become trapped at a local minimum. Thus, mathematically, the SVR model has more attractive properties than the NN model. The second advantage is that the design and training for the SVR model are relatively more straightforward and systematic as compared with those for the NN model. The third advantage is that it is relatively easier to achieve good generalization when using SVR as compared with NNs. Finally, the SVR is a type of model that is optimized so that prediction error and model complexity are simultaneously minimized. In short, the formulation of SVR captures the main insight of statistical learning theory in order to obtain a good generalization so that both training error and model complexity are controlled, by explaining the data with a simple model [22-24]. Oviedo is the capital city of the Principality of Asturias in northern Spain. It is also the name of the municipality that contains the city. Oviedo, which is the administrative and commercial centre of the region, also hosts the annual Prince of Asturias Awards. This prestigious event, held in the city's Campoamor Theatre, recognizes international achievement in eight categories. Oviedo University's international campus attracts many foreign scholars from all over the globe. The city of Oviedo has a population of 221,202 inhabitants. It covers a land area of

186.65 km², it has an altitude of 232 meters above sea level and a density of 1,185.12 inhabitants per square kilometer. The climate of Oviedo, as with the rest of northwest Spain, is more varied than that of southern parts of Spain. Summers are generally humid and warm, with considerable sunshine, but also some rain. Winters are cold with some very cold snaps and very rainy. The cold is especially felt in the mountains surrounding the city of Oviedo, where snow is present from October till May. Both rain and snow are regular weather features of Oviedo's winters. On the other hand, there is a coal power plant located seven kilometers south from the city of Oviedo: the Soto de Ribera's coal power plant (see Figure 1 below). Such plant provides most of the electrical energy used in the city of Oviedo. Figure 1. presents the geographical location of the three meteorological stations and the Soto de Ribera's coal-fired central power plant. The Soto de Ribera's coal power plant is located seven kilometers south from the city of Oviedo in the district of Ribera de Arriba and at an altitude of 126.50 meters above sea level. The data taking part in learning and testing have been collected within three years: from 2006 to 2008. The results of numerical experiments based on the application of SVR technique have confirmed good accuracy of monthly modelling for all considered pollutants. These detailed results will be presented and discussed in the paper.

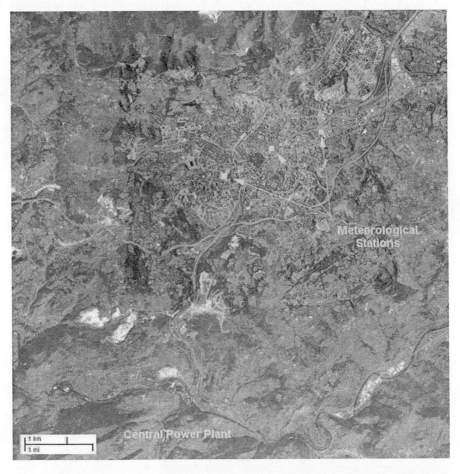

Figure 1. Photograph of the study area showing the location of the metereological stations in the city of Oviedo and the coal-fired power plant.

2. SOURCES AND TYPES OF AIR POLLUTION

Primary pollutants are emitted directly from identifiable sources. They pollute the air immediately upon being emitted. Secondary pollutants, in contrast, are produced in the atmosphere when certain chemical reactions take place among primary pollutants. The chemicals that make up smog are important examples. In some cases, the impact of primary pollutants on human health and the environment is less severe than the effects of the secondary pollutants they form [25-27].

2.1. Primary Pollutants

It accounts for nearly half of our pollution by weight. In addition to highway vehicles, this category includes trains, ships, and airplanes. Still, the tens of millions of cars and trucks on roads are, without a doubt, the greatest contributors in this category. A brief survey and description of the major primary pollutants is given below [28-31]:

- Aerosols or 'particulate matter': this is the general term used for a mixture of solid particle and liquid droplets found in the air. Some particles are large or dark enough to be seen as soot or smoke. Others are so small they can be detected only with an electron microscope. These particles, which come in a wide range of sizes, originate from many different stationary and mobile sources as well as from natural sources. Fine particles (particles less than 2.5 micrometers known as $PM_{2.5}$) result from fuel combustion from motor vehicles, power generation, and industrial facilities, as well as from residential fireplaces and wood stoves. Coarse particles (PM_{10}) are generally emitted from sources such as vehicles travelling on unpaved roads, material handling, and crushing and grinding operations, as well as windblown dust. Some particles are emitted directly from their sources, such as smokestacks and cars. In other cases, gases such as sulphur dioxide interact with other compounds in the air to form particles. Aerosols are frequently the most obvious form of air pollution because they reduce visibility and leave deposits of dirt on the surfaces with which they come in contact. Inhalable particulate matter includes both fine and coarse particles. These particles can accumulate in the respiratory system and are associated with numerous health effects [1, 29-30]. Exposure to coarse particles is primarily associated with the aggravation of respiratory conditions, such as asthma. Fine particles are most closely associated with such health effects as increased hospital admissions and emergency room visits for heart and lung disease, increased respiratory symptoms and disease, decreased lung function, and even premature death.
- Sulphur dioxide (SO_2): is a colourless and corrosive gas that originates largely from the combustion of sulphur-containing fuels, primarily coal and oil. Important sources include power plants, smelters, petroleum refineries, and pulp and paper mills. Once SO_2 is in the air, it is frequently transformed into sulphur trioxide (SO_3), which reacts with water vapour or water droplets to form sulphuric acid (H_2SO_4). It contributes to a serious environmental problem known as acid precipitation. High concentrations of

SO_2 can result in temporary breathing impairment for asthmatic children and adults who are active outdoors. Short-term exposures of asthmatic individuals to elevated SO_2 levels while at moderate exertion may result in reduced lung function that may be accompanied by such symptoms as wheezing, chest tightness, or shortness of breath [10]. Long-term exposures to high concentrations of SO_2 give place to respiratory illness and aggravation of existing cardiovascular disease.

- Nitrogen oxides: are gases that form during the high-temperature combustion of fuel when nitrogen in the fuel or the air reacts with oxygen. Power plants and motor vehicles are the primary sources. These gases also form naturally when certain bacteria oxidize nitrogen-containing compounds. The initial product formed is nitric oxide (NO). When NO oxidizes further in the atmosphere, nitrogen dioxide (NO_2) forms. Commonly, the general term NO_x is used to describe these gases. Nitrogen dioxide has a distinctive reddish, brown colour that frequently tints polluted city air and reduces visibility. When concentrations are high, NO_2 can also contribute to lung and heart problems. When air is humid, NO_2 reacts with water vapour to form nitric acid (HNO_3). Like sulphuric acid, this corrosive substance also contributes to the acid-rain problem. Moreover, because nitrogen oxides are highly reactive gases, they play an important part in the formation of smog [7-9].

- Carbon monoxide (CO): is a colorless, odorless, and poisonous gas produced by incomplete burning of carbon in fuels. It is the most abundant primary pollutant, with about two-thirds of the emissions coming from transportation sources, mainly highway vehicles. Carbon monoxide enters the bloodstream through the lungs and reduces oxygen delivery to the body's organs and tissues. In small amounts, it causes drowsiness, slows reflexes, and impairs judgment. If concentrations are sufficiently high, CO can cause death [10,30].

2.2. Secondary Pollutants

Recall that secondary pollutants are not emitted directly into the air, but form in the atmosphere when reactions take place among primary pollutants. Many reactions that produce secondary pollutants are triggered by strong sunlight and so are called photochemical reactions.

When certain volatile organic compounds are present, the result is the formation of a number of undesirable secondary products that are very reactive, irritating, and toxic. Collectively, this noxious mixture of gases and particles is called photochemical smog. The major component in photochemical smog is *ozone* [28-31]. The negative effects of ozone are well documented [32-34].

Short-term exposure to elevated levels of ozone causes eye and lung irritations. Moreover, there is mounting evidence of chronic effects from longer term or recurring exposures to more moderate levels.

Because the reactions that create ozone are stimulated by strong sunlight, the formation of this pollutant is limited to daylight hours. Peaks occur in the afternoon following a series of hot, sunny, calm days. As we might expect, ozone levels are highest during the warmer summer months.

Table 1. National ambient air quality standards by United States Environmental Protection Agency (USEPA) [10]

Pollutant	Maximum allowable concentrations
Carbon monoxide (CO)	
8-hour average	9 ppm (10 mg/m^3)
1-hour average	35 ppm (40 mg/m^3)
Nitrogen dioxide (NO$_2$)	
Annual arithmetic mean	0.053 ppm (100 μ g/m^3)
Ozone (O$_3$)	
1-hour average	0.12 ppm (235 μ g/m^3)
8-hour average	0.08 ppm (157 μ g/m^3)
Particulate <10 micrometers (PM$_{10}$)	
Annual arithmetic mean	50 μ g/m^3
24-hour average	150 μ g/m^3
Particulate <2.5 micrometers (PM$_{2.5}$)	
Annual arithmetic mean	15 μ g/m^3
24-hour average	65 μ g/m^3
Sulphur dioxide (SO$_2$)	
Annual arithmetic mean	0.03 ppm (80 μ g/m^3)
24-hour average	0.14 ppm (365 μ g/m^3)

2.3. Trends in Air Quality

The Clean Air Act of 1970 mandated the setting of standards for four of the primary pollutants (aerosols, sulphur dioxide, carbon monoxide, and nitrogen oxides) as well as the secondary pollutant ozone. At the time, these five pollutants were recognized as being the most widespread and objectionable. Today, with the addition of lead, they are known as the criteria pollutants and are covered by the United States National Ambient Air Quality Stardards (see Table 1 below) [7-9,28-31]. The primary standard for each pollutant shown in Table 1. is based on the highest level that can be tolerated by humans without noticeable ill effects, minus a 10 to 50 percent margin for safety.

3. MATHEMATICAL MODEL

The SVM is a learning method with a theoretical root in statistical learning theory [22-24]. The SVM was originally developed for classification, and was later generalized to solve regression problems [19-21,35]. This method is called support vector regression (SVR). The model produced by support vector classification only depends on a subset of the training data, because the cost function for building the model does not care about training points that lie beyond the margin. Analogously, the model produced by SVR only depends on a subset of the training data, because the cost function for building the model ignores any training data that are close (within a threshold ε) to the model prediction. The basic idea of SVR is briefly described here. Instead of attempting to classify new unseen variables $\hat{\vec{x}}$ into one of two categories $\hat{y} = \pm 1$, we now wish to predict a real-valued output for y' so that our training data is of the form $\{\vec{x}_i, y_i\}$, where $i = 1, 2, ..., L$, $y \in \Re$, $\vec{x} \in \Re^D$ [19-21,35]:

$$y_i = \vec{w} \cdot \vec{x}_i + b \tag{1}$$

The regression SVM will use a more sophisticated penalty function, not allocating a penalty if the predicted value y_i is less than a distance ε away from the actual value t_i, i.e. if $|t_i - y_i| < \varepsilon$. Referring to Figure 2, the region bound by $y_i \pm \varepsilon$ $\forall i$ is called an ε-insensitive tube. The other modification to the penalty function is that output variables which are outside the tube are given one of two slack variable penalties depending on whether they lie above (ξ^+) or below (ξ^-) the tube (where $\xi^+ > 0, \xi^- > 0$ $\forall i$):

$$t_i \leq y_i + \varepsilon + \xi^+ \tag{2}$$

$$t_i \geq y_i - \varepsilon - \xi^- \tag{3}$$

The error function for SVM regression can then be written as [21,24,35]:

$$C \sum_{i=1}^{L} \left(\xi_i^+ + \xi_i^- \right) + \frac{1}{2} \|\vec{w}\|^2 \tag{4}$$

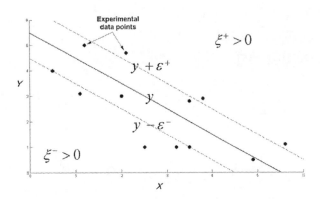

Figure 2. Regression with ε − insensitive tube.

This needs to be minimized subject to the constraints $\xi^+ \geq 0, \xi^- \geq 0$ $\forall i$ and (2) and (3). In order to do this we introduce Lagrange multipliers $\alpha_i^+ \geq 0, \alpha_i^- \geq 0, \mu_i^+ \geq 0, \mu_i^- \geq 0$ $\forall i$:

$$L_P = C\sum_{i=1}^{L}\left(\xi_i^+ + \xi_i^-\right) + \frac{1}{2}\|\vec{w}\|^2 - \sum_{i=1}^{L}\left(\mu_i^+\xi_i^+ + \mu_i^-\xi_i^-\right) - \sum_{i=1}^{L}\alpha_i^+\left(\varepsilon + \xi_i^+ + y_i - t_i\right)$$
$$-\sum_{i=1}^{L}\alpha_i^-\left(\varepsilon + \xi_i^- - y_i + t_i\right)$$

$$(5)$$

Substituting for y_i, differentiating with respect to $\vec{w}$, b, ξ^+ and ξ^- and setting the derivatives to 0 [19-20,24,35]:

$$\frac{\partial L_P}{\partial \vec{w}} = 0 \Rightarrow \vec{w} = \sum_{i=1}^{L}\left(\alpha_i^+ - \alpha_i^-\right)\vec{x}_i \tag{6}$$

$$\frac{\partial L_P}{\partial b} = 0 \Rightarrow \sum_{i=1}^{L}\left(\alpha_i^+ - \alpha_i^-\right) = 0 \tag{7}$$

$$\frac{\partial L_P}{\partial \xi_i^+} = 0 \Rightarrow C = \alpha_i^+ + \mu_i^+ \tag{8}$$

$$\frac{\partial L_P}{\partial \xi_i^-} = 0 \Rightarrow C = \alpha_i^- + \mu_i^- \tag{9}$$

Substituting (6) and (7) in, we now need to maximize L_D with respect to α_i^+ and α_i^- ($\alpha_i^+ \geq 0$, $\alpha_i^- \geq 0$ $\forall i$) where:

$$L_D = \sum_{i=1}^{L}\left(\alpha_i^+ - \alpha_i^-\right)t_i - \varepsilon\sum_{i=1}^{L}\left(\alpha_i^+ - \alpha_i^-\right) - \frac{1}{2}\sum_{i,j}\left(\alpha_i^+ - \alpha_i^-\right)\left(\alpha_j^+ - \alpha_j^-\right)\vec{x}_i \cdot \vec{x}_j \tag{10}$$

Using $\mu_i^+ \geq 0$ and $\mu_i^- \geq 0$ together with (8) and (9) means that $\alpha_i^+ \leq C$ and $\alpha_i^- \leq C$. We therefore need to find [19-21,35]:

$$\max_{\alpha^+,\alpha^-}\left[\sum_{i=1}^{L}\left(\alpha_i^+ - \alpha_i^-\right)t_i - \varepsilon\sum_{i=1}^{L}\left(\alpha_i^+ - \alpha_i^-\right) - \frac{1}{2}\sum_{i,j}\left(\alpha_i^+ - \alpha_i^-\right)\left(\alpha_j^+ - \alpha_j^-\right)\vec{x}_i \cdot \vec{x}_j\right] \tag{11}$$

such that $0 \leq \alpha_i^+ \leq C$, $0 \leq \alpha_i^- \leq C$ and $\sum_{i=1}^{L}\left(\alpha_i^+ - \alpha_i^-\right) = 0$ $\forall i$.

Substituting (6) into (1), new predictions y' can be found using:

$$\hat{y} = \sum_{i=1}^{L}\left(\alpha_i^+ - \alpha_i^-\right)\vec{x}_i \cdot \hat{\vec{x}} + b \tag{12}$$

A set S of Support Vectors $\vec{x}_s$ can be created by finding the indices i where $0 < \alpha < C$ and $\xi_i^+ = 0$ (or $\xi_i^- = 0$). This gives us:

$$b = \vec{t}_s - \varepsilon - \sum_{m \in S}^{L} \left(\alpha_m^+ - \alpha_m^- \right) \vec{x}_m \cdot \vec{x}_s \tag{13}$$

As before it is better to average over all the indices i in S [24,35]:

$$b = \frac{1}{N_s} \sum_{s \in S} \left[t_s - \epsilon - \sum_{m \in S}^{L} \left(\alpha_m^+ - \alpha_m^- \right) \vec{x}_m \cdot \vec{x}_s \right] \tag{14}$$

3.1. Non-Linear Support Vector Machines

When applying our SVM to linearly separable data we have started by creating a matrix H from the dot product of our input variables [22-24,35]:

$$H_{ij} = y_i y_j k \left(\vec{x}_i, \vec{x}_j \right) = \vec{x}_i \cdot \vec{x}_j = \vec{x}_i^T \vec{x}_j \tag{15}$$

$k \left(\vec{x}_i, \vec{x}_j \right)$ is an example of a family of functions called *kernel functions* ($k \left(\vec{x}_i, \vec{x}_j \right) = \vec{x}_i^T \vec{x}_j$ being known as a linear kernel). The set of kernel functions is composed of variants of Eq. (16) in that they are all based on calculating inner products of two vectors. This means that if the functions can be recast into a higher dimensionality space by some potentially non-linear feature mapping function $\vec{x} \mapsto \phi(\vec{x})$, only inner products of the mapped inputs in the feature space need be determined without us needing to explicitly calculate ϕ. The reason that this *kernel trick* is useful is that there are many regression problems that are not linearly regressable in the space of the inputs $\vec{x}$, which might be in a higher dimensionality feature space given a suitable mapping $\vec{x} \mapsto \phi(\vec{x})$.

Referring to Figure 3, if we define our kernel to be [24,35]:

$$k \left(\vec{x}_i, \vec{x}_j \right) = e^{-\left(\frac{\| \vec{x}_i - \vec{x}_j \|^2}{2\sigma^2} \right)} \tag{16}$$

Then a data set that it not linearly separable in the two dimensional data space (as in the left hand side of Figure 3) is separable in the non-linear feature space (right hand side of Figure 3) defined implicitly by this non-linear kernel function known as *radial basis function*. Other popular kernels for classification and regression are the *polynomial kernel* [24,35]:

$$k \left(\vec{x}_i, \vec{x}_j \right) = \left(\vec{x}_i \cdot \vec{x}_j + a \right)^b \tag{17}$$

and the *sigmoidal kernel* [19,24,35]:

$$k\left(\vec{x}_i, \vec{x}_j\right) = \tanh\left(a\vec{x}_i \cdot \vec{x}_j - b\right)$$ (18)

where a and b are parameters defining the kernel's behaviour.

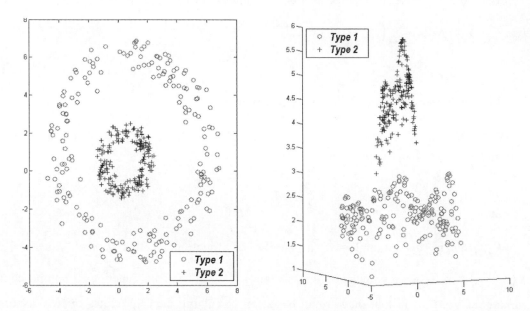

Figure 3. Dichotomous data re-mapped using radial basis functions (RBF) kernel.

In summary, in order to use an SVM to solve a regression problem on data that is not linearly separable, we need to first choose a kernel and relevant parameters which you expect might map the non-linearly separable data into a feature space where it is linearly separable. This is more of an art than an exact science and can be achieved empirically, e.g. by trial and error. Sensible kernels to start with are the radial basis, polynomial and sigmoidal kernels. Therefore, the first step consists of choosing our kernel and hence the mapping $\vec{x} \mapsto \phi\left(\vec{x}\right)$.

4. EXPERIMENTAL DATA SET

The Section of Industry and Energy from the government of Asturias has three meteorological stations distributed throughout the city of Oviedo (see Figure 1. above). These three stations measure every fifteen minutes the following primary and secondary pollutants: sulphur dioxide (SO_2), nitrogen oxides (NO and NO_2), carbon monoxide (CO), particulate matter less than 10 micrometers (PM_{10}) and ozone (O_3). This data set is collected, processed and delivered on average for the entire city every month. Therefore, we have data for the pollutants listed above each month from January 2006 to December 2008. This data set is shown in Table 2.

Table 2. Monthly average air pollution concentrations in Oviedo from January 2006 to December 2008

Month of year	SO2 (μ g m-3)	NO (μ g m-3)	NO2 (μ g m-3)	CO (mg m-3)	PM10 (μ g m-3)	O3 (μ g m-3)
Jan. 2006	20.186	28.710	31.427	0.592	50.231	13.298
Feb. 2006	22.661	31.429	36.503	0.580	67.655	11.821
Month of year	SO2 (μ g m-3)	NO (μ g m-3)	NO2 (μ g m-3)	CO (mg m-3)	PM10 (μ g m-3)	O3 (μ g m-3)
Mar. 2006	17.212	20.890	33.723	0.549	53.285	14.936
Apr. 2006	12.983	14.892	29.475	0.512	56.114	16.658
May. 2006	23.239	14.763	33.102	0.445	67.906	17.788
Jun. 2006	22.175	15.700	29.008	0.368	67.725	46.444
Jul. 2006	21.452	15.546	26.530	0.324	59.844	43.930
Aug. 2006	21.944	15.965	25.618	0.354	61.360	43.586
Sep. 2006	20.900	21.394	31.039	0.457	54.444	37.625
Oct. 2006	26.266	45.941	38.742	0.621	59.094	26.505
Nov. 2006	27.828	44.967	39.108	0.636	54.228	24.572
Dec. 2006	51.202	73.624	53.204	0.851	71.344	17.411
Jan. 2007	41.922	69.798	52.841	0.856	71.699	22.454
Feb. 2007	27.830	36.857	41.220	0.606	58.973	35.571
Mar. 2007	25.500	28.105	43.976	0.593	66.218	38.339
Apr. 2007	26.692	23.894	44.192	0.540	66.711	52.597
May. 2007	18.409	17.680	35.304	0.406	51.879	53.847
Jun. 2007	19.406	15.200	34.144	0.385	62.275	46.831
Jul. 2007	15.516	12.863	28.565	0.356	60.806	41.411
Aug. 2007	13.177	13.277	27.755	0.310	54.395	45.258
Sep. 2007	19.517	24.583	36.286	0.470	58.125	37.392
Oct. 2007	22.145	22.578	23.009	0.415	46.583	36.215
Nov. 2007	25.125	37.336	34.850	0.551	51.278	29.594
Dec. 2007	24.051	52.984	38.551	0.619	56.258	31.573
Jan. 2008	22.766	36.949	36.906	0.586	51.164	35.148
Feb. 2008	25.655	32.491	37.711	0.526	58.634	37.015
Mar. 2008	23.868	26.992	39.575	0.537	74.860	39.266
Apr. 2008	13.558	16.017	30.558	0.459	52.922	58.700
May. 2008	18.734	17.661	29.831	0.403	52.847	56.815
Jun. 2008	23.597	16.042	30.808	0.374	57.453	46.950
Jul. 2008	23.508	16.511	28.350	0.346	52.078	43.806
Aug. 2008	33.925	17.737	36.855	0.431	69.274	46.468
Sep. 2008	33.458	21.625	40.125	0.410	52.458	41.325
Oct. 2008	20.180	24.374	34.489	0.339	41.745	33.530
Nov. 2008	38.039	52.894	44.586	0.442	53.006	23.647
Dec. 2008	30.387	49.024	41.903	0.458	50.516	27.089

Then, we can study the trend in emissions of the preceding pollutants in the years 2006, 2007 and 2008 [7-10,26-31]. In the first place, Figure 4. shows the sulphur dioxide emissions each month during the years 2006, 2007 and 2008. It is possible to observe that the emission peaks occurring during late autumn and early winter, namely from November to February each year, reaching the maximum emission during the Christmas of 2006: 51.20 $\mu g/m^3$. Similarly minimum emissions (13.17 $\mu g/m^3$ in august 2007) occur during the summer months, because there are lower power consumption and less traffic in the city. This trend is general throughout the years studied, and it is within the logic. From the point of standard air quality view, following the USEPA Air Quality Standards (see Table 1 above), the maximum allowable concentration of SO_2 expressed as annual arithmetic mean is 80 $\mu g/m^3$. The annual arithmetic means for this gas during the years 2006, 2007 and 2008 were 24.0, 23.27 and 24.31 $\mu g/m^3$ respectively. Therefore, the emissions of this gas were below the maximum permitted and meet air quality standards for a healthy person during these three years, including emission peaks.

Secondly, Figure 5. shows the nitric oxide emissions each month during the years 2006, 2007 and 2008. It is also possible to observe again that the emission peaks occurring during late autumn and early winter, reaching the maximum emission in December 2006: 73.62 $\mu g/m^3$. Similarly minimum emissions (12.86 $\mu g/m^3$ in July 2007) occur during the summer months. The same trend that for the previous gas is observed throughout the years studied. Although the initial product of the combustion is nitric oxide (NO), this gas is rapidly oxidized and converted to NO_2. Its residence time in the atmosphere is very short and the USEPA Air Quality Standards does not consider it.

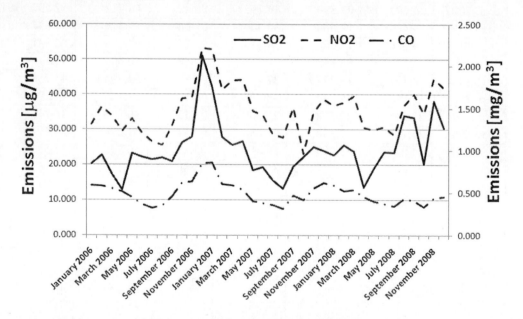

Figure 4. Monthly trend of sulphur dioxide (SO_2), nitrogen dioxide (NO_2) and carbon monoxide (CO) emissions during the years 2006, 2007 and 2008 in the city of Oviedo.

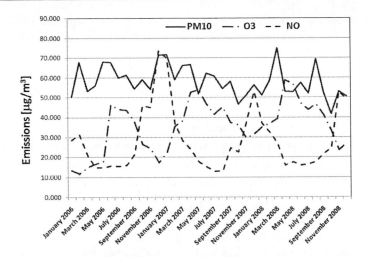

Figure 5. Monthly trend of nitric oxide (NO), particulate matter (PM$_{10}$) and ozone (O$_3$) emissions during the years 2006, 2007 and 2008 in the city of Oviedo.

Thirdly, the nitrogen dioxide (NO$_2$) emissions each month during the years 2006, 2007 and 2008 are also shown in Figure 4. Note that the emission peak occurring from November to February each year, reaching the maximum emission in December 2006: 53.20 µg/m^3. Similarly minimum emissions occur in August 2006 and October 2007 with values of 25.61 µg/m^3 and 23.00 µg/m^3 respectively. Following the USEPA Air Quality Standards (see Table 1 above), the maximum allowable concentration of NO$_2$ expressed as annual arithmetic mean is 100 µg/m^3. The annual arithmetic means for this gas during the years 2006, 2007 and 2008 were 33.96, 36.72 and 35.97 µg/m^3 respectively. Thus, the nitrogen dioxide (NO$_2$) emissions are also below the maximum permitted and meet air quality standards for a healthy person during these three years, including emission peaks. It is also important to highlight a certain flattening of the emissions of this gas in time.

Fourthly, Figure 4. also shows the carbon monoxide (CO) emissions each month during the years 2006, 2007 and 2008. The main emission peak occurs in December 2006 and January 2007 with a value of 0.85 mg/m^3. Similarly minimum emissions occur during the summer months: 0.32 mg/m^3 in July 2006, 0.31 mg/m^3 in August 2007 and 0.35 mg/m^3 in July 2008, respectively. This trend is quasi- sinusoidal with peaks and valleys, although the height of the peaks and valleys appears to be decreasing in time. Similarly, following the USEPA Air Quality Standards (see Table 1 above), the maximum allowable concentration of CO expressed as annual arithmetic mean is 3.33 mg/m^3. The annual arithmetic means for this gas during the years 2006, 2007 and 2008 were 0.52, 0.50 and 0.44 mg/m^3 respectively. Hence the emissions of CO were below the highest level that can be tolerated by humans according to USEPA Air Quality Standards during these three years, including emission peaks.

Fifthly, Figure 5. shows the particulate matter PM$_{10}$ emissions each month during the years 2006, 2007 and 2008. It is possible to observe that the emission peaks occur in December 2006, January 2007, March 2008 and August 2008 with values 71.34 µg/m^3, 71.70 µg/m^3, 74.86 µg/m^3 and 69.27 µg/m^3, respectively. However, the quasi-sinusoidal trend is lost here in general in case of the particulate matter. All aerosol emissions are kept in a band or range of concentrations between approximately 50 and 70 µg/m^3, regardless of the month and the season. From the point of standard air quality view, following the USEPA Air Quality Standards (see Table 1 above), the maximum allowable concentration of PM_{10} expressed as annual arithmetic mean is 50 $\mu g/m^3$. The annual arithmetic means for this pollutant during the years 2006, 2007 and 2008 were 60.27, 58.77 and 55.58 $\mu g/m^3$ respectively. Therefore, the aerosol emissions are above the allowable maximum for a healthy person during these three years, including emission peaks. This behaviour can give place to serious health problems for the population such as chronic diseases and deaths.

Figure 5. also shows the ozone emissions each month during the years 2006, 2007 and 2008. Note that there is a variation of the ozone concentration in the form of an oscillating sawtooth in time, reaching maximum values during summer months: 46.44 $\mu g/m^3$ in June 2006, 53.85 $\mu g/m^3$ in May 2007, and 58.7 $\mu g/m^3$ in April 2008. This trend is general throughout the years studied, since ozone is associated with photochemical reactions, and these ones require the presence of strong sunlight. The Clean Air Act directs the USEPA to set National Ambient Air Quality Standards for several pollutants, including ground-level ozone, and cities out of compliance with these standards are required to take steps to reduce their levels.

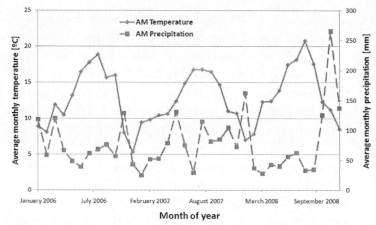

Figure 6. Meteorological data: average monthly temperature and average monthly precipitation in the city of Oviedo from January 2006 to December 2008.

In May 2008, the USEPA lowered its ozone standard from 80 $\mu g/m^3$ to 75 $\mu g/m^3$. This proved controversial, since the Agency's own scientists and advisory board had recommended lowering the standard to 60 $\mu g/m^3$, and the World Health Organization recommends 51 $\mu g/m^3$. Many public health and environmental groups also supported the 60 $\mu g/m^3$ standard. The annual arithmetic means for this gas in the city of Oviedo during the years 2006, 2007 and 2008 were 26.21, 39.26 and 40.81 $\mu g/m^3$ respectively. Therefore, the emissions of this gas were below the maximum permitted and meet air quality standards during these three years, including emission peaks. In April 2008, a peak was reached very close to the allowable limit. This fact was very dangerous for the health of the population of Oviedo. There is a great deal of evidence to show that high concentrations of ozone, created by high concentrations of pollution and daylight UV rays at the Earth's surface, can harm lung function and irritate the respiratory system. Exposure to ozone and the pollutants that produce it has been linked to premature death, asthma, bronchitis, heart attack, and other cardiopulmonary problems. According to scientists of the United States Environmental

Protection Agency (USEPA), susceptible people can be adversely affected by ozone levels as low as 40 $\mu g/m^3$. Finally, in order to explain the peaks of SO_2, NO_2, NO and CO emissions during the period November 2006 to January 2007, it is necessary to take into account the role of meteorology. In this sense, Figure 6. shows the average monthly temperature as well as the average monthly precipitation in the city of Oviedo from January 2006 to December 2008. It is possible to observe that the temperature during this period (November 2006 to January 2007) is lower than in the other years. This means that the electricity and heating consumptions were greater and therefore the emissions of these pollutants were also increased in this period.

5. METHODOLOGY

In order to obtain a relationship of dependency among the concentrations of the six pollutants measured, a regression analysis was carried out. The results corresponding to this analysis are indicated below. In this work the SVM technique with several types of kernels is applied, working in the regression mode [21-22] as model of pollution. This choice is accepted after trying other neural type solutions, like the MLP structure [11]. The main advantage of the SVM over MLP is its good generalization ability, acquired at relatively small number of learning data and at large number of input nodes (high dimensional problem). Due to very specific problem formulation the learning task is simplified to the solution of the quadratic problem of a single minimum point (global minimum). The most known kernel functions used in practice are radial (Gaussian), polynomial, spline or even sigmoidal functions [21-22]. The most important is the choice of coefficients ε and C. The constant ε determines the margin within which the error is neglected. The smaller its value the higher accuracy of learning is required, and more support vectors will be found by the algorithm. The regularization constant C is the weight, determining the balance between the complexity of the network, characterized by the weight vector, and the error of approximation, measured by the slack variables and the value of ε. For the normalized input signals the value of ε is usually adjusted in the range $10^{-3} - 10^{-2}$, and C is much bigger than 1. Support vector machines (SVMs) are a set of related supervised learning methods used for classification and regression. A support vector machine constructs a hyperplane or set of hyperplanes in a high-dimensional space, which can be used for classification, regression or other tasks. Intuitively, a good separation is achieved by the hyperplane that has the largest distance to the nearest training datapoints of any class (so-called functional margin), since in general the larger the margin the lower the generalization error of the classifier. With respect to the implementation of the method, the parameters of the maximum-margin hyperplane are derived by solving the optimization. There exist several specialized algorithms for quickly solving the QP problem that arises from SVMs, mostly reliant on heuristics for breaking the problem down into smaller, more-manageable chunks. A common method for solving the QP problem is the Platt's Sequential Minimal Optimization (SMO) algorithm [19-24], which breaks the problem down into two-dimensional sub-problems that may be solved analytically, eliminating the need for a numerical optimization algorithm such as conjugate gradient methods. Another approach is to use an interior point method that uses Newton-like iterations to find a solution of the Karush-Kuhn-Tucker conditions of the primal and dual problems.

Instead of solving a sequence of broken down problems, this approach directly solves the problem as a whole [36]. To avoid solving a linear system involving the large kernel matrix, a row rank approximation to the matrix is often used to use the kernel trick. Cross-validation is a technique for assessing how the results of a statistical analysis will generalize to an independent data set [37-38]. It is mainly used in settings where the goal is prediction, and one wants to estimate how accurately a predictive model will perform in practice. One round of cross-validation involves partitioning a sample of data into complementary subsets, performing the analysis on one subset (called the training set), and validating the analysis on the other subset (called the validation set or testing set). To reduce variability, multiple rounds of cross-validation are performed using different partitions, and the validation results are averaged over the rounds. In K-fold cross-validation, the original sample is randomly partitioned into K subsamples. Of the K subsamples, a single subsample is retained as the validation data for testing the model, and the remaining $K-1$ subsamples are used as training data. The cross-validation process is then repeated K times (the folds), with each of the K subsamples used exactly once as the validation data. The K results from the folds then can be averaged (or otherwise combined) to produce a single estimation. The advantage of this method over repeated random sub-sampling is that all observations are used for both training and validation, and each observation is used for validation exactly once. 10-fold cross-validation is commonly used [37-38].

6. RESULTS AND DISCUSSION

Taking into account that the relationship among pollutants is highly nonlinear and very complex, it was necessary to use more accurate analysis tools based on statistical learning such as the above mentioned support vector regression (SVR) and the well-known technique of the multilayer perceptron (MLP) [11-13]. For the all normalized data samples we have used a tolerance value $\varepsilon = 0.01$. Therefore, taking several types of kernels is as follows [19-24, 35-36]:

> The SMO model with linear kernel: The concentrations of pollutants are normalized.

$$C_{SO_2} = 0.3742C_{NO} + 0.341C_{NO_2} - 0.1116C_{CO} + 0.1899C_{PM} - 0.0265C_{O_3} - 0.0773$$
$$C_{NO} = 0.1798C_{SO_2} + 0.194C_{NO_2} + 0.3683C_{CO} - 0.1188C_{PM} - 0.0539C_{O_3} - 0.0089$$
$$C_{NO_2} = 0.4516C_{SO_2} + 0.3331C_{NO} + 0.299C_{CO} + 0.1335C_{PM} + 0.0059C_{O_3} + 0.2108$$
$$C_{CO} = -0.1789C_{SO_2} + 0.5842C_{NO} + 0.2528C_{NO_2} + 0.1246C_{PM} - 0.0676C_{O_3} + 0.0321 \quad (19)$$
$$C_{PM} = 0.4434C_{SO_2} - 0.281C_{NO} + 0.3073C_{NO_2} + 0.3407C_{CO} + 0.0635C_{O_3} + 0.0545$$
$$C_{O_3} = -0.2777C_{SO_2} - 0.5779C_{NO} - 0.0047C_{NO_2} - 0.3535C_{CO} + 0.215C_{PM} + 0.4992$$

Table 3. Coefficient correlations corresponding to SMO models with linear, quadratic, RBF and PUK kernel and multilayer perceptron (MLP) of the six pollutants measured in the meteorological stations located in the city of Oviedo

Technique/pollutant	SO2	NO	NO2	CO	PM10	O3
SMO linear kernel	0.8144	0.8435	0.8617	0.8184	0.6698	0.5572
SMO quad. kernel	0.8202	0.8921	0.8704	0.7921	0.6991	0.5330
SMO RBF kernel	0.8088	0.8479	0.8619	0.8101	0.6552	0.5493
SMO PUK kernel	0.8248	0.9088	0.9018	0.8336	0.7080	0.6237
Multilayer perceptron (MLP)	0.7203	0.8952	0.8819	0.7457	0.6342	0.5159

Table 4. Mean absolute error (MAE), root mean squared error (RMSE), relative absolute error (RAE) and root relative squared error (RRSE) corresponding to SMO models with linear, quadratic, RBF and PUK kernel, and multilayer perceptron (MLP) of the six pollutants measured in the meteorological stations located in the city of Oviedo

Technique	Type of Error	SO_2	NO	NO_2	CO	PM_{10}	O_3
SMO linear kernel	MAE	6.7769	8.3540	4.6409	0.0806	9.9601	11.1971
	RMSE	9.4547	13.6439	6.0047	0.1080	13.1714	14.1691
	RAE	55.0915	51.1073	49.7634	55.9775	72.2458	77.7730
	RRSE	59.1431	57.1136	50.8522	57.7103	74.7004	83.0093
Technique	Type of Error	SO_2	NO	NO_2	CO	PM_{10}	O_3
SMO quadratic kernel	MAE	6.6128	6.931	4.5054	0.0854	9.4854	11.5416
	RMSE	9.2956	10.8146	5.821	0.1146	12.7137	14.4333
	RAE	53.7569	42.402	48.3105	59.3383	68.8028	80.1664
	RRSE	58.1481	45.2699	49.2971	61.2231	72.1045	84.5569
SMO RBF kernel	MAE	6.8705	8.3915	4.7161	0.0840	10.1383	11.3834
	RMSE	9.7596	14.2428	6.0189	0.1107	13.6301	14.2804
	RAE	55.8519	51.3369	50.5696	58.3865	73.5381	79.0675
	RRSE	61.0504	59.6205	50.9727	59.1258	77.3018	83.6612
SMO PUK kernel	MAE	6.4571	6.1281	3.9251	0.0748	9.4624	10.1365
	RMSE	9.123	9.9771	5.1055	0.1035	12.5021	13.4015
	RAE	52.4915	37.4899	42.0874	51.9527	68.6356	70.4067
	RRSE	57.0682	41.7641	43.2375	55.2749	70.9047	78.5119
Multilayer perceptron (MLP)	MAE	8.9386	7.2569	4.4816	0.102	10.7088	11.511
	RMSE	11.6342	10.6594	5.6912	0.1298	13.7977	14.8296
	RAE	72.6645	44.3958	48.0556	70.8714	77.6763	79.9536
	RRSE	72.7772	44.6204	48.1976	69.3685	78.2524	86.8788

Since the correlation coefficient of ozone (O_3) is low with respect to the coefficients of the other pollutants (see Table 3 above) and ozone is always accompanied by a smaller factor in terms of fitting (see Eq. (19) above), we can conclude that the concentration of this pollutant has little influence on the concentrations of other pollutants, that is to say, the concentration of this pollutant is almost independent. Less marked, the particulate matter

PM$_{10}$ has similar behavior to ozone. Furthermore, the root mean squared errors for the particulate matter PM$_{10}$ and ozone (O$_3$) are greater than the remaining pollutants analyzed in this work (see Table 4 above). This trend will be kept in all the remaining SMO models with different kernels.

> ➢ The SMO model with quadratic kernel: Tables 3 and 4 show the coefficient correlations and root mean squared errors for this kind of kernel. Some correlation coefficients are greater than the SMO model with linear kernel (for SO$_2$, NO, NO$_2$ and PM$_{10}$) and the remaining ones (CO and O$_3$) are slightly smaller. The results are shown in Table 3 above.

> ➢ The SMO model with radial basis functions (RBF) kernel: In the same way, Tables 3 and 4 show the coefficient correlations and root mean squared errors for this kind of kernel. On the one hand, the correlation coefficients are lower for this kernel than the SMO model with linear kernel except for NO and NO$_2$. On the other hand, the root mean squared errors are greater than the SMO model with linear kernel. Therefore, this fitting is worse than the other fittings. We can conclude that the SMO model with RBF kernel is the worst one.

> ➢ The SMO model equipped with the recently proposed Pearson VII universal (PUK) kernel [39]: the PUK function has the flexibility to change easily from Gaussian into a Lorentzian shape and into intermediate shapes as well. This flexibility results in a higher mapping power for PUK in comparison to the commonly used linear, polynomial and RBF kernel functions. The PUK kernel contains two parameters, namely σ and ω. The parameters σ and ω control the width (also named Pearson width) and the actual shape (tailing behaviour) of the Pearson VII function. In order to use SVM, both the kernel parameters and the SVM regularization constant, C, need to be defined by the user. In this paper, those parameters were defined by means of a grid search optimisation. To decrease the number of parameter possibilities (time saving) an internal scaling factor β was introduced, according to Melssen et al. [40].

> A good performance was achieved using the SVM method combined with the Pearson VII universal kernel (PUK) function. In fact, the correlation coefficients are greater and the root mean squared errors are smaller than the previous remaining SMO models with linear, quadratic and RBF kernels (see Tables 3 and 4). Therefore, this fitting is the best one. The optimal values for σ, ω and C in this work were 1.0, 1.0 and 100, respectively [39-40].

> ➢ The MLP model: an artificial neural networks (ANN) is an abstract computational model of the human brain. The most important example of global network is the multilayer perceptron (MLP), employing the sigmoidal activation function of neurons. In MLP the neurons are arranged in layers, counting from the input layer (the set of input nodes), through the hidden layers, up to the output layer. The best structure of the neural network selected in this work has four neurons in the hidden layer. On the one hand, the correlation coefficients are similar to the SMO models with linear, quadratic and RBF kernels, but less than the previous SMO model with the PUK kernel. On the other hand, the root mean squared errors are greater than all the previous remaining SMO models (see Tables 3 and 4). As a result the acquired generalization ability of MLP technique was not good enough and this was the main reason of its inferior testing performance (see Figure 7. below). It is evident that the results of SVM are much closer to the actual values of pollutants than that generated by MLP technique for this nonlinear problem. Therefore, the best fitting is the previous SMO model equipped with the PUK kernel.

Next, the number of iterations and CPU time employed in each technique in order to solve this highly non-linear problem are shown in Table 5:

Finally, Figure 7. represents the correlation coefficients for the SMO regression models using linear, quadratic, RBF and PUK kernels as well as for the multilayer perceptron (MLP) used here, respectively for the six different pollutants studied in this work. This graph also demonstrated the flexibility of SVM using the PUK function in building models with better predictive abilities than those obtained from linear, quadratic and RBF kernels for the air quality's problem here studied.

The curve corresponding to the best fit is the SMO with PUK kernel. From this curve, it is possible to do two groups of pollutants. On the one hand, the first group includes the pollutants with a correlation coefficient greater than 0.8, and consists of the following gases: SO_2, NO, NO_2 and CO [7-10,30-31].

Table 5. The CPU time and number of iterations employed in each technique in order to get convergence and to solve the non-linear problem

Item/technique	SMO with linear kernel	SMO with quadratic kernel	SMO with RBF kernel	SMO with PUK kernel	Multilayer perceptron (MLP)
CPU time (s)	1.46	1.70	2.98	2.77	1.39
No. iterations	599,330	599,330	599,330	599,330	500,000

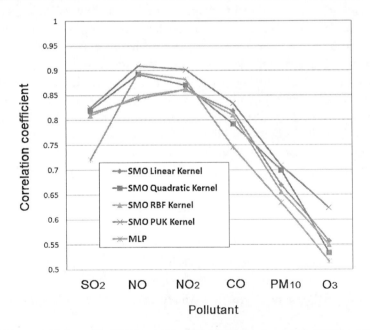

Figure 7. Correlation coefficients for SMO models with the linear, quadratic, RBF and PUK kernels and the multilayer perceptron (MLP) for the six pollutants studied.

On the other hand, the second group has a correlation coefficient less than 0.8, and consists of the following pollutants [7-10,30-31]: PM_{10} and O_3. This behaviour shows that there is greater dependence between the gases in the first group, whereas ozone and particulate matter act more independently. This trend was shown previously in the experimental curves for the gases of the first group, since they were almost similar. However, the curves of ozone and particulate matter have a completely different shape and independent variation.

CONCLUSION

This work presents the application of the SVM technique to estimate highly nonlinear source-receptor relationships between precursor emission and pollutant concentrations. Such model is identified to be used for the resolution of the multi-objective air quality control problem in the city of Oviedo (Spain). SVR is a type of modelling approach that is optimized so that prediction error and model complexity are simultaneously minimized. Because of its universal approximation ability, SVR can be used to model highly nonlinear processes. Choosing optimal hyper-parameters for the models is important step in the identification stage. Further, 10-fold cross-validation is reliable way to determine the optimal hyper-parameters in this paper [37-38]. The optimal values are firstly searched in coarse grids, and then searched in finer grids. The final models are obtained after training the SVRs using these optimal hyper-parameters. The models obtained this way are found to have good generalization property. In this work, the SVR method is used for finding approximate solution of the complex nonlinear problem consists on modelling the air quality in the city of Oviedo. The SVR model reproduces quite accurately the mechanism of the dependence between the main pollutants both primary and secondary pollutants in Oviedo. In this sense, the key step in engineering analysis is therefore choosing appropriate mathematical models. These models will clearly be selected depending on what phenomena are to be predicted, and it is most important to select mathematical models that are *reliable* and *effective* in predicting the quantities sought [22-24]. In this paper, we have constructed a model to study pollutant substances in the city of Oviedo taking into account the compliance of the requirements of air quality to ensure the health of healthy people by means of the SVR technique with success. This model can be applied to other similar cities without the direct intervention of an expert, although expert supervision would be desirable. Moreover, the SVR model provides an estimation of the decision rule used to determine the level of risk according to the limit values of the main pollutants in the atmosphere (NAAQS).

The outcome of this study can be summarized in a few points:

- An air quality modelling by SVR in the city of Oviedo (Spain).
- An effective support for proper actions by managers and relevant authorities.
- Warnings for sensitive groups such as elderly people, children, asthmatics who should stay at home on the months with dangerous levels of air pollution.

The problem was solved using the popular suite of machine learning software written in Java called Weka and developed at the University of Waikato [41]. Further, we have used an iMac computer with a 2.66 GHz Intel Core 2 Duo, 4 GB RAM memory and 640 GB hard disk. The total CPU time employed for each load case analyzed ranges from 1.39 s for the multilayer perceptron (MLP) to about 3 s for the SMO model with radial basis functions (RBF) kernel and the total number of iterations in order to get convergence varies between 500,000 for the multilayer perceptron and 599,330 for the other SMO models analyzed.

As a general rule, emissions of pollutants grow as the economy and population are increased and they decline during economic downturns. In any case, the methodology used in this work can be applied successfully to other cities with similar or different sources of pollutants, but it is always necessary to take into account the specificities of each. This work shows that the city of Oviedo has been modelled with success with respect to the air quality.

Finally, there is an increasing interest to use mathematical models with good physical properties to understand the behaviour of the pollutants in the atmosphere in order to improve the air quality and to reduce the number of deaths. From this point of view, the administration and the government of Asturias can use the results shown in this work in order to obtain the best way to attack and to solve this serious problem according to the Air Quality Standard rule requirements.

ACKNOWLEDGMENTS

The authors wish to acknowledge the computational support provided by the Departments of Mathematics, Construction and Computer Science at University of Oviedo as well as pollutant data in the city of Oviedo supplied by the Section of Industry and Energy from the government of Asturias. This research has also been supported partially by MEC and FEDER grant TIN2007-61273. We would like to thank Anthony Ashworth for his revision of English grammar and spelling of the manuscript.

REFERENCES

[1]   García Nieto, P. J. (2001). Parametric study of selective removal of atmospheric aerosol by coagulation, condensation and gravitational settling. *International Journal of Environmental Health Research*, 11, 151-162.

[2]   García Nieto, P. J. (2006). Study of the evolution of aerosol emissions from coal-fired power plants due to coagulation, condensation, and gravitational settling and health impact. *Journal of Environmental Management*, 79(4), 372-382.

[3]   Akkoyunku, A. and Ertürk, F. (2003). Evaluation of air pollution trends in Istanbul. *International Journal of Environmental Pollution*, 18, 388-398.

[4]   Karaca, F., Alagha, O. and Ertürk, F. (2005). Statistical characterization of atmospheric PM_{10} and PM2.5 concentrations at a non-impacted suburban site of Istanbul, Turkey. *Chemosphere*, 59(8), 1183-1190.

[5]   Elbir, T. and Muezzinoglu, A. (2000). Evaluation of some air pollution indicators in Turkey. *Environment International*, 26(1-2), 5-10.

[6]   Comrie, A. C. and Diem, J. E. (1999). Climatology and forecast modelling of ambient carbon monoxide in Phoenix. *Atmospheric Environment*, 33, 5023-5036.

[7]   Godish, T. Air Quality. Boca Raton: Lewis Publishers; 2004.

[8]   Cooper, C. D. and Alley, F. C. *Air Pollution Control*. New York: Waveland Press; 2002.

[9]   Wang, L. K., Pereira, N. C. and Hung, Y. T. *Air Pollution Control Engineering*. New York: Humana Press; 2004.

[10]   Lutgens, F. K. and Tarbuck, E. J. T*he Atmosphere: An Introduction to Meteorology*. New York: Prentice Hall; 2001.

[11]   Haykin, S. Neural Networks. *Comprehensive Foundation*. New York: Prentice Hall; 1999.

[12]   Boznar, M., Lesjack, M. and Mlakar, P. (1993). A neural network based method for short-term predictions of ambient SO_2 concentrations in highly polluted industrial areas of complex Terrain. *Atmospheric Environment*, 270, 221-230.

[13]   Hooyberghs, J., Mensink, C., Dumont, D., Fierens, F. and Brasseur, O. (2005). A neural network forecast for daily average PM_{10} concentrations in Belgium. *Atmospheric Environment*, 39(18), 3279-3289.

[14]   Kukkonen, J., Partanen, L., Karpinen, A., Ruuskanen, J., Junninen, H., Kolehmainen, M., Niska, H., Dorling, S., Chatterton, T., Foxall, R. and Cawley, G. (2003). Extensive evaluation of neural networks models for the prediction of NO_2 and PM_{10} concentrations, compared with a deterministic modelling system and measurements in central Helsinki. *Atmospheric Environment*, 37, 4539-4550.

[15]   Bianchini, M., Di Iorio, E., Maggini, M., Mocenni, C. and Pucci, A. A cyclostationary neural network model for the prediction of the NO_2 concentration. In: *Proceedings of ESANN*, Bruges (Belgium); April 2006; pp. 67-72.

[16]   Chaloulakou, A., Saisana, M. and Spyrellis, N. (2003). Comparative assessment of neural networks and regresión models for forecasting summertime ozone in Athens. *Science of the Total Environm*ent, 313, 1-13.

[17]   Gardner, M. W. and Dorling, S. R. (1999). Neural network modelling and prediction of hourly NO_x and NO_2 concentrations in urban air in London. *Atmospheric Environment*, 33(5), 709-719.

[18]   Karaca, F., Nikov, A. and Alagha, O. (2006). NN-AirPol: a neural-network-based method for air pollution evaluation and control. *International Journal of Environmental Pollution*, 28(3-4), 310-325.

[19]   Shawe-Taylor, J. and Cristianini, N. Kernel Methods for Pattern Analysis. New York: Cambridge University Press; 2004.

[20]   Bishop, C. M. *Pattern Recognition and Machine Learning*. New York: Springer; 2006.

[21]   Schölkopf, B. and Smola, A. J. Learning with Kernels: Support Vector Machines, Regularization, Optimization and Beyond. Cambridge (MA): The MIT Press; 2002.

[22]   Vapnik, V. The Nature of Statistical Learning Theory. New York: Springer; 1999.

[23]   Bishop, C. M. Pattern Recognition and Machine Learning. New York: Springer; 2006.

[24]   Steinwart, I. and Christmann, A. Support Vector Machines. New York: Springer; 2008.

[25]   Monteiro, A., Lopes, M., Miranda, A.I., Borrego, C. and Vautard, R. (2005). Air pollution forecast in Portugal: a demand from the new air quality framework directive. *International Journal of Environmental Pollution*, 5, 1-9.

[26]   Wark, K., Warner, C. F. and Davis, W. T. Air Pollution: Its Origin and Control. New York: Prentice Hall; 1997.

[27]   Schnelle, K. B. and Brown, C. A. *Air Pollution Control Technology Handbook*. Boca Raton: CRC Press; 2001.

[28] Friedlander, S. K. Smoke, *Dust and Haze: Fundamentals of Aerosol Dynamics*. New York: Oxford University Press; 2000.

[29] Vincent, J. H. *Aerosol Sampling: Science, Standards, Instrumentation and Applications*. New York: Wiley; 2007.

[30] Colbeck, I. *Environmental Chemistry of Aerosol*. New York: Wiley-Blackwell; 2008.

[31] Hewitt, C. N. and Jackson, A. V. *Atmospheric Science for Environmental Scientists*. New York: Wiley-Blackwell; 2009.

[32] Weinhold, B. (2008). Ozone nation: EPA standard panned by the people. *Environmental Health Perspectives*, 116(7), A302–A305.

[33] Anderson, W., Prescott, G. J., Packham, S., Mullins, J., Brookes, M. and Seaton, A. (2001). Asthma admissions and thunderstorms: a study of pollen, fungal spores, rainfall, and ozone. *The Quarterly Journal of Medicine*, 94(8), 429–433.

[34] Jerrett, M., Burnett, R. T., Arden Pope III, C., Ito, K., Thurston, G., Krewski, D., Shi, Y., Calle, E. and Thun, M. (2009). Long-term ozone exposure and mortality. *The New England Journal of Medicine*, 360 (11), 1085-1095.

[35] Fletcher, T. Support Vector Machines Explained: Introductory Course. Internal Report. London: University College London; 2009.

[36] Ferris, M. and Munson, T. (2002). Interior-point methods for massive support vector machines. *SIAM Journal on Optimization*, 13, 783-804.

[37] Picard, R. and Cook, D. (1984). Cross-validation of regression models. *Journal of the American Statistical Association*, 79(387), 575-583.

[38] Efron, B. and Tibshirani, R. (1997). Improvements on cross-validation: the .632 + bootstrap method. *Journal of the American Statistical Association*, 92(438), 548-560.

[39] Üstün, B., Melssen, W. J. and Buydens, L. M. C. (2006). Facilitating the application of support vector regression by using a universal Pearson VII function based kernel. Chemometrics and Intelligent Laboratory Systems, 81, 29–40.

[40] Melssen, W. J., Üstün, B. and Buydens, L. M. C. (2006). SOMPLS: A supervised self-organising map partial least squares algorithm for multivariate regression problems, Chemometrics and Intelligent Laboratory Systems, 86, 299–309.

[41] Halle, M., Frank, E., Holmes, G., Pfahringer, B., Reutemann, P. and Witten, I. H. (2009). The WEKA data mining software: an update. Special Interest Group on Knowledge Discovery and Data Mining Explorations, 11(1), 10-18.

Reviewed by Prof. Dr. Celestino Ordóñez Galán, Departament of Natural Resources and Environment, University of Vigo, 36310 Vigo, Spain. (Email: cgalan@uvigo.es).

In: Support Vector Machines
Editor: Brandon H. Boyle

ISBN: 978-1-61209-342-0
© 2011 Nova Science Publishers, Inc.

Chapter 3

IMAGE INTERPOLATION USING SUPPORT VECTOR MACHINES

Liyong Ma, Yi Shen and Jiachen Ma*

School of Information Science and Engineering,
Harbin Institute of Technology at Weihai, Weihai, 264209, P. R. China

ABSTRACT

Image interpolation has a wide range of applications in remote sense, medical diagnoses, multimedia communication, and other image processing fields. Support vector machines (SVMs) have been used successfully for various supervised classification tasks, regression tasks, and novelty detection tasks. In this chapter, support vector machines based image interpolation schemes for image zooming and color filter array interpolation are discussed.

Firstly, a local spatial properties based image interpolation scheme using SVMs is introduced. After the proper neighbor pixels region is selected, SVMs are trained with local spatial properties that include the mean and the variations of gray value of the neighbor pixels in the selected region. The support vector regression machines are employed to estimate the gray value of unknown pixels with the neighbor pixels and local spatial properties information. Some interpolation experiments show that the proposed scheme is superior to the linear, cubic, neural network and other SVMs based interpolation approaches.

Secondly, a SVMs based color filter array interpolation scheme is proposed to effectively reduce color artifacts and blurring of the CFA interpolation. Support vector regression (SVR) is used to estimate the color difference between two color channels with applying spectral correlation of the R, G, B channels.

The neighbor training sample models are selected on the color difference plane with considering spatial correlation, and the unknown color difference between two color channels is estimated by the trained SVR to get the missing color value at each pixel. Simulation studies indicate that the proposed scheme produces visually pleasing full-color images and obtains higher PSNR results than other conventional CFA interpolation algorithms.

---

* E-mail: maliyong@hit.edu.cn

1. INTRODUCTION OF IMAGE INTERPOLATION

In recent years there has been considerable interest in image interpolation. Image interpolation has a wide range of applications in remote sense, medical diagnoses, multimedia communication and other image processing fields.

Some typical applications of image interpolation include enlarging an image for display, image registration, error concealment for real-time video communication, digital scan conversion for ultrasound or radar imaging, and color filter array interpolation [1-6].

1.1. Linear and Cubic Image Interpolation

Image interpolation is an old problem, but there are many new solutions for it. Some valuable review papers about image interpolation can be found in literature, such as [1], [2] and [3]. The well-known approaches to image interpolation are linear interpolation algorithm and cubic interpolation algorithm [1-4].

Let x denote the coordinate value to be interpolated. Assume that x_{k-1}, x_k, x_{k+1} and x_{k+2} are the nearest available neighbors of x, where $x_k \leq x < x_{k+1}$. Let $f(x_{k-1})$, $f(x_k)$, $f(x_{k+1})$ and $f(x_{k+2})$ denote the available gray value of x_{k-1}, x_k, x_{k+1} and x_{k+2}, respectively. Then the distance between x and neighbors can be defined as

$$s = x - x_k, \; 1 - s = x_{k+1} - x \; (0 \leq s \leq 1).$$

We have one-dimensional linear interpolation of x

$$\hat{f}(x) = (1-s)f(x_k) + sf(x_{k+1}) \tag{1}$$

Similarly, we have one-dimensional cubic interpolation of x

$$\hat{f}(x) = [f(x_{k-1})((3+s)^3 - 4(2+s)^3 + 6(1+s)^3 - 4s^3) + f(x_k)((2+s)^3 - 4(1+s)^3 + 6s^3) \tag{2}$$
$$+ f(x_{k+1})((1+s)^3 - 4s^3) + f(x_{k+2})s^3]/6$$

For an image that is two dimensions, we can apply one-dimensional linear interpolation or cubic interpolation above to the image along the rows firstly, and then the interpolation is applied to the image along the columns. And this two-dimensional interpolation is called bilinear interpolation or bicubic interpolation.

However, the linear and cubic interpolation methods blur result images, particularly in edge regions [1-3]. Some other learning based interpolation methods have been developed for image interpolation recently [5, 7-9].

An efficient neural network based interpolation method was developed in [7] where multi-layer perceptron was employed to perform interpolation estimation after being trained with a group of image pixels.

1.2. Support Vector Regression

The training set of SVMs in which each example is described by a d-dimensional vector, $x \in R^d$, consists of n training examples. The labels are used to describe categories that training examples belonging to. Following training, the result SVMs are able to classify previously unseen and unlabeled instances into categories based on examples learnt from the training set.

Support vector regression (SVR) is a function approximation approach applied with SVMs. A training data set consists of n points $\{x_i, y_i\}, i = 1,2,...,n$, $x_i \in R^d$, $y_i \in R^d$, where x_i is the i-th input pattern and y_i is the i-th output pattern. The aim of SVR is to find a function $f(x) = w \cdot x + b$, under the constrains $y_i - w \cdot x - b \leq \varepsilon$ and $w \cdot x + b - y_i \leq \varepsilon$ to allow for some deviation ε between the eventual targets y and the function $f(x)$ to model the data. By minimizing $\|w\|^2$ to penalize over-complexity and introducing the slack variables ξ_i, ξ_i^* for the two types of training errors, the regression weight results can be reached. For a linear ε-insensitive loss function this task therefore refers to minimize

$$\|w\|^2 + C\sum_{i=1}^{n} \xi_i + \xi_i^*, \tag{3}$$

subject to $y_i - w \cdot x - b \leq \varepsilon + \xi_i$ and $w \cdot x + b - y_i \leq \varepsilon + \xi_i^*$, where all the slack variables are positive.

For linearly non-separable case, a mapping function $\varphi : R^d \rightarrow R^d$ can be found to map the current space into a higher dimensional one in which the data point is separable. The dot product in the mapped space is avoided by kernel function $\psi(x, y)$ that can be selected as linear kernel, polynomial kernel, radial basis function kernel or two layer neural kernel [10, 11]. In this chapter SVR is employed for image interpolation learning and estimation.

2. SUPPORT VECTOR MACHINES BASED IMAGE INTERPOLATION

In [8] the image interpolation error was trained with SVR, and the interpolation result images were corrected with the interpolation error that was estimated by SVR. And in [5] this SVR based interpolation error compensation approach was successfully used for video error concealment .But this approach was provided for interpolation error compensation not directly for image interpolation. Next three SVR based image interpolation approaches will be introduced. These SVR based interpolation approaches are data fitting image interpolation approach, neighbor pixels image interpolation approach and local spacial properties image interpolation approach.

2.1. Data Fitting Image Interpolation Approach

When we regard the position of every pixel in a digital image that is two dimensions as the coordinate value, the gray value of every pixel is the corresponding curve surface value. And we can perform image interpolation by data fitting approach employing SVR estimation.

Let q denote the pixel to be interpolated. We can select a neighbor area which includes the known pixels around q with the size of 4×4 or 5×5. And SVR is trained employing relative coordinate value of the known neighbor pixels around q in the selected area as input pattern, and the gray value of these known neighbor pixels are collected as output pattern. After the training of SVR, the pixel gray value of pixel q can be estimated with this trained SVR. In this estimation process, the input pattern of SVR is the relative coordinate value of q and the output pattern the interpolation result of q.

2.2. Neighbor Pixel Image Interpolation Approach

In the neighbor pixels approach every pixel in the known source image is used as sample for SVR training. The gray value of every pixel is employed as SVR output pattern of training sample, and the gray value of its neighbor pixels are collected as SVR input pattern during the training process. In this approach the coordinate of pixels are not used at all. After the training, interpolation result image can be obtained with every pixel to be interpolated is estimated by trained SVR. During the estimation process the gray value of neighbor pixels around the pixel to be interpolated are employed as SVR input patterns. And the output pattern of SVR is the gray value of the pixel to be estimated.

2.3. Local Spatial Properties Image Interpolation Approach

All the two approaches above employ the gray value of the neighbor pixels as SVR patterns during SVR training and estimation. However, little information about the spatial local properties of the pixel to be interpolated is used. The interpolation results relate to some spatial local properties of the pixel to be interpolated, such as the smooth properties of the region around the pixel and the directional information of the edges. We can expect to obtain high quality interpolation result image by using the local spatial properties in SVR input patterns during the training and estimation. The gray value of the pixel to be interpolated is associated with the average gray value of the region around the pixel. And the pixel gray value to be estimated is also associated with the difference between gray value of ambient pixels of the pixel to be interpolated along various directions. Local spatial properties interpolation scheme can employ the average gray value of the region around the pixel to be interpolated and the gray value difference of various directional around this pixel as input patterns of SVR. And we can obtain the local spatial properties based SVR interpolation scheme as described below. Firstly an ambient region around the pixel to be interpolated needs to be decided before the interpolation calculation. This ambient region is selected according to the pixel numbers to be interpolated between two known pixels.

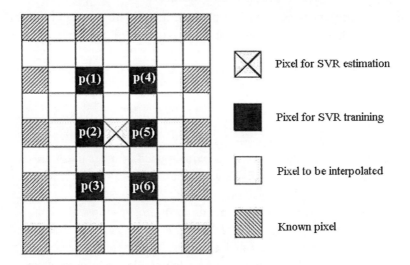

Pixel for SVR estimation

Pixel for SVR tranining

Pixel to be interpolated

Known pixel

Figure 1. Ambient Region for Local Spatial Properties SVR Interpolation.

For example, the region for image zooming in with the magnifying factor 2 is illustrated in Figure 1. In the selected region the gray value of known pixels is denoted as $p(i)$, where $i = 1, 2, ..., 6$.

Secondly the SVR training is performed. In this step every pixel in the source image is employed as the input sample of SVR. The input patterns of SVR include the pixel gray value of the neighbor known pixels in the selected region, i.e. $p(i)$ in Figure 1. Other input patterns include average gray value of neighbor known pixels and some other local spatial properties in the selected ambient region. The average gray value of neighbor known pixels in the selected region in Figure 1. is calculated as

$$\bar{v} = \frac{1}{6} \sum_{i=1}^{6} p(i) \tag{4}$$

Other local spatial properties employed as input patterns of SVR are calculated as

$$v_1 = p(1) - p(3)$$
$$v_2 = p(4) - p(6)$$
$$v_3 = p(1) - p(4)$$
$$v_4 = p(2) - p(5)$$
$$v_5 = p(3) - p(6)$$
$$v_6 = p(1) - p(6)$$
$$v_7 = p(3) - p(4) \tag{5}$$

Then the input patterns of SVR are 14 dimensions. And the output pattern is the gray value of the central pixel to be estimated in Figure 1. After the training, the trained SVR can be employed to estimate unknown gray value of the pixels to be interpolated.

Finally the trained SVR is employed to perform interpolation calculation for every pixel to be estimated. In this estimate process the input patterns of SVR are calculated with the known pixels in the selected ambient region around the pixel to be interpolated. And the output pattern of SVR is the estimated gray value of the pixel to be interpolated.

2.4. Conclusion

Some standard test images that have been widely used in other literatures are used in the experiments. These test images include Lena, Cameraman, Elaine, etc. The test images are down-sampled to 1/8, 1/4 and 1/2 of the original size. Then these reduced images are zoomed in with various interpolation approaches to obtain result images those have the same size with the original images. The zooming in interpolation with the magnifying factor 2 is used here as in [7], that is double expanding rows and columns. Result images are compared with the original images those are used as standard images to calculate normalized mean square error (NMSE) and peak signal to noise ratio (PSNR). Let I and $\tilde{I}$ be the original standard image and the interpolated result image respectively, where I and $\tilde{I}$ with the same size of $M \times N$. The pixel in I and the pixel in $\tilde{I}$ is denoted as $I(m,n)$ and $\tilde{I}(m,n)$ respectively, where $1 \le m \le M$, $1 \le n \le N$. For 8 bits gray value images, NMSE and PSNR are calculated as follows.

$$MSE = \frac{1}{MN} \sum_{m=1}^{M} \sum_{n=1}^{N} \left| I(m,n) - \tilde{I}(m,n) \right|^2 \tag{6}$$

$$NMSE = \frac{\sum_{m=1}^{M} \sum_{n=1}^{N} \left[x(m,n) - \tilde{x}(m,n) \right]^2}{\sum_{m=1}^{M} \sum_{n=1}^{N} \left[x(m,n) \right]^2} \tag{7}$$

$$PSNR = 10 \log_{10} \frac{255^2}{MSE} \tag{8}$$

The interpolation approaches tested in our experiments include linear interpolation, cubic interpolation, multi-layer perceptron neural network interpolation, data fitting based SVR interpolation, neighbor pixels based SVR interpolation and local spatial properties based SVR interpolation. The experiments are performed in Matlab and the SVM tools for Matlab [12] is used. The ε-SVR with RBF kernel is employed in the SVR interpolation experiments.

Some interpolation results of the interpolation experiments are listed in Table 1 where the size of the source image to be interpolated is 64×64 and the size of the enlarged destination image is 128×128. It is shown that the local spatial properties based SVR interpolation scheme obtains the least NMSE value and the highest PSNR value. It means that the local spatial properties based SVR interpolation scheme can obtain the best result image.

Table 1. Comparison of result images with different interpolation approaches

Test Image	Cameraman		Lena	
	NMSE	PSNR	NMSE	PSNR
Linear Interpolation	0.026	21.42	0.013	23.26
Cubic Interpolation	0.031	20.72	0.019	22.86
Neural Network Interpolation	0.026	21.51	0.015	24.05
Data Fitting SVR Interpolation	0.038	19.84	0.030	20.86

Some result images of different interpolation approaches applied to image Cameraman are illustrated in Figure 2. It can be observed that the linear interpolation and cubic interpolation blur image edges. The data fitting SVR interpolation blurs more edge regions in result image. The near neighbor SVR interpolation makes the most regions of result image dark and blur. The neural network interpolation blurs the edges and the continue lines in result image. The local space properties based SVR interpolation obtains the best result image. These observation results are consistent with the calculation results in Table 1.

Some residual images of different interpolation approaches applied to image Cameraman are showed in Figure 3. The near neighbor SVR interpolation has the greatest resident in result image. The residual in the result images of data fitting SVR interpolation, near neighbor SVR interpolation and neural network interpolation is distributed in all image regions. And the residual in the result images of the linear interpolation and the cubic interpolation are centrally distributed in edge regions. The local space properties based SVR interpolation scheme has less residual in result image. These observation results are also consistent with the calculation results in Table 1.

(a)   (b)   (c)

(d)   (e)   (f)   (g)

Figure 2. Result Images of Different Interpolation Approaches. (a) Standard Image (b) Linear Interpolation (c) Cubic Interpolation (d) Data Fitting SVR Interpolation, (e) Near Neighbour SVR Interpolation (f) Neural Network Interpolation (g) Local Properties Interpolation.

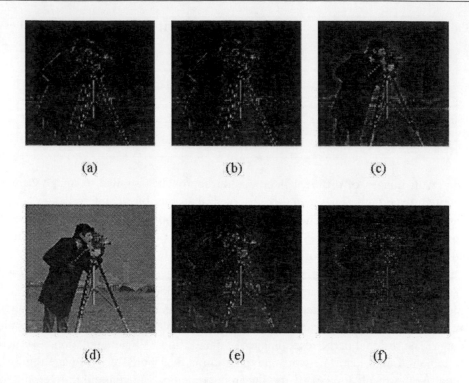

Figure 3. Residual Images of Different Interpolation Approaches, (a) Standard Image (b) Linear Interpolation (c) Cubic Interpolation (d) Data Fitting SVR Interpolation, (e) Near Neighbour SVR Interpolation (f) Neural Network Interpolation (g) Local Properties Interpolation.

3. SUPPORT VECTOR MACHINES BASED INTERPOLATION FOR COLOR FILTER ARRAY

3.1. Introduction to Color Filter Array Interpolation

As one of most popular devices to capture real scenes in color, digital camera for still images needs to reproduce color images that contain samples from three channels, i.e., Red, Green, and Blue. Digital color cameras transmit the image scenes through Red (R), Green (G) and Blue (B) color filters and acquire sample data using three electronic sensors. These sample data from three sensors are rearranged according to the corresponding color channel to obtain the result color images. To produce a color image, three CCD or CMOS sensors are needed to obtain R, G and B channel pixel value at the same time. This is a very expensive solution, and actually it is only used in few professional digital still cameras. Designers employ a single sensor overlaid with a color filter array (CFA) to acquire the color image. With this scheme, only one pixel value of the three primary color channels is obtained. To restore a full-color image form CFA samples, the two missing color value at each pixel need to be estimated from the adjacent pixels. This process is commonly known as CFA interpolation or demosaicking. The well known CFA pattern is Bayer CFA.

Bilinear interpolation is the simplest method for CFA interpolation, in which the missing color value is filled with the average of its neighboring CFA samples in the same color channel. It introduces errors in the edge region with blurred result images and produces color artifacts. To obtain more accurate and visually pleasing results, many sophisticated CFA interpolation methods have been proposed. In [13] an effective color interpolation algorithm (ECI) using signal correlation information to get better image quality is provided. The frequency response of this approach is better than the conventional methods especially in high frequency. Another enhanced ECI interpolation approach (EECI) which effectively uses both the spatial and the spectral correlations is proposed in [14], and it provides effective scheme to enhance two existing state-of-the-art interpolation methods. In [15] a universal demosaicking algorithm (UD) is provided employing an edge-sensing mechanism and a post-processor to unify existing interpolation solutions.

3.2 Color Filter Array Interpolation Using SVR

Generally, images have strong spatial and spectral correlations. Image spatial correlation refers to the fact that within a homogeneous image region, neighboring pixels share similar color value, while spectral correlation dictates that there is a high correlation between the R, G and B image planes, resulting in that the difference (or radio) between two color planes is likely to be a constant within a local image neighborhood [13].

The image acquired from Bayer pattern sensor filter is showed in Figure 4, one of the R, G or B channel is sampled in every pixel from the original full color image. The full color image has the size of M rows and N columns. The R, G and B channel value of the pixel in the position of row i and column j are denoted as $R_{i,j}$, $G_{i,j}$ and $B_{i,j}$, respectively, where $1 \le i \le M$, and $1 \le j \le N$. Image edge can be expanded with symmetry copy method in image processing, that is copy the image edge row or column to expand a new image row or column.

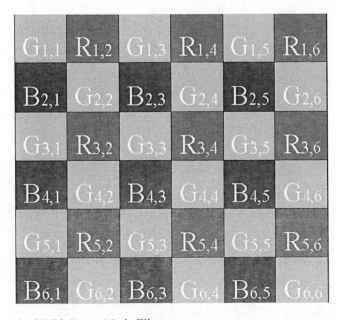

Figure 4. Image Acquired With Bayer Mode Filter.

The proposed scheme of CFA interpolation using SVR is described as follows.

Step 1: Construct Plane of Kr
The Kr plane is defined as

$$Kr = G - R \tag{9}$$

The value in Kr plane of the pixel in the row i and column j is denoted as $Kr_{i,j}$, and the value of $Kr_{i,j}$ where $G_{i,j}$ is known can be calculated as

$$Kr_{i,j} = G_{i,j} - (R_{i,j-1} + R_{i,j+1})/2 \qquad \text{when } i \text{ is odd}$$

$$Kr_{i,j} = G_{i,j} - (R_{i-1,j} + R_{i+1,j})/2 \qquad \text{when } i \text{ is even}$$

Then we obtain all the value of Kr in the pixels where the value of G channel is known. Then SVR training is performed in the Kr plane. The training samples are selected when $Kr_{i-2,j}$, $Kr_{i+2,j}$, $Kr_{i,j-2}$, $Kr_{i,j+2}$ and $Kr_{i,j}$ are known, or $Kr_{i-1,j-1}$, $Kr_{i-1,j+1}$, $Kr_{i+1,j-1}$, $Kr_{i+1,j+1}$ and $Kr_{i,j}$ are known, as showed in Figure 5. Where $Kr_{i,j}$ is collected as output pattern of the training sample, and others are collected as input pattern. All the training samples are collected as training sample set, and this sample set is used for SVR training. This trained SVR can be employed for interpolation estimation after the training.

The $Kr_{i,j}$ value of the pixels where $R_{i,j}$ is known can be estimated employing the trained SVR. As showed in Figure 6, $Kr_{i,j-1}$, $Kr_{i-1,j-1}$, $Kr_{i,j+1}$ and $Kr_{i+1,j+1}$ are collected as input pattern when using trained SVR to estimate the value of $Kr_{i,j}$.

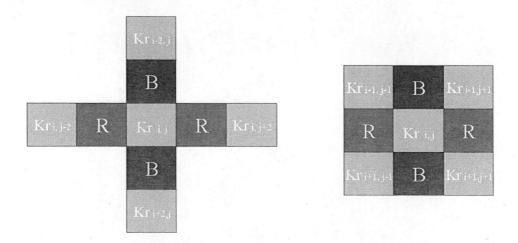

Figure 5. SVR Training Samples of the Kr Plane.

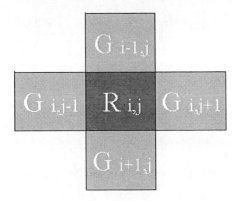

Figure 6. SVR Estimation when R is known in the Kr Plane.

Step 2: Construct Plane Kb
The Kb plane is defined as

$$Kb = G - B \tag{10}$$

The value of $Kb_{i,j}$ where $G_{i,j}$ is known can be calculated as

$$Kb_{i,j} = G_{i,j} - (B_{i,j-1} + B_{i,j+1})/2 \qquad \text{when } i \text{ is even}$$

$$Kb_{i,j} = G_{i,j} - (B_{i-1,j} + B_{i+1,j})/2 \qquad \text{when } i \text{ is odd}$$

Then we obtain all the value of Kb in the pixels where the value of G channel is known. Then SVR training is performed in the Kb plane. The training samples are selected when $Kb_{i-2,j}$, $Kb_{i+2,j}$, $Kb_{i,j-2}$, $Kb_{i,j+2}$ and $Kb_{i,j}$ are known, or $Kb_{i-1,j-1}$, $Kb_{i-1,j+1}$, $Kb_{i+1,j-1}$, $Kb_{i+1,j+1}$ and $Kb_{i,j}$ are known.. Where $Kb_{i,j}$ is collected as output pattern of the training sample, and others are collected as input pattern. All the training samples are collected as training sample set, and this sample set is used for SVR training.

The $Kb_{i,j}$ value of the pixels where $B_{i,j}$ is known can be estimated employing the trained SVR. $Kb_{i,j-1}$, $Kb_{i-1,j-1}$, $Kb_{i,j+1}$ and $Kb_{i+1,j+1}$ are collected as input pattern when using trained SVR to estimate the value of $Kb_{i,j}$.

Step 3: Interpolation of channel G
The value of $G_{i,j}$ where $R_{i,j}$ is known can be calculated as

$$G_{i,j} = R_{i,j} + Kr_{i,j} . \tag{11}$$

And the value of $G_{i,j}$ where $B_{i,j}$ is known can be calculated as

$$G_{i,j} = B_{i,j} + Kb_{i,j} \qquad (12)$$

Step 4: Interpolation of channel R

The value of $Kr_{i,j}$ in the pixels where $B_{i,j}$ is known can be estimated employing the trained SVR in step 1 with $Kr_{i,j-1}$, $Kr_{i-1,j-1}$, $Kr_{i,j+1}$ and $Kr_{i+1,j+1}$ around $B_{i,j}$ are collected as input pattern. And R channel can be estimated as

$$R_{i,j} = G_{i,j} - Kr_{i,j} \qquad (13)$$

Step 4: Interpolation of channel B

The value of $Kb_{i,j}$ in the pixels where $R_{i,j}$ is known can be estimated employing the trained SVR in step 2 with $Kb_{i,j-1}$, $Kb_{i-1,j-1}$, $Kb_{i,j+1}$ and $Kb_{i+1,j+1}$ around $R_{i,j}$ are collected as input pattern. And B channel of the pixels where the B channel is unknown can be estimated as

$$B_{i,j} = G_{i,j} - Kb_{i,j} \qquad (14)$$

Step 5: Interpolation of channel B

The value of $Kr_{i,j}$ in the pixels where $B_{i,j}$ is known can be estimated employing the trained SVR in step 1 with $Kr_{i,j-1}$, $Kr_{i-1,j-1}$, $Kr_{i,j+1}$ and $Kr_{i+1,j+1}$ around $B_{i,j}$ are collected as input pattern. And R channel of the pixels where the R channel is unknown can be estimated as

$$R_{i,j} = G_{i,j} - Kr_{i,j} \qquad (15)$$

3.3. Experiments

Some standard test images are used in our experiments to verify the effect of the above SVR CFA interpolation algorithm. Part of the images is showed in Figure 7. The result images are compared with the original images to calculate the peak signal to noise radio (PSNR). In all the experiments, γ-SVR and RBF is used. PSNR of different CFA interpolation result images in the marked areas of Figure 7. is listed in Table 2 to describe the detail restore capability of different approaches. It is obvious that the proposed SVR based CFA interpolation obtains the best PSNR value.

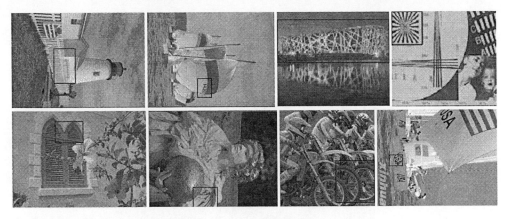

Figure 7. Test Images with Marked Area for CFA Interpolation.

Table 2. PSNR of result images with different CFA interpolation approach

Image	Bilinear	UD	ECI	EECI	SVR
Lighthouse	16.27	19.32	19.17	21.51	27.92
Sails	14.79	17.33	18.65	19.24	20.52
Nest	13.51	15.24	18.07	17.36	22.04
Faces	9.85	12.80	16.02	14.44	22.59
Window	23.91	29.32	24.67	26.12	31.87
Statue	23.32	26.60	25.86	26.33	31.56
Bike	19.20	21.27	24.03	23.32	28.28
Sailboat	15.51	18.39	19.09	20.53	29.01

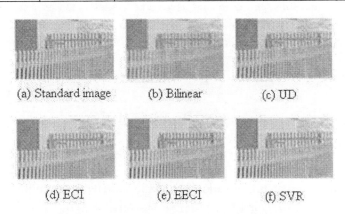

Figure 8. Details of image Lighthouse with different CFA Interpolation.

To better observe the details of image result, result images of different interpolation approaches for Lighthouse are illustrated in Figure 8. It can be observed that the bilinear interpolation blurs the image edges. And it is clearly that bilinear interpolation, ECI, EECI and UD approach produce visible artifacts in the fence area. SVR based CFA interpolation approach obtains the best result image without too much artifacts.

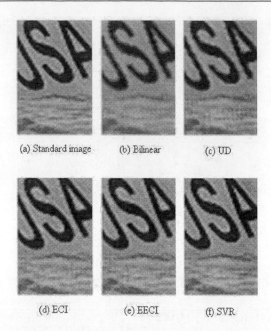

(a) Standard image   (b) Bilinear   (c) UD

(d) ECI   (e) EECI   (f) SVR

Figure 9. Details of image Sail with different CFA Interpolation.

Result images of different interpolation approaches for Sail are illustrated in Figure 9. We can also find that the bilinear interpolation is quite unacceptable as it blurs the edge area. And all the bilinear, ECI, EECI and UD CFA interpolation approaches produce visible artifacts clearly. The results show that SVR based CFA interpolation algorithm produce visually pleasing full-color images. In this chapter we discussed SVR based image interpolation approach, and two algorithms are detailed. Image interpolation using SVMs has just been developed recently, and there are many undiscovered issues, such as, the selection of kernel function, construction a problem-oriented kernel to get better regression results, the parameters selection, and real time implementation. All these issues need to be studied in the future.

ACKNOWLEDGMENT

This work was partially supported by the Natural Science Foundation of China (No.60874054 and No.30800240), China Postdoctoral Science Foundation (20100471057), the Natural Scientific Research Innovation Foundation in Harbin Institute of Technology and the Fundamental Research Funds for the Central Universities (HIT.NSRIF.2009151), and the Research Fund of Harbin Institute of Technology at Weihai (HIT(WH)ZB200802).

REFERENCES

[1]   Thevenaz P, Blu T, Unser M. Interpolation Revisited. *IEEE Transactions on Medical Imaging*, 2000, 19(7), 739-758.

[2] Lehmann T, Gonner C, Spitzer K. Survey: Interpolation Methods in Medical Image Processing. *IEEE Transactions on Medical Imaging*, 1999, 18(11), 1049-1075.

[3] Meijering E. A Chronology of Interpolation: From Ancient Astronomy to Modern Signal and Image Processing. *Proceedings of IEEE*, 2002, 90(3), 319-342.

[4] Russ J. *The Image processing Handbook*, 4th edn. CRC Press, 2002.

[5] Ma L, Sun Y, Feng N. Error Compensation Based Directional Interpolation Algorithm for Video Error Concealment. *Advances in Soft Computing*, 2009, 52:107-114.

[6] Ma L, Ma J, Shen Y. Local Activity Levels Guided Adaptive Scan Conversion Algorithm. *Proceedings of the 27th Annual International Conference of the IEEE Engineering in Medicine and Biology Society*, 2005, 6718-6720.

[7] Plaziac N. Image Interpolation Using Neural Networks. *IEEE Transactions on Image Processing*, 1999, 8(11), 1647-1651.

[8] Ma L, Ma J, Shen Y. Support Vector Machines Based Image Interpolation Correction Scheme, *Lecture Notes in Artificial Intelligent*, 2006, 4062: 679-684.

[9] Ma L, Shen Y, Ma J. Local Spatial Properties Based Image Interpolation Scheme Using SVMs. *Journal of Systems Engineering and Electronics*, 2008, 19(3), 618-623.

[10] Vapnik V. *Statistical Learning Theory*. John Wiley, New York, 1998.

[11] Cristiani N, Shawe-Taylor J. *An Introduction to Support Vector Machines and Other Kernel-based Learning Methods*. Cambridge University Press, Cambridge, 2000.

[12] Chang C, Lin C. LIBSVM: Introduction and Benchmarks. http://www.csie. ntu.tw/~cjlin/papers, 2001.

[13] Pei S, Tam I. Effective Color Interpolation in CCD Color Filter Arrays Using Signal Correlation. *IEEE Transactions on Circuits and Systems for Video Technology*, 2003, 13 (6), 503-513.

[14] Chang L, Tan Y. Effective Use of Spatial and Spectral Correlations for Color Filter Array Demosaicking. *IEEE Transactions on Consumer Electronics*, 2004, 50 (1), 355-365.

[15] Lukac R, Plataniotis K. Universal Demosaicking for Imaging Pipelines with an RGB Color Filter Array. *Pattern Recognition*, 2005, 38(11), 2208-2212.

In: Support Vector Machines
Editor: Brandon H. Boyle

ISBN: 978-1-61209-342-0
© 2011 Nova Science Publishers, Inc.

Chapter 4

UTILIZATION OF SUPPORT VECTOR MACHINE (SVM) FOR PREDICTION OF ULTIMATE CAPACITY OF DRIVEN PILES IN COHESIONLESS SOILS

Pijush Samui[1] *and S.K. Sekar[2]*

[1]Associate Professor, Centre for Disaster Mitigation and Management,
VIT University, Vellore-632014, India
[2]Senior Professor and Director, Centre for Disaster Mitigation and Management, VIT
University, Vellore- 632014, India

ABSTRACT:

This chapter examines the capability of Support Vector Machine (SVM) for prediction of ultimate capacity (Q) of driven piles in cohesionless soils. SVM that is firmly based on the theory of statistical learning theory, uses regression technique by introducing ε-insensitive loss function has been adopted. SVM achieves good generalization ability by adopting a structural risk minimization (SRM) induction principle that aims at minimizing a bound on the generalization error of a model rather than the minimizing the error on the training data only. SVM is trained with optimization of a convex, quadratic cost function, which guarantees the uniqueness of the SVM solution. In this chapter, the developed SVM model outperforms the artificial neural network (ANN) model based on root-mean-square-error (RMSE) and mean-absolute-error (MAE) performance criteria. An equation has been developed for the prediction of Q of driven piles based on the developed SVM model. A sensitivity analysis has been also done to determine the effect of each input parameter on Q. This chapter shows that the developed SVM model is a robust model for prediction of Q of driven piles in cohesionless soils.

Keywords: pile foundation; Support Vector Machine; Artificial Neural Network; Sensitivity analysis; prediction.

---

[*] Email: pijush.phd@gmail.com, Tel: 91-416-2202283, Fax: 91-416-2243092

INTRODUCTION

Piles are structural members of timber, concrete, and/or steel that are used to transmit surface loads to lower levels in the soil mass. So, the determination of ultimate capacity (Q) of driven piles in cohesionless soil is an imperative task in geotechnical engineering. There are several methods available for the determination of ultimate capacity of driven piles in cohesionless soils (Meyerhof, 1976; Coyle and Castello, 1981; RP2A,1984; Randolph,1985; Randolph at al.,1994). However, most of the available methods simplify the problem by incorporating several assumptions associated with the factors that affect the ultimate capacity of driven piles in cohesionless soils. Recently, geotechnical engineers have successfully applied artificial neural network (ANN) in different problems (Ghaboussi, 1992; Mayoraz and Vulliet, 2002; Samui and Kumar, 2006). ANN has been also used for pile foundation analysis successfully (Chow et al., 1995; Chan et al., 1995; goh, 1995; Lee and Lee, 1996; Kiefa, 1998). But, ANN has some limitations. The limitations are listed below:

- Unlike other statistical models, ANN does not provide information about the relative importance of the various parameters (Park and Rilett, 1999).
- The knowledge acquired during the training of the model is stored in an implicit manner and hence it is very difficult to come up with reasonable interpretation of the overall structure of the network (Kecman, 2001).
- In addition, ANN has some inherent drawbacks such as slow convergence speed, less generalizing performance, arriving at local minimum and over-fitting problems.

As a result, alternative methods are needed, which can predict ultimate capacity of driven piles in cohesionless soils accurately.

In this study, as an alternative method SVM has been adopted to predict Q. This study uses the database collected by Kiefa(1998). It provides a new, efficient novel approach to improve the generalization performance and can attain a global minimum. In general, SVMs have been used for pattern recognition problems. Recently it has been used to solve non-linear regression estimation and time series prediction by introducing ε-insensitive loss function (Mukherjee et al. 1997; Muller et al. 1997; Vapnik 1995; Vapnik et al. 1997, Samui, 2008; Samui et al., 2008). The SVM implements the structural risk minimization principle (SRMP), which has been shown to be superior to the more traditional Empirical Risk Minimization Principle (ERMP) employed by many of the other modelling techniques (Osuna et al. 1997; Gunn 1998). SRMP minimizes an upper bound of the generalization error whereas, ERMP minimizes the training error. In this way, it produces the better generalization than traditional techniques. The paper has the following aims:

1. To investigate the feasibility of the SVM model for predicting Q of pile.
2. To develop an equation for prediction of Q of pile based on the developed SVM model
3. To make a comparative study between SVM and ANN model developed by Kiefa (1998).
4. To explore the relative importance of the factors affecting the Q prediction by carrying out a sensitivity analysis.

DETAILS OF SVM MODEL

Support Vector Machine (SVM) has originated from the concept of statistical learning theory pioneered by Boser et al. (1992). An interesting property of SVM approach is that it is an approximate implementation of the structural risk minimization (SRM) induction principle which tells that the generalization ability of learning machines depend more on capacity concept than merely the dimensionality of the space or the number of free parameters of the loss function. This study uses the SVM as a regression technique by introducing a ε-insensitive loss function. In this section, a brief introduction on how to construct SVM for regression problem is presented. More details can be found in many publications (Boser et al. 1992; Cortes and Vapnik 1995; Gualtieri et al. 1999; Vapnik 1998). The ε-insensitive loss function can be described in the following way

$$L_\varepsilon(y) = 0 \text{ for } |f(x) - y| < \varepsilon \text{ otherwise } L_\varepsilon(y) = |f(x) - y| - \varepsilon \tag{1}$$

Consider the problem of approximating the set of data,

$$D = \{(x_1, y_1)....(x_1, y_1)\}, \ x \in R^N, \ y \in r \tag{2}$$

where x is the input, y is the output, R^N is the N-dimensional vector space and r is the one dimensional vector space. In this study, the input parameters are the length of the pile (L), cross sectional area of pile (A), angle of shear resistance of the soil around the shaft (ϕ_{shaft}), angle of shear resistance of the soil at the tip of the pile (ϕ_{tip}) and the effective overburden pressure at the tip of the pile(σ'_v) and the output of the model is Q.

So, $x = \left[L, A, \phi_{tip}, \phi_{shaft}, \sigma'_v\right]$ and $y = [Q]$.

The main aim in SVM is to find a function $f(x)$ that gives a deviation of ε from the actual output and at the same time is as flat as possible. Let us assume a linear function

$$f(x) = (w.x) + b \ \ w \in R^n, \qquad b \in r$$
$$\tag{3}$$

where, $w =$ is an adjustable weight vector and $b =$ scalar threshold.

Flatness in the case of (3) means that one seeks a small w. One way of obtaining this is by minimizing the Euclidean norm $\|w\|^2$. This is equivalent to the following convex optimization problem

Minimize: $\dfrac{1}{2}\|w\|^2$

Subjected to: $y_i - \left(\left\langle w.x_i \right\rangle + b\right) \le \varepsilon$, $i = 1, 2,...,l$

$\left(\left\langle w.x_i \right\rangle + b\right) - y_i \le \varepsilon$, $i = 1, 2,...,l$ (4)

In order to allow for some errors, the slack variables ξ_i and ξ_i^* (see Figure 1) are introduced in (4). The formulation can then be restated as

Minimize: $\dfrac{1}{2}\|w\|^2 + C\displaystyle\sum_{i=1}^{l}\left(\xi_i + \xi_i^*\right)$

Subjected to: $y_i - \left(\left\langle w.x_i \right\rangle + b\right) \le \varepsilon + \xi_i$, $i = 1, 2,...,l$

$\left(\left\langle w.x_i \right\rangle + b\right) - y_i \le \varepsilon + \xi_i^*$, $i = 1, 2,...,l$

$\xi_i \ge 0$ and $\xi_i^* \ge 0$, $i = 1, 2,...,l$ (5)

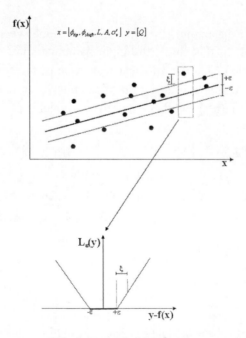

Figure 1. Prespecified Accuracy ε and Slack Variable ξ in support vector regression [Scholkopf (1997)].

The constant $0 < C < \infty$ determines the trade-off between the flatness of f and the amount up to which deviations larger than ε are tolerated (Smola and Scholkopf 2004). In practice, the C value is selected by trail and error. A large C assigns higher penalties to errors so that the

SVM is trained to minimize error with lower generalization while a small C assigns fewer penalties to errors; this allows the minimization of margin with errors, thus higher generalization ability.

If C goes to infinitely large, SVM would not allow the occurrence of any error and result in a complex model, whereas when C goes to zero, the result would tolerate a large amount of errors and the model would be less complex. The above constrained optimization problem Eq.(5) is solved by using the method of Lagrange multipliers. Lagrangian function is constructed in the following way

$$L\left(w,\xi,\xi^*,\alpha,\alpha^*,\gamma,\gamma^*\right) = \frac{\|w\|^2}{2} + C\left(\sum_{i=1}^{1}\left(\xi_i + \xi_i^*\right)\right) - \sum_{i=1}^{1}\alpha_i\left[\varepsilon + \xi_i - y_i + \langle w.x_i\rangle + b\right]$$

$$- \sum_{i=1}^{1}\alpha_i^*\left[\varepsilon + \xi_i^* + y_i - \langle w.x_i\rangle - b\right] - \sum_{i=1}^{1}\left(\gamma_i\xi_i + \gamma_i^*\xi_i^*\right) \tag{6}$$

where α, $\alpha*$, γ and γ^* are the Lagrangian multipliers. The solution to the constrained optimization problem is determined by the saddle point of the Lagrangian function $L\left(w,\xi,\xi^*,\alpha,\alpha^*,\gamma,\gamma^*\right)$, which has to be minimized with respect to w, b, ξ and ξ^*. The minimum with respect to w, b, ξ and ξ^* of the Lagrangian, L is given by,

Condition 1: $\dfrac{\partial L}{\partial w} = 0 \Rightarrow w = \sum_{i=1}^{1} x_i\left(\alpha_i - \alpha_i^*\right)$

Condition 2: $\dfrac{\partial L}{\partial b} = 0 \Rightarrow \sum_{i=1}^{1}\alpha_i = \sum_{i=1}^{1}\alpha_i^*$

Condition 3: $\dfrac{\partial L}{\partial \xi} = 0 \Rightarrow \sum_{i=1}^{1}\gamma_i = \sum_{i=1}^{1}\left(C - \alpha_i\right)$

Condition 4: $\dfrac{\partial L}{\partial \xi^*} = 0 \Rightarrow \sum_{i=1}^{1}\gamma_i^* = \sum_{i=1}^{1}\left(C - \alpha_i^*\right)$ $\qquad(7)$

Substituting (7) into (6) yields the dual optimization problem
Maximize:

$$-\varepsilon\sum_{i=1}^{1}\left(\alpha_i^* + \alpha_i\right) + \sum_{i=1}^{1}y_i\left(\alpha_i^* - \alpha_i\right) - \frac{1}{2}\sum_{i=1}^{1}\sum_{j=1}^{1}\left(\alpha_i^* - \alpha_i\right)\left(\alpha_j^* - \alpha_j\right)\left(x_i.x_j\right)$$

Subjected to: $\sum_{i=1}^{1}\alpha_i = \sum_{i=1}^{1}\alpha_i^*$; $0 \leq \alpha_i^* \leq C$ and $0 \leq \alpha_i \leq C$ $\qquad(8)$

The coefficients α_i, α_i^* are determined by solving the above optimization problem Eq. (8). From the Karush-Kuhn-Tucker (KKT) optimality condition, it is known that some of α_i, α_i^* will be zero. The non-zero α_i, α_i^* are called support vectors. So Eq. (3) can be written as

$$f(x) = \sum_{\text{support vectors}} \left(\alpha_i - \alpha_i^*\right)\left(x_i . x\right) + b$$

$$\text{where } b = -\left(\frac{1}{2}\right) w.\left[x_r + x_s\right] \tag{9}$$

where, x_r and x_s is support vector. From (7) it is clear that w has been completely described as a linear combination of training patterns.

So, the complexity of a function representation by support vectors is independent of the dimensionality of input space and it depends only on the number of support vectors.

When linear regression is not appropriate, then input data has to be mapped into a high dimensional feature space through some nonlinear mapping (Boser et al. 1992)(see Figure 2). After replacing x by its mapping in the feature space $\Phi(x)$ into the optimization problem (8) Maximize:

$$-\varepsilon \sum_{i=1}^{l}\left(\alpha_i^* + \alpha_i\right) + \sum_{i=1}^{l} y_i\left(\alpha_i^* - \alpha_i\right) - \frac{1}{2}\sum_{i=1}^{l}\sum_{j=1}^{l}\left(\alpha_i^* - \alpha_i\right)\left(\alpha_j^* - \alpha_j\right)\left(\Phi\left(x_i\right)\Phi\left(x_j\right)\right)$$

$$\text{Subjected to: } \sum_{i=1}^{l} \alpha_i = \sum_{i=1}^{l} \alpha_i^* \; ; 0 \le \alpha_i^* \le C \text{ and } 0 \le \alpha_i \le C \tag{10}$$

The concept of kernel function $[K\left(x_i, x_j\right) = \Phi\left(x_i\right)\Phi\left(x_j\right)]$ has been introduced to reduce the computational demand (Cristianini and Shwae-Taylor 2000; Cortes and Vapnik 1995). So optimization problem can be written as:

Maximize:

$$-\varepsilon \sum_{i=1}^{l}\left(\alpha_i^* + \alpha_i\right) + \sum_{i=1}^{l} y_i\left(\alpha_i^* - \alpha_i\right) - \frac{1}{2}\sum_{i=1}^{l}\sum_{j=1}^{l}\left(\alpha_i^* - \alpha_i\right)\left(\alpha_j^* - \alpha_j\right)\left(K\left(x_i . x_j\right)\right)$$

$$\text{Subjected to: } \sum_{i=1}^{l} \alpha_i = \sum_{i=1}^{l} \alpha_i^* \; ; 0 \le \alpha_i^* \le C \text{ and } 0 \le \alpha_i \le C \tag{11}$$

The final form of regression is given by (by putting the value of w(

$$w = \sum_{i=1}^{l}\left(\alpha_i - \alpha_i^*\right)K\left(x_i, x\right) \text{ in Eq.3)}$$

$$f(x) = \sum_{i=1}^{l}\left(\alpha_i - \alpha_i^*\right)K\left(x_i, x\right) + b \tag{12}$$

Where $b = -\dfrac{1}{2}\sum_{i=1}^{l}\left(\alpha_i - \alpha_i^{*}\right)\left\{K\left(x_i x_r\right) + K\left(x_i x_s\right)\right\}$

Some common kernels have been used such as polynomial (homogeneous), polynomial (nonhomogeneous), radial basis function, Gaussian function, sigmoid etc for non-linear cases. Figure 3. shows a typical architecture of SVM for Q prediction.

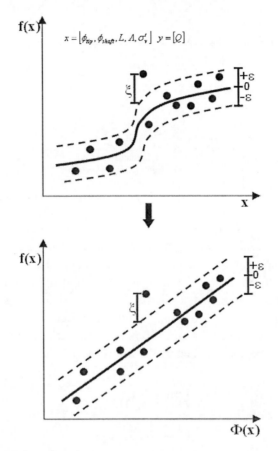

Figure 2. Concept of nonlinear regression.

This chapter uses the above SVM model for prediction of Q of driven piles in cohesionless soil. The data set consists of 59 case studies pile foundation. The input parameters that have been selected are related to the geotechnical parameters and the geometry of pile foundation. More specifically, L, A, ϕ_{shaft}, ϕ_{tip} and σ'_v are considerd as input. The output from the model is Q. In carrying out the formulation, the data has been divided into two sub-sets: such as

(a) A training dataset: This is required to construct the model. In this study, 41 out of the possible 59cases of pile are considered for training dataset.

(b) A testing dataset: This is required to estimate the model performance. In this study, the remaining 18 data are considered as testing dataset.

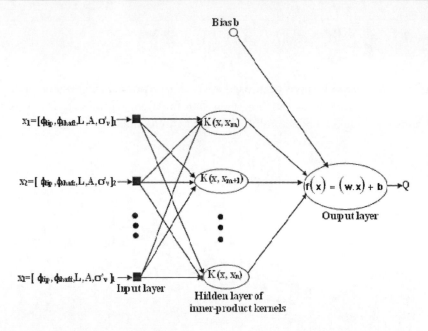

Figure 3. Architecture of SVM for Q prediction.

The data is scaled between 0 and 1. To train the SVM model, radial basis function has been used as kernel function. In training process, a simple trial-and-error approach has been used to select the design value of C, ε and width (σ) of radial basis function. In this study, a sensitivity analysis has been done to extract the cause and effect relationship between the inputs and outputs of the SVM model. The basic idea is that each input of the model is offset slightly and the corresponding change in the output is reported. The procedure has been taken from the work of Liong et al (2000). According to Liong et al (2000), the sensitivity(S) of each input parameter has been calculated by the following formula

$$S(\%) = \frac{1}{41} \sum_{j=1}^{41} \left(\frac{\% \text{ change in ouput}}{\% \text{ change in input}} \right)_j \times 100 \qquad (13)$$

where N is the number of data points. The analysis has been carried out on the trained model by varying each of input parameter, one at a time, at a constant rate of 30%. In the present study, training, testing and sensitivity analysis of SVM has been carried out by using MATLAB.

RESULTS AND DISCUSSION

The coefficient of correlation(R) is the main criterion that is used to evaluate the performance of the SVM models developed in this work. The design value of C, ε and σ is 130, 0.01 and 0.7 respectively. Number of support vector is 37. Figure 4. shows the performance of the SVM model for training dataset. In order to evaluate the capabilities of the SVM model, the model is validated with new data that are not part of the training dataset.

Figure 5. shows the performance of the SVM model for testing dataset. A comparative study has been made between the developed SVM model and ANN model proposed by Kiefa(1998) for testing data set. Table 1 shows root-mean-square-error (RMSE) and mean absolute-error (MAE) of the ANN and SVM model. It is clear from Table 1 that SVM is better model than the ANN model. The use of the SRM principle in defining cost function provided more generalization capacity with the SVM compared to the ANN, which uses the

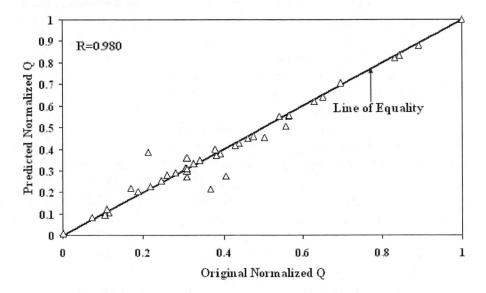

Figure 4. Performance of SVM for training dataset.

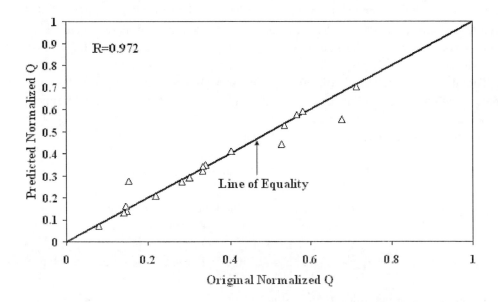

Figure 5. Performance of SVM for testing dataset.

Table 1. Comparison between ANN and SVM model

Model	RMSE(kN)	MAE(kN)
SVM	257.0084	149.1723
ANN(Kiefa,1998)	368.9784	274.5

empirical risk minimization principle. SVM uses only three parameters (radial basis function: σ, C and ε; polynomial kernel: degree of polynomial, C and ε).

In ANN, there are a larger number of controlling parameters, including the number of hidden layers, number of hidden nodes, learning rate, momentum term, number of training epochs, transfer functions, and weight initialization methods.

Obtaining an optimal combination of these parameters is a difficult task as well. Another major advantage of the SVM is its optimization algorithm, which includes solving a linearly constrained quadratic programming function leading to a unique, optimal, and global solution compared to the ANN. In SVM, the number of support vectors has determined by algorithm rather than by trial-and-error which has been used by ANN for determining the number of hidden nodes.

The loss of performance with respect to the testing set addresses SVM's susceptibility to overtraining. There is a marginal reduction in performance on the testing dataset (i.e., there is a difference between SVM performance on training and testing) for the SVM model. So, SVM has the ability to avoid overtraining, and hence it has better generalization capability than ANN. In prediction models, there are infinitely many functions that may provide an accurate fit to the finite testing set. Notwithstanding this, SVM formulation does not try to fit data.

Instead, it tries to capture underlying functions from which the data were generated irrespective of the presence of noise. For SVM, this insensitivity to noise in the data is attributed to the ε-insensitive loss function in the model formulation. This feature also provides control over model complexity in ways that alleviate the problems of over- and under-fitting.

The determination of Q of driven piles in cohesionless is a complex problem in geotechnical engineering. For most mathematical models that attempt to solve this problem, the lack of physical understanding is usually supplemented by either simplifying the problem or incorporating several assumptions into the models.

In contrast, as shown in this study, SVM uses the data alone to determine the parameters of the model. In this case, there is no need to simplify the problem or to incorporate any assumptions.

Moreover, SVM can always be updated to obtain better results by presenting new training examples as new data become available. The following equation (by putting

$$K(x_i, x) = \exp\left\{ -\frac{(x_i - x)(x_i - x)^T}{2\sigma^2} \right\}$$,s=0.7,b=0 and l=41 in has been developed for the

prediction of Q of driven piles based on the SVM model.

$$Q = \sum_{i=1}^{41} \left(\alpha_i - \alpha_i^* \right) \exp \left\{ - \frac{\left(x_i - x \right)\left(x_i - x \right)^T}{0.98} \right\} \tag{13}$$

Figure 6. shows the value of $\left(\alpha_i - \alpha_i^* \right)$.

In case of sensitivity studies, the analysis has been done for training dataset. The result of sensitivity analysis has been shown in Figure 7. From Figure 7, it is clear that L has the most significant effect on the predicted Q followed by A, ϕ_{tip}, ϕ_{shaft} and σ'_v.

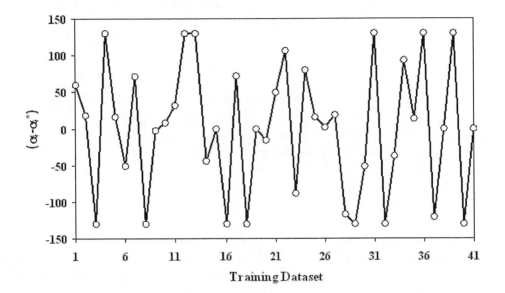

Figure 6. Values of $\left(\alpha_i - \alpha_i^* \right)$.

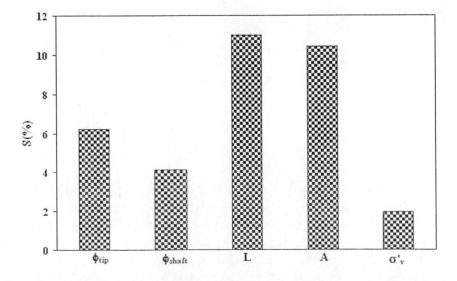

Figure 7. Sensitivity analysis of input parameters.

CONCLUSION

In this paper, SVM approach for the prediction of ultimate capacity of driven piles in cohesionless soil has been presented. 59 pile load tests data have been utilized to construct the model. SVM training consists of solving a – uniquely solvable – quadratic optimization problem and always finds a global minimum. The results indicate that SVM has the ability to predict Q of piles with an acceptable degree of accuracy. This study also gives a formula for prediction of ultimate capacity of driven piles in cohesionless soil. The sensitivity analysis indicates that L is the most important factor affecting Q of pile. The main drawback of SVM is the determination of proper parameters C and ε is still a heuristic process. However, despite the aforementioned limitation, the results of this study indicate that SVM is a powerful and practical tool for Q prediction of driven piles in cohesionless soil.

REFERENCES

Kiefa, M.A. General Regression Neural Networks for driven piles in cohesionless soils. *Journal of geotechnical and geoenviromental engineering*. 1998, 124(12), 1177-1185.

Boser, B.E.; Guyon, I.M.; Vapnik, V.N. A training algorithm for optimal margin classifiers. In D. Haussler, editor, 5th Annual ACM Workshop on COLT, Pittsburgh, PA, ACM Press, 1992, 144-152.

Chan, W.T.; Chow, Y.K.; Liu, L.F. Neural Network: An Alternative to pile driving formula. *Computers and geotechnics*. 1995, 17, 135-156.

Chow, Y.K.; Chan, L.F.; Liu, L.F.; Lee, S.L. Prediction of pile capacity from stress-wave measurements: A neural network approach. *International journal of numerical and analytical methods in geomechani*cs.1995, 19, 107-126.

Cortes, C; Vapnik, V.N. *Support vector networks. Machine Learning*. 1995, 20, 273-297.

Coyle, H.M; Castello, R.R. New design correlations for piles in sand. *Journal of Geotechnical Engineering*. 1981, 107(7), 965-986.

Cristianini, N.; Shawe-Taylor, J. (2000). An introduction to Support vector machine, Cambridge University press, London.

Ghaboussi, J. Potential application of neuro-biological computational models in geotechnical engineering. Numerical models in geomechanices 1992, G.N. Pande and S. Pietruszezak, eds., Balkemma, Rotterdam, The Netherlands, 543-555.

Goh, A.T.C. Empirical design in geotechnics using neural networks. *Geotechnique*. 1995, 45(4), 709-714.

Gualtieri, J.A.; Chettri, S.R.; Cromp, R.F.; Johnson, L.F. (1999). Support vector machine classifiers as applied to AVIRIS data. In the Summaries of the Eighth JPL Airbrone Earth Science Workshop.

Gunn, S. (1998). Support vector machines for classification and regression, Image. *Speech and Intelligent Systems Tech*. Rep., University of Southampton, U.K.

Kecman, V. Learning and Soft Computing: Support Vector Machines, Neural Networks, And Fuzzy Logic Models, the MIT press: Cambridge, Massachusetts, London, England, 2001.

Lee, I.M.; Lee, J.H. Prediction of pile bearing capacity using artificial neural network. *Computers and geotechnics*. 1996, 18(3), 189-200.

Liong, S.Y.; Lim, W.H.; Paudyal, G.N. River stage forecasting in Bangladesh: neural network approach. *Journal of computing in civil engineering*. 2000, 14(1), 1-8.

Mayoraz, F; Vulliet, L. Neural Networks for Slope Movement Prediction. *International Journal of Geomechanics*. 2002, 2, 153-173.

Meyerhof, G.G. Bearing capacity and settlement of pile foundation. *Journal of Geotechnical Engineering*. 1976, 102(3), 196-228.

Mukherjee, S.; Osuna, E.; Girosi, F. Nonlinear prediction of chaotic time series using support vector machine. *Proc., IEEE Workshop on Neural Networks for Signal Processing 7, Institute of Electrical and Electronics Engineers*, New York. 1997, 511–519.

Muller, K.R.; Smola, A.; Ratsch, G.; Scholkopf, B.; Kohlmorgen, J.; Vapnik, V. (1997). Predicting time series with support vector machines. Proc., International Conference on Artificial Neural Networks, Springer-Verlag, Berlin, 999.

Osuna, E.; Freund, R.; Girosi, F. An improved training algorithm for support vector machines. Proc., IEEE Workshop on Neural Networks for Signal Processing 7, Institute of Electrical and Electronics Engineers, New York. 1997, 276–285.

Pal, M.; Deswal, S. Modeling pile capacity using support vector machines and generalized regression neural network. *Journal of Geotechnical and Geoenvironmental Engineering*. 2008, 134 (7), 1021-1024.

Park, D; Rilett, L.R. Forecasting freeway link ravel times with a multi-layer feed forward neural network. *Computer Aided Civil and Znfa Structure Engineering*. 1999, 14, 358 - 367.

Park, H.I.; Seok, J.W.; Hwang, D.J. Hybrid neural network and genetic algorithm approach to the prediction of bearing capacity of driven piles. *Proceedings of the 6th European Conference on Numerical Methods in Geotechnical Engineering - Numerical Methods in Geotechnical Engineering*. 2006, 671-676.

Pooya Nejad, F.; Jaksa, M.B.; Kakhi, M.; McCabe, B.A. *Prediction of pile settlement using artificial neural networks based on standard penetration test data. Computers and Geotechnics*. 2009, 36 (7), 1125-1133.

Randolph, M.F.; Dolwin, J; Beck, R. Design of driven piles in sand. *Ge'otechnique*. 1994, 44(3), 427-448.

Randolph, M.F. Capacity of piles driven into dense sand. Rep. Soils TR 171, Engg. Dept., Cambridge University, 1985.

RP2A: Recommended practice for planning, designing and constructing fixed offshore platforms. American petroleum Institute, Washington, D.C., 1984, 15th Ed.

Samui, P; Kumar, B. Artificial Neural Network Prediction of Stability Numbers for Two-layered Slopes with Associated Flow Rule. *The Electronic Journal of Geotechnical Engineering*. 2006, 11.

Samui, P. Prediction of friction capacity of driven piles in clay using the support vector machine. *Canadian Geotechnical Journal*. 2008, 45 (2), 288-295.

Scholkopf, B. (1997). Support vector learning, R. Oldenbourg, Munich.

Smola, A.J.; Scholkopf, B. A tutorial on support vector regression. Statistics and Computing. 2004, 14, 199-222.

Vapnik, V.N. (1995). The nature of statistical learning theory. Springer, New York.

Vapnik, V.N. (1998). *Statistical learning theory*. New York, Wiley.

Vapnik, V.N.; Golowich, S.; Smola, A. (1997). Support method for function approximation regression estimation and signal processing. *Advance in neural information processing system 9*, Mozer M. and Petsch T., Eds. Cambridge, Ma:MIT press.

In: Support Vector Machines
Editor: Brandon H. Boyle

ISBN 978-1-61209-342-0
© 2011 Nova Science Publishers, Inc.

Chapter 5

SUPPORT VECTOR MACHINES IN MEDICAL CLASSIFICATION TASKS

David Gil[1] *and Magnus Johnsson*[2]
[1]Computing Technology and Data Processing,
University of Alicante, Spain
[2]Lund University Cognitive Science, Sweden

1. Introduction

The terms diagnosis and classification imply the procedure to discern or to distinguish. In the medical field both terms are used indistinctly. For this reason the implementation of classifier systems in medical diagnosis is rising progressively, taking advantage of the interactive computer programs. Undoubtedly the evaluation of patient data and the experts decisions are the most important factors in diagnosis. However, expert systems or decision support systems and diverse artificial intelligence procedures for classification have a huge potential of being good supportive tools for the expert. Classification systems help in improving accuracy and reliability of diagnoses and reducing possible errors, as well as making the diagnoses faster [1].

Some of the related work in the field of the medical diagnosis has been developed basically by means of Artificial Neural Networks (ANNs) [18] [54]. A particular advantage of SVMs over other classifiers is that they can achieve better performance when applied to real world problems [23]. Some classifiers, such as ANNs suffer from the overfitting problem. In the case of the SVM overfitting is unlikely to occur. Overfitting is caused by too much flexibility in the decision boundary.

Since their introduction in the late seventies [51], Support vector machines (SVMs) marked the beginning of a new era in the learning from examples paradigm [4] [24]. SVMs have focussed recent attention from the pattern recognition community due to a number of theoretical and computational merits derived from the Statistical Learning Theory (SLT) [50] [49] developed by Vladimir Vapnik at AT&T. Moreover, recent developments in defining and training statistical classifiers make it possible to build reliable classifiers in very small sample size problems [10] since pattern recognition systems based on SVM circumvent the curse of dimensionality, and even may find nonlinear decision boundaries for small

training sets. These techniques have been successfully used in a number of applications
[5] [47] including voice activity detection [12] [13] [41] [42], content-based image retrieval
[46], texture classification [28] and medical imaging diagnosis [16] [37] [56].

2. Support Vector Machines

Support Vector Machines (SVM) is a supervised learning algorithm developed by Vladimir
Vapnik [50]. SVM creates a hyperplane or a set of hyperplanes in a high dimensional (or
even infinite dimensional) space which can be used in classification or regression problems.
The main idea behind SVM is to get good separation between classes in order to achieve a
correct classification.

SVMs have been successfully applied to a wide variety of applications, e.g. including
pattern recognition, biology and financial domains [45] [17]. by its ability to learn from
experimental data. The reason is that SVM often performs better than other conventional
parametric classifiers [24, 19].

For a classification problem, it is necessary to first try to estimate a function $f : \Re^N \to \{\pm 1\}$ using training data, which are l N-dimensional patterns x_i and class labels y_i, where

$$(x_1, y_1), ..., (x_l, y_l) \in \Re^N \times \{\pm 1\} \tag{1}$$

such that f will classify new samples (x, y) correctly.

Given this classification problem the SVM classifier, as described by [50] [21] [6],
satisfies the following conditions:

$$\begin{cases} \mathbf{w}^T \varphi(x_i) + b \geq +1 & if \quad y_i = +1, \\ \mathbf{w}^T \varphi(x_i) + b \leq -1 & if \quad y_i = -1, \end{cases} \tag{2}$$

which is equivalent to

$$y_i[\mathbf{w}^T \varphi(x_i) + b] \geq 1, \quad i = 1, 2, ..., l. \tag{3}$$

Here training vectors x_i are mapped into a higher dimensional space by the function φ.
The equations of (2) construct a hyperplane $\mathbf{w}^T \varphi(x_i) + b = 0$ in this higher dimensional
space that discriminates between the two classes shown in figure 1. Each of the two half-
spaces defined by this hyperplane corresponds to one class, H_1 for $y_i = +1$ and H_2 for
$y_i = -1$. Therefore the SVM classifier corresponds to decision functions:

$$y(x) = sign[\mathbf{w}^T \varphi(x_i) + b] \tag{4}$$

Thus the SVM finds a linear separating hyperplane with the maximal margin in this
higher dimensional space. The margin of a linear classifier is the minimal distance of any
training point to the hyperplane which is the distance between the dotted lines H_1 and
H_2 and the solid line shown in figure 1. The points x which lie on the solid line satisfy
$\mathbf{w}^T \varphi(x_i) + b = 0$, where $\mathbf{w}$ is normal to the hyperplane, $|b|/\|\mathbf{w}\|$ is the perpendicular
distance from the hyperplane to the origin, and $\|\mathbf{w}\|$ is the Euclidean norm of w. $1/\|\mathbf{w}\|$
is the shortest distance from the separating hyperplane to the closest positive (negative)
example. Therefore, the margin of a separating hyperplane will be $1/\|\mathbf{w}\| + 1/\|\mathbf{w}\|$. To

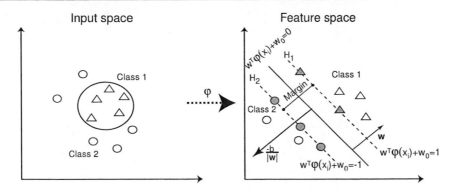

Figure 1. The mapping between input space and feature space in a two class problem with the SVM. Mapping the training data non-linearly into a higher dimensional feature space via function φ. H_1 and H_2 are parallel since they have the same normal $\mathbf{w}$ and perpendicular distance from the origin, $|\pm 1 - b|/\|\mathbf{w}\|$, and that no training points fall between them. The support vectors are the gray triangles and circles respectively located on H_1 and H_2. The distance from $\mathbf{w}$ to these support vectors is $1/\|\mathbf{w}\|$ and the margin is simply $2/\|\mathbf{w}\|$.

calculate the optimal separating plane is equivalent to maximizing the separation margin or distance between the two dotted lines H_1 and H_2.

It has to be considered that $H_1 : \mathbf{w}^T \varphi(x_i) + b = 1$ and $H_2 : \mathbf{w}^T \varphi(x_i) + b = -1$ are parallel since they have the same normal $\mathbf{w}$ and perpendicular distance from the origin, $|1 - b|/\|\mathbf{w}\|$ for H_1 and $|-1 - b|/\|\mathbf{w}\|$ for H_2, and that no training points fall between them. Thus we expect the solution for a typical two dimensional problem to have the form shown in figure 1. Those training points which gives equality in (3) are lying on one of the hyperplanes H_1 and H_2 are called support vectors and they are indicated in figure 1 by means of a gray color.

In practice, a separating hyperplane may not exist, i.e. if a high noise level causes a large overlap of the classes. To allow for the possibility of examples violating the edges of the margin (when perfect separation is not possible) [35], one introduces slack variables [44] [6] [50] [3].

$$\xi_i \geq 0, \quad i = 1, 2, ..., l. \tag{5}$$

in order to relax the constraints to

$$y_i[\mathbf{w}^T \varphi(x_i) + b] \geq 1 - \xi_i, \ i = 1, 2, ..., l. \tag{6}$$

A classifier which generalizes well is then found by controlling both the classifier capacity (via $\mathbf{w}$) and the sum of the slacks $\sum_i \xi_i$. The latter is done as it can be shown to provide an upper bound on the number of training errors which leads to a convex optimization problem. One possible realization, called C-SVC, of a soft margin classifier is minimizing the objective function

$$\min_{w,b,\xi} \quad J(\mathbf{w}, b, \xi) = \frac{1}{2}\mathbf{w}^T\mathbf{w} + C\sum_{i=1}^{l} \xi_i \tag{7}$$

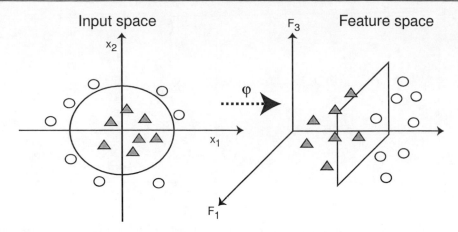

Figure 2. This figure illustrates the nonlinear transformation where the 2-D input space is mapped to a 3-D feature space. Note that, all the points belonging to a given class remain at a given side of the separating hyperplane and the data become linearly separable. In the input space, the hyperplane corresponds to a non-linear decision function whose form is determined by the kernel.

subject to the constraints (5) and (6). The constant $C > 0$ determines the trade-off between the flatness of a function and the amount up to which deviations are tolerated from the actually obtained targets y_i for all the training data. The positive real constant C is a tuning parameter in the algorithm. Therefore $C \sum_{i=1}^{l} \xi_i$ minimizes the misclassification error.

Figure 1 shows the basic idea of SVM, which is to map the data into some other dot product space (called the feature space) F via a nonlinear map

$$\Phi : \Re^N \to F \qquad (8)$$

and perform the above linear algorithm in F. This is also shown in Figure 2 that supplement Figure 1 illustrating this process. As can be seen, this only requires the evaluation of dot products.

$$K(x, x') = (\Phi(x).\Phi(x')) \qquad (9)$$

Clearly, if F is high-dimensional. this approach is not feasible and we have to find a computationally cheaper way. The key observation then is to substitute it for a simple kernel K that can be evaluated efficiently.

Kernel substitution is a method for using a linear classifier algorithm to solve a non-linear problem by mapping the original non-linear observations into a higher-dimensional space (as it is indicated in figure 1), where the linear classifier is subsequently used; this makes a linear classification in the new space equivalent to non-linear classification in the original space.

That transformation is done using Mercer's theorem [52], which states that any continuous, symmetric, positive semi-definite kernel function $K(x, x')$ can be expressed as a dot product in a high-dimensional space.

In that point the tools to construct nonlinear classifiers are defined. We substitute $\Phi(x_i)$ for each training example x_i, and perform the optimal hyperplane algorithm in F. Because we are using kernels, we will thus end up with nonlinear decision function of the form

$$y(x) = sign\left[\sum_{i=1}^{l} y_i K(x, x') + b\right].$$
(10)

where $K(x, x')$ is called the Kernel function, whose value is equal to the inner product of two vectors x and x' in the feature space; namely, $K(x, x') = \varphi(x)^T \varphi(x')$. Through the Kernel function, all computations are performed in the low-dimensional input space. Any function that satisfies the Mercers condition [7] can be used as the Kernel function.

There are many possibilities to define a function to be used as a Kernel. However, typical examples of kernels used in SVM, which have been successfully applied to a wide variety of applications, are linear, polynomials, radial basic functions and hyperbolic tangent:

$$Linear\ Kernel : k(\mathbf{x}, x') = x \cdot x'$$
(11)

$$Polynomial\ Kernel : k(x, x') = (x \cdot x' + c)^d$$
(12)

$$RBF\ Kernel : k(x, x') = \exp\left(-\frac{\gamma(x - x')^2}{\sigma}\right)$$
(13)

$$Sigmoid\ Kernel : k(x, x') = \tanh(\gamma x \cdot x' + c)$$
(14)

In this study, Radial Basis Functions Kernel (RBF) function has been adopted because we believe that it is a suitable choice for our problem. The RBF kernel nonlinearly maps samples into a higher dimensional space, so it, unlike the linear kernel, can handle the case when the relation between class labels and attributes is nonlinear.

Furthermore, the linear kernel is a special case of RBF as [25] shows that the linear kernel with a penalty parameter C has the same performance as the RBF kernel with some parameters (C, γ). In addition, the sigmoid kernel behaves like RBF for certain parameters [32]. Moreover, the number of hyperparameters influences the complexity of model selection. The polynomial kernel has more hyperparameters than the RBF kernel. Finally, the RBF kernel has less numerical difficulties. One key point is $0 < K_{ij} \leq 1$ in contrast to polynomial kernels of which kernel values may go to infinity ($\gamma x_i^T x_j + r > 1$) or zero ($\gamma x_i^T x_j + r < 1$) while the degree is large.

3. Experimentation

In this section we experiment with different data sets; in particular Breast Cancer, Parkinson and Urological databases.

The Breast Cancer and Parkinson databases used in this study are taken from the University of California at Irvine (UCI) machine learning repository [2] [34] [33]. The reason to use these sets of data is that the data sets of this website have been donated from hospitals.

These data have been studied by many professionals of artificial intelligence departments and they have been widely verified.

In contrast to these two databases, we conducted a study using a proprietary database. This has been obtained after several years of cooperation with the urology team of the Alicante University Hospital.

These databases have been used both for training and testing experiments. Frequently, the complete data set is divided into two subsets: the training set and the test set. Here, the training set is used to determine the system parameters, and the test set is used to evaluate the diagnosis accuracy and the network generalization. Cross-validation has been widely used to assess the generalization of a network. The cross-validation estimate of accuracy which is dctcrmincdby the overall number of correct classifications divided by the total number of examples in thedataset.

$$Acc_{cv} = \frac{1}{n} \sum_{x_i \in S} \delta(I(S_i, x_i), y_i) \qquad (15)$$

where n is the size of the dataset S, x_i is the example of S, y_i is the target of x_i, and S_i is the probable target of x_i by the classifier. Therefore:

$$\delta(i,j) = \begin{cases} 1 & if \quad i \in N_c(t) \\ 0 & otherwise \end{cases} \qquad (16)$$

Specifically, for this study we have applied a five-fold cross-validation method for the performance assessment of every network. The data has been divided in five sets (S1, S2, S3, S4, S5) and the five experiments performed were:
Experiment 1 - Training: S1, S2, S3, S4; Test: S5
Experiment 2 - Training: S1, S2, S3, S5; Test: S4
Experiment 3 - Training: S1, S2, S4, S5; Test: S3
Experiment 4 - Training: S1, S3, S4, S5; Test: S2
Experiment 5 - Training: S2, S3, S4, S5; Test: S1

The sets of data used for the process of constructing the model (the training data) were of 565, 195 and 380 registers for Breast Cancer, Parkinson and Urological respectively. The other set of data used to validate the model (the test data) was of 113, 39 and 76 registers also for Breast Cancer, Parkinson and Urological respectively. The test data are chosen randomly from the initial data and the remaining data form the training data. The method is called 5-fold cross validation since this process has been performed five times. The function approximation fits a function using the training set only. Then the function approximation is asked to predict the output values for the data in the testing set. The errors it makes are accumulated to provide the mean absolute test set error, which is used to evaluate the model. The results are presented using confusion matrices.

SVMs have empirically been shown to have good generalization performance on a wide variety of problems. However, the use of SVMs is still limited to a small group of researchers. One possible reason is that training algorithms for SVMs are slow, especially for large problems. Another explanation is that SVM training algorithms are complex, subtle, and difficult for an average engineer to implement. Training a SVM requires the solution of a very large Quadratic Programming (QP) optimization problem.

For these particular reasons we have used a new algorithm for training the SVM: Sequential Minimal Optimization (SMO) which is a faster training method for SVMs. SMO breaks this large QP problem into a series of smallest possible QP problems [39] [40] [26]. This implementation globally replaces all missing values and transforms nominal attributes into binary ones. It also normalizes all attributes by default.

These small QP problems are solved analytically, which avoids using a time-consuming numerical QP optimization as an inner loop. The amount of memory required for SMO is linear in the training set size, which allows SMO to handle very large training sets. Because matrix computation is avoided, SMO scales somewhere between linear and quadratic in the training set size for various test problems, while the standard SVM algorithm scales somewhere between linear and cubic in the training set size. SMOs computation time is dominated by SVM evaluation, hence SMO is fastest for linear SVMs and sparse data sets. On realworld sparse data sets, SMO can be more than 1000 times faster than the standard SVM algorithm [39].

The method to evaluate the efficiency of the SVM system is to obtain some measures as classification accuracy, sensitivity, specificity, positive predictive value, negative predictive value and confusion matrix. A confusion matrix [30] contains information about actual and predicted classifications done by a classification system. Moreover, we will present the receiver operating characteristic (ROC) [11], or simply ROC curves for every diagnosis. ROC curve is a graphical plot of the sensitivity, or true positives, vs. (1 - specificity), or false positives, for a binary classifier system as its discrimination threshold is varied. ROC analysis has been used successfully in medicine, radiology, and other areas for many decades, and it has been introduced relatively recently in other areas like machine learning and data mining. For example, ROC curves were employed in psychophysics to assess human (and occasionally non-human animal) detection of weak signals [20]. In medicine, ROC analysis has been extensively used in the evaluation of diagnostic tests [57, 38].

Figure 3 shows the ROC space with various measures that help to understand how to interpret the curve. From the above point to the left (indicating a perfect classification) and also with reference to the dashed line "random guess", we can establish that the larger the area that lies below the line is, the greater is the accuracy. The area under the ROC curve, also called AUC, the probability that a classifier will rank a randomly chosen positive instance higher than a randomly chosen negative one [14].

3.1. Breast Cancer Database

The Breast Cancer dataset consist of 32 attributes; 30 real-valued input features, an ID number and the Diagnosis (M = malignant, B = benign). This is defined in table 1.

The equations 17 to 21 define classification accuracy, sensitivity, specificity, positive predictive value and negative predictive value. Then, the confusion matrix is provided in table 2 and the ROC curve in figure 4.

$$Classif.\ accuracy(\%) = \frac{TP + TN}{TP + FP + FN + TN} \times 100 = 97,89\% \qquad (17)$$

$$Sensitivity(\%) = \frac{TP}{TP + FN} \times 100 = 99.71\% \qquad (18)$$

ROC Space

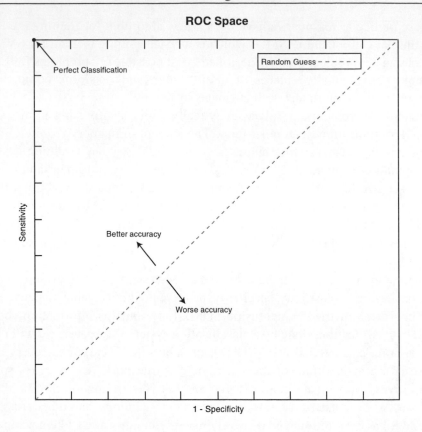

Figure 3. The receiver operating characteristic (ROC) present general information about the ROC curve. It shows the ROC space with various measures that help to understand how to interpret the curve. From the above point to the left (indicating a perfect classification) and also with reference to the dashed line "random guess", we can establish that the larger the area that lies below the line is, the greater is the accuracy.

$$Specificity(\%) = \frac{TN}{FP + TN} \times 100 = 94.81\% \qquad (19)$$

$$Positive\,predictive\,value(\%) = \frac{TP}{TP + FP} \times 100 = 97\% \qquad (20)$$

$$Negative\,predictive\,value(\%) = \frac{TN}{FN + TN} \times 100 = 99.5\% \qquad (21)$$

3.2. Parkinson Database

The dataset is composed of a range of biomedical voice measurements from 31 people, 23 with PD. Each column in table 3 is a particular voice measure, and each row corresponds to one of 195 voice recordings of these individuals ("name" column). Table 3 shows the fields of this database and a brief description of each input variable.

Table 1. List of real-valued features computed for each cell nucleus.

Field name	Description
radius	mean of distances from center to points on the perimeter
texture	standard deviation of gray-scale values
perimeter	for each cell nucleus
area	for each cell nucleus
smoothness	local variation in radius lengths
compactness	perimeter^2 / area - 1.0
concavity	severity of concave portions of the contour
concave points	number of concave portions of the contour
symmetry	for each cell nucleus
fractal dimension	"coastline approximation" - 1

Table 2. Definition of the confusion matrix (for the Breast Cancer dataset) with the values for every measure of the SVM classifier and linear kernel.

Actual	Predicted	
	Positive	Negative
Positive	True positive (TP)=356	False negative (FN)=1
Negative	False positive (FP)=11	True negative (TN)=201

Now, we present the results of applying SVM to the Parkinson database as we performed in the previous section with the Breast Cancer one by means of the equations 22 to 26. They define classification accuracy, sensitivity, specificity, positive predictive value and negative predictive value. Then, the confusion matrix is provided in table 4 and the ROC curve in figure 5.

$$Classif.\,accuracy(\%) = \frac{TP + TN}{TP + FP + FN + TN} \times 100 = 91.79\% \qquad (22)$$

$$Sensitivity(\%) = \frac{TP}{TP + FN} \times 100 = 99.32\% \qquad (23)$$

$$Specificity(\%) = \frac{TN}{FP + TN} \times 100 = 68.75\% \qquad (24)$$

$$Positive\,predictive\,value(\%) = \frac{TP}{TP + FP} \times 100 = 90.68\% \qquad (25)$$

$$Negative\,predictive\,value(\%) = \frac{TN}{FN + TN} \times 100 = 97.06\% \qquad (26)$$

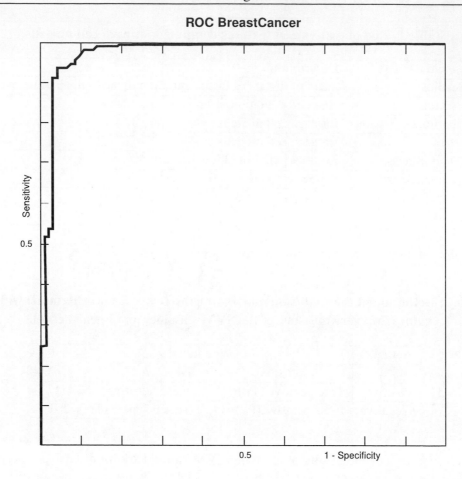

Figure 4. ROC curve for the Breast Cancer diagnosis by using SVM.

3.3. Urological Database

In the current section, with the urological database, we will implement a more extensive process. This is because this is a new database, created from scratch by the urologists.

Firstly, we examine the input data, which are the data collected by the urologist. Then, this information is normalized (in order to get similar characteristics to those of the two previous databases) which is shown in Table 5. Then, we discussed the improvements that occur when we perform a dimensionality reduction using two different techniques very effective. On this last modified urological database we it will be applied the SVM method.

The preparation of the data gets significantly improve accuracy. However, as we expected the results are worse than the ones obtained with the two previous databases.

The input data in the system starts when a patient reports to a physician. Then, a large number of information to be considered during the diagnosis will be saved in a database. In this study, an exhaustive urological exploration with 20 different measurements has been carried out by using 381 patients with dysfunctions in the Lower Urinary Tract (LUT). The 20 input variables (table 5) that are essential to the

Table 3. List of measurement methods applied to acoustic signals recorded from each subject.

Field name	Description
name	ASCII subject name and recording number
MDVP:Fo(Hz)	Average vocal fundamental frequency
MDVP:Fhi(Hz)	Maximum vocal fundamental frequency
MDVP:Flo(Hz)	Minimum vocal fundamental frequency
MDVP:Jitter(%)	Five measures of variation in fundamental frequency
MDVP:Jitter(Abs)	
MDVP:RAP	
MDVP:PPQ	
Jitter:DDP	
MDVP:Shimmer	Six measures of variation in amplitude
MDVP:Shimmer(dB)	
Shimmer:APQ3	
Shimmer:APQ5	
MDVP:APQ	
Shimmer:DDA	
NHR	Two measures of ratio of noise to tonal components in the voice
HNR	
RPDE	Two nonlinear dynamical complexity measures
D2	
DFA	Signal fractal scaling exponent
spread1	Three nonlinear measures of fundamental frequency variation
spread2	
PPE	
Status	Output - Health of the subject (1) - Parkinson's, (0) - healthy

Table 4. Definition of the confusion matrix (for the Parkinson dataset) with the values for every measure of the SVM classifier and linear kernel.

Actual	Predicted	
	Positive	Negative
Positive	True positive (TP)=146	False negative (FN)=1
Negative	False positive (FP)=15	True negative (TN)=33

diagnosis of the LUT diseases of interest are extracted from the urological database. The table 5 helps us to understand the dimension of the problem to deal with (different types of data, ranges and incomplete fields). These variables can be divided into five classes:

(a) General information about a patient, in our case only the age, normally the gender is also included but we use only female patients (the urological service is specialized in

ROC Parkinson

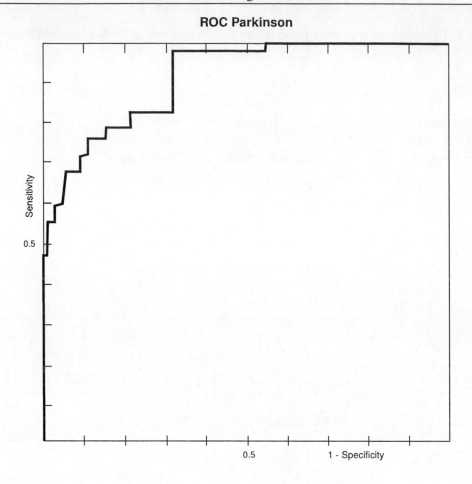

Figure 5. ROC curve for the Parkinson diagnosis by using SVM.

female incontinence).

(b) Neurological Physical Examination (3 features in total).

(c) Free flowmetry analysis (5 features in total).

(d) Cystometry (3 features in total) and

(e) Test pressure / flow (8 features in total).

Moreover, the 20 input variables (categorized into 3 groups or classes) are prearranged using the following structures:

(a) Numerical variables such as age, volume of urine and micturition time are normalized onto the interval (0, 1). For instance, the patients ages may span from 0 to 100 years old. However, in practice the oldest is 86, and thereby the age of a 86-year-old patient can be normalized to the value of 86/86=1 whereas a 63-year-old patient can be normalized to the value of 63/86=0.73.

(b) The variables with only two independent attributes are prearranged with binary values (0, 1). We only have the representation of anal tone where 1 means normal and 0 denotes relaxed.

(c) The variables with three independent attributes, such as perineal and perianal sensitivity, detrusor contraction or abdominal pressure are prearranged using the ternary values (-1, 0, 1). For example, the abdominal pressure will take -1 for the absence, 0 represents weak and 1 represents normal.

Table 5. Fields of the urological database and their consequent values normalized on to the interval between parenthesis.

	Input variables	Values normalized
General Information	Age	(0, 1)
Neurological Physical Examination	Perineal and perianal sensitivity	(-1, 0, 1)
	Anal tone	(0, 1)
	Voluntary control of the anal sphincter	(-1, 0, 1)
Free Flowmetry	Volume of urine	(0, 1)
	Post void residual	(0, 1)
	Maximum flow rate	(0, 1)
	Average flow rate	(0, 1)
	Micturition time	(0, 1)
Cystometry	Bladder storage	(0, 1)
	Detrusor pressure filling	(0, 1)
	First sensation of bladder filling	(0, 1)
Test pressure / flow	Detrusor contraction	(-1, 0, 1)
	Abdominal pressure	(-1, 0, 1)
	Volume of urine in micturition	(0, 1)
	Post void residual	(0, 1)
	Maximum pressure detrusor	(0, 1)
	Maximum flow rate	(0, 1)
	Average flow rate	(0, 1)
	Micturition time	(0, 1)

3.3.1. Dimensionality Reduction

Research indicates that application of data dimensionality reduction as a pre-step to the classification procedure does improve the classification accuracy [43] [15]. Furthermore, feature selection can also provide a better understanding of the underlying process that generated the data [22]. It is beneficial, and also demanded in many cases, to limit the number of input features when building classification systems in order to have a good predictive and less computationally intensive model [55]. In the area of medical diagnosis, a small feature subset means lower test and diagnostic costs. There are several approaches to go about the dimensionality reduction process. The wrapper and the filter approach are two of the most important. These select the most significant attributes [31]. The wrapper approach uses the selected data mining algorithm in its search for the attribute subsets [29] while in the

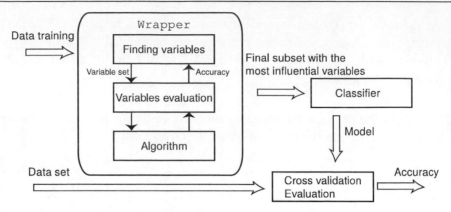

Figure 6. Wrapper approach in variables selection. The wrapper method requires one predetermined learning algorithm and uses the performance of the learning algorithm to evaluate and determine which features are selected. Thus, with this method a high accuracy is obtained.

filter approach, undesirable attributes are filtered out of the data before classification begins [9]. Feature wrappers use induction learning in order to evaluate a feature subset whereas feature filters use a heuristic in order to do the same task. Feature filters are known to be faster than feature wrappers. However, since wrappers use the performance function as the evaluation function, they are known to outperform filters in terms of accuracy. Therefore, the decision between filter or wrapper selection depends on the problem. If data analysis needs to be performed in high dimensional space, selecting the filter approach seems to be a better alternative in order to avoid computational cost. However, if accuracy is important and computational cost is manageable, then wrappers should be utilized [48]. The wrapper approach uses a predetermined learning algorithm along with a statistical re-sampling technique (usually cross-validation) to determine a feature (variable) subset that results in the most accurate model. Wrapper methods integrate feature selection with the machine learning process. The wrapper approach includes a target classifier as a black box for performance evaluation. In other words, a computation-intensive evaluator is performed many times on candidate feature subsets to choose relevant features. When wrappers are included in the training process, they are often called as embedded methods. The wrapper model requires one predetermined learning algorithm and uses the performance of the learning algorithm to evaluate and determine which features are selected. An algorithm commonly used by the wrapper is a genetic algorithm (GA), which is employed to search optimal feature subsets under the assessment of the classifiers predictive accuracy [36] [27]. Thanks to this integration with the training process wrapper is a beneficial approach considering that we immediately see the result of the reduction of the feature space being translated into the corresponding classification with our subset of features selection. Figures 6 and 7 illustrate both methods. Recently, some researchers proposed a hybrid approach for feature selection [8] [53]. The basic idea is to select a small number of variable subsets based on variable correlation and then determine the best subset by explicitly evaluating the loss function.

In this work the wrapper approach has been selected to decide the importance degree

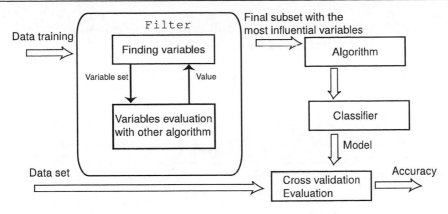

Figure 7. Filter approach in variable selection. The filter method does not require a particular learning algorithm. It use a heuristic to evaluate a feature subset. Features filters are known to be faster than feature wrappers because heuristics are faster than induction learning.

of every input data. In particular, an SVM classifier which evaluates the worth of every attribute. Then, the results in table 6 indicates this order of importance of each of them.

3.3.2. Architecture of the SVM

Each selected attribute of the urological data studied in the previous section constituted the input nodes of the SVM-based structure shown in Figure 8 which shows the architecture of SVM.

Finally, in this section we present the results of applying SVM to the Urological database as we performed in the previous sections with the Breast Cancer and Parkinson by means of the equations 27 to 31. They define classification accuracy, sensitivity, specificity, positive predictive value and negative predictive value. Then, the confusion matrix is provided in table 7 and the ROC curve in figure 9.

$$Classif.\ accuracy(\%) = \frac{TP + TN}{TP + FP + FN + TN} \times 100 = 84.25\% \qquad (27)$$

$$Sensitivity(\%) = \frac{TP}{TP + FN} \times 100 = 92.92\% \qquad (28)$$

$$Specificity(\%) = \frac{TN}{FP + TN} \times 100 = 33.92\% \qquad (29)$$

$$Positive\ predictive\ value(\%) = \frac{TP}{TP + FP} \times 100 = 89.08\% \qquad (30)$$

$$Negative\ predictive\ value(\%) = \frac{TN}{FN + TN} \times 100 = 45.23\% \qquad (31)$$

Table 6. Fields in order of worth. This will be used to decide what variables will constitute the input data in the SVM classifier.

Ranked attributes:	
Number	Name
8	AverageFlow
7	MaxFlow
15	VolumeUrineMicturition
16	PostVoidResidual
4	VoluntaryControlAnal
6	PostVoidResidual
18	MaximumFlowRate
12	FirstSensationBladderFilling
1	Age
2	PerinealAndPerianalSensitivity
10	BladderStorage
9	MicturitionTime
5	VolUrina
13	DetrusorContraction
20	MicturitionTime
14	AbdominalPressure
11	DetrusorPressureFilling
3	AnalTone
19	AverageFlowRate
17	MaximumPressureDetrusor
Selected attributes:	
8,7,15,16,4,6,18,12,1,2,10,9,5,13,20,14,11,3,19,17 : 20	

Table 7. Definition of confusion matrix (for the Urological dataset) with the value for every measure.

Actual	Predicted	
	Positive	Negative
Positive	True positive (TP)=302	False negative (FN)=23
Negative	False positive (FP)=37	True negative (TN)=19

The results of Sensitivity and Positive predictive are excellent. However, Specificity and Negative predictive are slightly low due to the skewed distribution of the output classes. This skewed distribution explains that positive predictive is rather high. That is, there are 325 samples of healthy patients and 56 of illness patients.

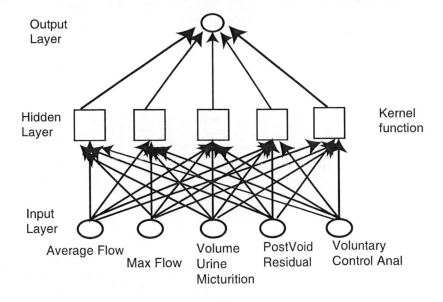

Figure 8. Architecture of the SVM. The input data correspond to the five highest values of worth of every input variable selected in table 6. In this study the RBF kernel function has been adopted.

4. Conclusions

In this work we have evaluated the performance of classifiers for medical tasks. It is constructed by means of the SVM method when applied to the diagnosis of certain dysfunctions. In particular we have used Breast Cancer, Parkinson and urological databases.

The experiment starts with a preprocessing of the medical databases. This preprocessing includes missing data treatment and normalization process. After that, data are provided to the SVM which determines whether there is a dysfunction or not. Data preprocessing is the stage in which the most time of the experimentation is spent. However, it is worth it because the accuracy of the system will increase notably approximately of 15%.

This is especially necessary for databases less refined as urological databases, as Breast Cancer and Parkinson have been used much more and have no missing data, and much more homogeneous values.

In these experiments we have obtained results very encouraging for Breast Cancer, Parkinson and urological databases with values of 97.89%, 91.79% and 84.25% respectively.

In some cases a bit less precision does not completely reflects the reality. This happens, for example, with urological database as well as other medical databases much less developed as those of Breast Cancer and Parkinson's. The problem is the skewed distribution of the output classes. It is necessary an intensive debug and cleaning process of

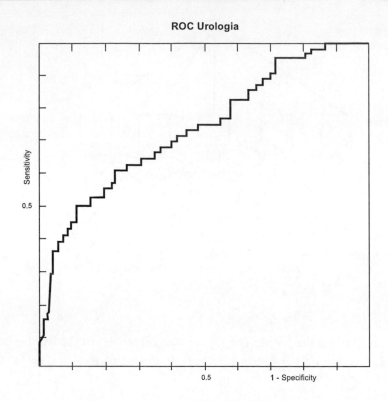

Figure 9. ROC curve for the Urological diagnosis by using SVM.

databases besides better distributions of the output classes before they are used successfully in machine learning.

We can conclude that the accuracy of the SVM has been tested and it shows a high degree of certainty. As a next and natural step in the procedure of a diagnosis,it would be very useful to show if it is able to distinguish and classify among the most common dysfunctions. For that reason the SVM has to be tested with more than two classes.

Acknowledgment

We would like to express our acknowledgement to the Spanish Ministry of Science and Innovation (Ministerio de Ciencia e Innovación - MICINN), more specifically the "José Castillejo" program and to the Swedish Research Council, the Swedish Linnaeus project Cognition, Communication and Learning (CCL) as funders of the work exhibited in this document.

References

[1] M.F. Akay. Support vector machines combined with feature selection for breast cancer diagnosis. *Expert Systems With Applications*, **36**(2, Part 2):3240 – 3247, 2009.

[2] A. Asuncion and D.J. Newman. UCI machine learning repository, 2007.

[3] K.P. Bennett and OL Mangasarian. Robust linear programming discrimination of two linearly inseparable sets. *Optimization Methods and Software*, **1**(1):23–34, 1992.

[4] C.J.C. Burges. A Tutorial on Support Vector Machines for Pattern Recognition. *Data Mining and Knowledge Discovery*, **2**(2):121–167, 1998.

[5] XB Cao, YW Xu, D. Chen, and H. Qiao. Associated evolution of a support vector machine-based classifier for pedestrian detection. *Information Sciences*, **179**(8):1070–1077, 2009.

[6] C. Cortes and V. Vapnik. Support-vector networks. *Machine Learning*, **20**(3):273–297, 1995.

[7] R. Courant and D. Hilbert. *Methods of mathematical physics. Volume I*. Interscience Publishers, 1953.

[8] S. Das. Filters, Wrappers and a Boosting-Based Hybrid for Feature Selection. In *MACHINE LEARNING-INTERNATIONAL WORKSHOP THEN CONFERENCE-*, pages 74–81, 2001.

[9] W. Duch. Filter Methods. *Studies in fuzziness and soft computing*, **207**:89, 2006.

[10] R.P.W. Duin. Classifiers in almost empty spaces. In *icpr*, page 2001. Published by the IEEE Computer Society, 2000.

[11] J.P. Egan. *Signal detection theory and ROC-analysis*. Academic Pr, 1975.

[12] D. Enqing, L. Guizhong, Z. Yatong, and Z. Xiaodi. Applying support vector machines to voice activity detection. In *2002 6th International Conference on Signal Processing*, pages 1124–1127, 2002.

[13] D. Enqing, Z. Heming, and L. Yongli. Low bit and variable rate speech coding using local cosine transform. In *TENCON'02. Proceedings. 2002 IEEE Region 10 Conference on Computers, Communications, Control and Power Engineering*, pages 423–426, 2002.

[14] T. Fawcett. An introduction to ROC analysis. *Pattern recognition letters*, **27**(8):861–874, 2006.

[15] X. Fu and L. Wang. Data dimensionality reduction with application to simplifying RBF network structure and improving classification performance. *Systems, Man and Cybernetics, Part B, IEEE Transactions on*, **33**(3):399–409, 2003.

[16] G. Fung and J. Stoeckel. SVM feature selection for classification of SPECT images of Alzheimer's disease using spatial information. *Knowledge and Information Systems*, **11**(2):243–258, 2007.

[17] D. Gil and M. Johnsson. Using support vector machines in diagnoses of urological dysfunctions. *Expert Systems with Applications*, **37**(6):4713 – 4718, 2010.

[18] D. Gil, M. Johnsson, J.M. Garcia Chamizo, A.S. Paya, and D.R. Fernandez. Application of artificial neural networks in the diagnosis of urological dysfunctions. *Expert Systems with Applications*, **36**(3P2):5754–5760, 2009.

[19] JM Górriz, J. Ramírez, A. Lassl, D. Salas-Gonzalez, EW Lang, CG Puntonet, I. Álvarez, M. López, and M. Gómez-Río. Automatic computer aided diagnosis tool using component-based SVM. In *IEEE Nuclear Science Symposium Conference Record, 2008. NSS'08*, pages 4392–4395, 2008.

[20] DM Green and JA Swets. Signal detection theory and psychophysics. New York. *NY: Wiley*, 1966.

[21] I. Guyon, B. Boser, and VN Vapnik. A training algorithm for optimal margin classifiers. In *Proc. of the 5th annual workshop of computational learning theory, ACM*, pages 144–152, 1992.

[22] I. Guyon and A. Elisseeff. An introduction to variable and feature selection. *The Journal of Machine Learning Research*, **3**:1157–1182, 2003.

[23] J. He, H.J. Hu, R. Harrison, P.C. Tai, and Y. Pan. Transmembrane segments prediction and understanding using support vector machine and decision tree. *Expert Systems With Applications*, **30**(1):64–72, 2006.

[24] T. Joachims. Text categorization with support vector machines: Learning with many relevant features. *Machine Learning: ECML-98*, pages 137–142, 1998.

[25] S.S. Keerthi and C.J. Lin. Asymptotic behaviors of support vector machines with Gaussian kernel. *Neural Computation*, **15**(7):1667–1689, 2003.

[26] SS Keerthi, SK Shevade, C. Bhattacharyya, and KRK Murthy. Improvements to Platt's SMO algorithm for SVM classifier design. *Neural Computation*, **13**(3):637–649, 2001.

[27] K. Kim. Toward Global Optimization of Case-Based Reasoning Systems for Financial Forecasting. *Applied Intelligence*, **21**(3):239–249, 2004.

[28] K.I. Kim, K. Jung, S.H. Park, and H.J. Kim. Support vector machines for texture classification. *IEEE Transactions on Pattern Analysis and Machine Intelligence*, **24**(11):1542–1550, 2002.

[29] R. Kohavi and G.H. John. Wrappers for feature subset selection. *Artificial Intelligence*, **97**(1-2):273–324, 1997.

[30] R. Kohavi and F. Provost. Glossary of terms. *Machine Learning*, **30**(2/3):271–274, 1998.

[31] Y. Li, Z.F. Wu, J.M. Liu, and Y.Y. Tang. Efficient feature selection for high-dimensional data using two-level filter. In *Machine Learning and Cybernetics, 2004. Proceedings of 2004 International Conference on*, volume 3, 2004.

[32] H.T. Lin and C.J. Lin. A study on sigmoid kernels for SVM and the training of non-PSD kernels by SMO-type methods. *Taipei: Department of Computer Science and Information Engineering, National Taiwan University*, 2003.

[33] M.A. Little, P.E. McSharry, E.J. Hunter, J. Spielman, and L.O. Ramig. Suitability of dysphonia measurements for telemonitoring of Parkinson? s disease. *IEEE transactions on bio-medical engineering*, 2008.

[34] M.A. Little, P.E. McSharry, S.J. Roberts, D.A.E. Costello, and I.M. Moroz. Exploiting Nonlinear recurrence and Fractal scaling properties for voice disorder detection. *BioMedical Engineering OnLine*, **6**(1):23, 2007.

[35] D.R. Martin, C.C. Fowlkes, and J. Malik. Learning to Detect Natural Image Boundaries Using Brightness and Texture. *ADVANCES IN NEURAL INFORMATION PROCESSING SYSTEMS*, pages 1279–1286, 2003.

[36] S.H. Min, J. Lee, and I. Han. Hybrid genetic algorithms and support vector machines for bankruptcy prediction. *Expert Systems With Applications*, **31**(3):652–660, 2006.

[37] B. Pang, D. Zhang, and K. Wang. Tongue image analysis for appendicitis diagnosis. *Information Sciences*, **175**(3):160–176, 2005.

[38] M.S. Pepe. *The statistical evaluation of medical tests for classification and prediction*. Oxford University Press, USA, 2004.

[39] J. Platt. Machines using sequential minimal optimization. *Advances in Kernel Methods-Support Vector Learning*, 1998.

[40] J. Platt. Sequential minimal optimization: A fast algorithm for training support vector machines. *Advances in Kernel Methods-Support Vector Learning*, **208**, 1999.

[41] F. Qi, C. Bao, and Y. Liu. A novel two-step SVM classifier for voiced/unvoiced/silence classification of speech. In *International Symposium on Chinese Spoken Language Processing*, pages 77–80, 2004.

[42] J. Ramírez, P. Yélamos, J. Górriz, C. Puntonet, and J. Segura. Svm-enabled voice activity detection. *Advances in Neural Networks-ISNN 2006*, pages 676–681, 2006.

[43] ML Raymer, WF Punch, ED Goodman, LA Kuhn, and AK Jain. Dimensionality reduction using genetic algorithms. *Evolutionary Computation, IEEE Transactions on*, **4**(2):164–171, 2000.

[44] B. Scholkopf, A.J. Smola, R.C. Williamson, and P.L. Bartlett. New Support Vector Algorithms, 2000.

[45] K.S. Shin, T.S. Lee, and H. Kim. An application of support vector machines in bankruptcy prediction model. *Expert Systems With Applications*, **28**(1):127–135, 2005.

[46] D. Tao, X. Tang, X. Li, and X. Wu. Asymmetric bagging and random subspace for support vector machines-based relevance feedback in image retrieval. *IEEE Transactions on Pattern Analysis and Machine Intelligence*, pages 1088–1099, 2006.

[47] H.H. Tsai and D.W. Sun. Color image watermark extraction based on support vector machines. *Information Sciences*, **177**(2):550–569, 2007.

[48] Ö. Uncu and IB Türkşen. A novel feature selection approach: Combining feature wrappers and filters. *Information Sciences*, **177**(2):449–466, 2007.

[49] V. Vapnik. Statistical learning theory., 1998.

[50] V.N. Vapnik. The Nature of Statistical Learning Theory [M], 1995.

[51] V.N. Vapnik and S. Kotz. *Estimation of dependences based on empirical data*. Springer-Verlag New York, 1982.

[52] R.C. Williamson, A.J. Smola, and B. Scholkopf. Generalization performance of regularization networks and support vector machines via entropy numbers of compact operators. *IEEE transactions on Information Theory*, **47**(6):2516–2532, 2001.

[53] E.P. Xing, M.I. Jordan, and R.M. Karp. Feature Selection for High-Dimensional Genomic Microarray Data. In *MACHINE LEARNING-INTERNATIONAL WORKSHOP THEN CONFERENCE-*, pages 601–608, 2001.

[54] H. Yan, Y. Jiang, J. Zheng, C. Peng, and Q. Li. A multilayer perceptron-based medical decision support system for heart disease diagnosis. *Expert Systems with Applications*, **30**(2):272–281, 2006.

[55] GP Zhang. Neural networks for classification: a survey. *Systems, Man and Cybernetics, Part C, IEEE Transactions on*, **30**(4):451–462, 2000.

[56] S.M. Zhou, J.Q. Gan, and F. Sepulveda. Classifying mental tasks based on features of higher-order statistics from EEG signals in brain-computer interface. *Information Sciences*, **178**(6):1629–1640, 2008.

[57] M.H. Zweig and G. Campbell. Receiver-operating characteristic (ROC) plots: a fundamental evaluation tool in clinical medicine. *Clin Chem*, **39**(4):561–577, 1993.

In: Support Vector Machines
Editor: Brandon H. Boyle
ISBN: 978-1-61209-342-0
© 2011 Nova Science Publishers, Inc.

Chapter 6

KERNEL LATENT SEMANTIC ANALYSIS USING TERM FUSION KERNELS

Alberto Muñoz, Javier González and Javier Arriero[*]
Carlos III University of Madrid

Abstract

Text mining is an interesting field in which complex data mining problems arise, such as document or term classification, topic extraction, web page recommendation and others. In recent years relevant research has focused on probabilistic models, such as Latent Dirichlet Allocation or Probabilistic Latent Semantic Analysis. The output of such models are probabilities that allow to solve classification problems, but these models do not provide explicit geometric representations of documents, terms or topics. In this work we follow a Regularization Theory approach to propose appropriate kernels for diverse Text Mining tasks that can be used to solve representation, regression and classification problems (via Support Vector Machines). One advantage of this proposal is the ability to combine different sources of information (for instance, the term by document matrix and the co-citation matrix) and to provide explicit term or document maps that incorporate all this information. In addition, the system provides explicit conditional probabilities, as the Latent Dirichlet Allocation model does, but avoiding the computational burden usually involved in the iterative step of probabilistic models. Finally we perform several experiments involving real data bases, showing the advantages of the new approach.

Keywords: Latent Semantic Analysis, Information Fusion, Asymmetric similarity, Regularization.

1. Introduction

Text mining is an interesting field in which non trivial data mining problems arise, such as document or term classification, topic extraction, web page recommendation and others. For instance, consider the task of term visualization. The primary source of information for

---

[*]E-mail address: {alberto.munoz,javier.gonzalez,javier.arriero}@uc3m.es

any visualization algorithm is a $n \times n$ matrix $\mathbf{D}$ made up of data point dissimilarities d_{ij}, where d is some predefined distance measure. Alternatively, a $n \times n$ matrix $\mathbf{S}$ made up of data point similarities s_{ij} can be used. Often distances (or similarities) are derived from a $n \times p$ data matrix $\mathbf{X}$, being n the number of data points and p the number of variables used to represent them.

However, the very high dimension causes the occurrence of problems related to the 'curse of dimensionality' phenomenon (see (4) for further details). In particular, nearest neighbours become often meaningless (see (1) for details) and visualization algorithms, being based on the use of the $\mathbf{S}$ matrix, will produce non accurate word or document maps (see Section 4.). Moreover, the use of non symmetric similarity (or distance) measures is advised in this case (details in (14)). In particular, considering word relationships, most people will relate, for instance, 'pattern' to 'recognition' more often than conversely. Therefore word relations should be modeled by asymmetric similarities.

Let $\mathbf{X}$ a $n \times p$ matrix representing a text database where $\mathbf{x}_{ij} = 1$ if the ith term appears in the document jth and 0 otherwise. Let $|\mathbf{x}_i|$ denote the number of documents indexed by term ith and $|\mathbf{x}_i \wedge \mathbf{x}_j|$ the number of documents indexed by both i and j terms. Consider the following asymmetric similarity measure ($s_{ij} \neq s_{ji}$):

$$s_{ij} = \frac{|\mathbf{x}_i \wedge \mathbf{x}_j|}{|\mathbf{x}_i|} = \frac{\sum_k min(x_{ik}, x_{jk})}{\sum_k x_{ik}}. \tag{1}$$

Measure s_{ij} can be interpreted as the degree in which topic represented by term i is a subset of topic represented by term j. This similarity measure has been used in a number of works related to Information Retrieval (see for instance (14),(13),(12))

Cocitation matrices are also examples of asymmetric matrices that arise in the context of Information Retrieval. Denote by $|\mathbf{x}_i|$ the number of cites received by author (or Web page) i; then $|\mathbf{x}_i \wedge \mathbf{x}_j|$ measures the number of authors (or Web pages) that simultaneously cite authors i and j and we can use again s_{ij} given in eq. 1.

In this work we propose a method to transform/combine asymmetric text mining matrices into symmetric positive-definite matrices. From these matrices we can easily obtain Mercer kernels that can be used to solve document (or term) classification tasks. In particular we will afford here the task of semantic latent classes extraction. To this aim we start from the document by term $n \times p$ matrix $\mathbf{X}$ and perform some clustering process to induce labels on the terms of the document base. This will allow to apply the proposed combination method to obtain an appropriate term kernel matrix. Using kernel factor analysis (3) or cluster analysis we will obtain a number of latent semantic classes in which the terms group that will be identified with latent semantic classes. Using a Gaussian mixture model on the terms represented in the space of latent classes we will assign explicit conditional probabilities $P(c_i|\mathbf{t}_j)$, where c_i indicates the latent semantic class i and $\mathbf{t}_j$ term j.

The rest of the paper is organized as follows. In Section 2. we detail how to transform asymmetric similarity matrices into kernel matrices for classification purposes. In Section 3. we propose a kernel latent semantic class model that takes advantage of the proposed classification matrices. In Section 4. we test the proposed model on a subset of 938 documents from ISI Web of Science against Latent Dirichlet Allocation (LDA) model. In Section 5. we conclude and outline some future lines of research.

2.   Kernel Combination for Text Mining Tasks

Given the asymmetric similarity matrix $\mathbf{S}$ of dimensions $p \times p$, where $(\mathbf{S})_{ij} = s_{ij}$, the similarity proposed in eq. 1 we consider the triangular decomposition of $\mathbf{S}$: let $\mathbf{S}_1$ and $\mathbf{S}_2$ be the two symmetric matrices built from the upper and lower triangular parts of S respectively. $\mathbf{S}_1$ corresponds to s_{ij} and $\mathbf{S}_2$ corresponds to s_{ji}. It is straightforward to check that $\frac{1}{2}(\mathbf{S}_1 + \mathbf{S}_2) = \frac{1}{2}(\mathbf{S} + \mathbf{S}^T)$, the symmetric part of the well known decomposition $\mathbf{S} = \frac{1}{2}(\mathbf{S} + \mathbf{S}^T) + \frac{1}{2}(\mathbf{S} - \mathbf{S}^T)$.

Consider there are q topics/semantic classes and define $\mathbf{S}_y$ the matrix whose components are given by

$$(\mathbf{S}_y)_{ij} = \sum_{k=1}^{q} y_{ki} y_{kj}, \tag{2}$$

where $y_{ki} = 1$ if the i-th term belongs to class k and 0 otherwise ($k \in 1, \ldots, q$). Thus $\mathbf{S}_y$ is a similarity matrix that identifies terms in the same class ($(\mathbf{S})_{ij} = 1$ if terms i and j belong to the same semantic class and $(\mathbf{S})_{ij} = 0$ otherwise).

Next we combine $\mathbf{S}_1$, $\mathbf{S}_2$ and $\mathbf{S}_y$ to obtain a fusion similarity matrix $\mathbf{S}^*$ by using the following fusion scheme:

$$\mathbf{S}^* = \frac{1}{2}(\mathbf{S}_1 + \mathbf{S}_2) + \tau \mathbf{S}_y, \tag{3}$$

where $\tau > 0$. Thus we are combining two different similarity measures for terms, $\mathbf{S}_1$ and $\mathbf{S}_2$ and using the matrix that incorporates the class label information, $\mathbf{S}_y$, to produce the fused matrix $\mathbf{S}^*$.

The underlying idea in eq. 3 is to increase similarities for terms in the same semantic class and decrease similarities for points with different class labels. As a consequence the separation among semantic classes will be increased. Similar fusion procedures have been used in (12).

Note that $\mathbf{S}^*$ in eq. 3 could be non-positive definite since $\mathbf{S}_1$ and $\mathbf{S}_2$ are not necessarily positive definite either. To turn $\mathbf{S}^*$ into positive-definite we will project it onto the convex cone of positive semi-definite matrices of size p defined by

$$\mathsf{K}_+^p = \{\mathbf{K} = \mathbf{K}^T \in \mathbb{R}^{p \times p} : K \geq 0\}, \tag{4}$$

where $\mathbf{K} \geq 0$ means that $\mathbf{K}$ is positive semi-definite. To this aim we consider the *orthogonal projection* of $\mathbf{S}^*$ onto K_+^p given by:

$$\Pi(\mathbf{S}^*) = \sum_{j=1}^{p} max(0, l_j) \mathbf{v}_j \mathbf{v}_j^T, \tag{5}$$

where $\mathbf{v}_j$ are the eigenvectors of $\mathbf{S}^*$ and l_j its corresponding eigenvalues (some of them could be negative). Matrix $\Pi(\mathbf{S}^*)$ is usually known as the positive part of $\mathbf{S}^*$.

To obtain the final fusion kernel we define distances $d_{ij}^* = 2(1 - \Pi(\mathbf{S}^*)_{ij})$ and then obtain the elements of $\mathbf{K}^*$ by solving (using Multidimensional Scaling) the system of equations $d_{ij}^{*2} = (\mathbf{K}^*)_{ii} + (\mathbf{K}^*)_{jj} - 2(\mathbf{K}^*)_{ij}$, where $i, j \in \{1, \ldots, p\}$.

The fusion scheme proposed in eq. 3 can be derived using a regularization theory approach, similar to the one used in the derivation of SVM classifiers (16). We consider the maximization of an error functional $F_\lambda(\tilde{\mathbf{S}})$ that is the sum of an error term plus a regularization term:

$$F_\lambda(\tilde{\mathbf{S}}) = \frac{1}{n} \sum_{i=1}^{p} \sum_{j=1}^{p} (\tilde{\mathbf{S}})_{ij} y_j y_i - \lambda \sum_{i=1}^{p} \sum_{j=1}^{p} \left((\frac{1}{2}(\mathbf{S}_1 + \mathbf{S}_2))_{ij} - (\tilde{\mathbf{S}})_{ij} \right)^2, \tag{6}$$

where $\lambda > 0$.

The maximization of the first term of $F_\lambda(\tilde{\mathbf{S}})$ is equivalent to the minimization (in the $\mathbf{z}_i$ variables) of a between-group separation criterion

$$\frac{1}{p} \sum_{k=1}^{q} \sum_{i=1}^{p} y_{ki} (\mathbf{z}_i - \mathbf{m}_k)^T (\mathbf{z}_i - \mathbf{m}_k), \tag{7}$$

where $\mathbf{m}_k$ is the centroid of class k, $\mathbf{z}_i \in \mathbb{R}^d$ is the Euclidean representation of term i using the decomposition $\tilde{\mathbf{S}} = \mathbf{Z}\mathbf{Z}^T$, $\mathbf{Z} = \mathbf{U}\Lambda^{\frac{1}{2}}$, $\mathbf{U}$ is the column matrix of eigenvectors of $\tilde{\mathbf{S}}$ and $\Lambda^{\frac{1}{2}}$ is the diagonal matrix of the corresponding eigenvalues.

The regularization term $F_\lambda(\tilde{\mathbf{S}})$ avoids the concentration of points belonging to the same class in a single point by favouring the choice of a modified similarity matrix similar to the original one. The choice of the regularization parameter λ is made for cross validation. The solution to regularization problem in eq. 6 is just the $\mathbf{S}^*$ of eq. 3, where $\tau = \frac{1}{2\lambda}$. See (9) for further details.

3. Application: Latent Semantic Class Extraction in Text Mining

Semantic classes contain words that share some semantic attribute. Semantic classes can be identified with topics. The knowledge of these semantic classes allows information retrieval methods not just to use the occurrence of query terms in a document as the basis to retrieve relevant documents, but also documents with words belonging to the same semantic class. Latent Semantic Analysis (6) uses the SVD as a technique for deriving a set of uncorrelated factors that are taken as semantic classes so that each term and document is represented by its vector of factor values.

Consider the $n \times p$ document by term $\mathbf{X}$ matrix. Documents $\mathbf{d}_i$ and terms $\mathbf{t}_j$ are represented by rows and columns of the $\mathbf{X}$ matrix, respectively. Matrix $\mathbf{X}^T\mathbf{X}$ contains the correlations among terms $\mathbf{t}_j$ and $\mathbf{t}_k$ (measured as $\mathbf{t}_j^T\mathbf{t}_k$) and $\mathbf{X}\mathbf{X}^T$ contains the correlations among documents $\mathbf{d}_i\mathbf{d}_s^T$. Using the SVD for $\mathbf{X}$, $\mathbf{X} = \mathbf{U}\Sigma\mathbf{V}^T$, we get that $\mathbf{X}\mathbf{X}^T = \mathbf{U}\Sigma\Sigma^T\mathbf{U}^T$ and $\mathbf{X}^T\mathbf{X} = \mathbf{V}\Sigma^T\Sigma\mathbf{V}^T$. The inmersion of the term $\mathbf{t}_j$ into the semantic class space is given by $\mathbf{t}_j^s = \Sigma^{-1}\mathbf{V}\mathbf{t}_j$ and the inmersion of document $\mathbf{d}_i$ in the same latent space is given by $\mathbf{d}_i^s = \Sigma^{-1}\mathbf{U}\mathbf{d}_i$.

The previous techique is implicitly using the Euclidean distance for terms given that $\|\mathbf{t}_j - \mathbf{t}_k\|^2 = \mathbf{t}_j^T\mathbf{t}_j + \mathbf{t}_k^T\mathbf{t}_k - 2\mathbf{t}_j^T\mathbf{t}_k$. It is well known that Euclidean distance is not appropriate for text mining tasks (involving terms) (14; 13) and this is in line with the convenience of using more than a metric for evaluating term similarities in Section 1. Another well known problem in using the Euclidean norm for terms is that large norm terms are ranked higher by retrieval engines than rare (very specific) terms (terms with very small norm).

Our approach to solve these problems is to use the fusion metric (proposed in previous section) that takes into account the two asymmetric similarities plus the labels. Suppose that we are able to find a suitable transformation $\phi : \mathbb{R}^n \longrightarrow \mathbb{R}^m$ so that the induced distance on terms $d_\phi(\mathbf{t}_j, \mathbf{t}_k)^2 = \|\phi(\mathbf{t}_j) - \phi(\mathbf{t}_k)\|^2$ corresponds to the obtained fusion kernel matrix $\mathbf{K}^*$. This means that

$$d_\phi(\mathbf{t}_j, \mathbf{t}_k)^2 = (\mathbf{K}^*)_{ii} + (\mathbf{K}^*)_{jj} - 2(\mathbf{K}^*)_{ij}, \tag{8}$$

where $i, j \in \{1, \ldots, p\}$. On the other hand:

$$d_\phi(\mathbf{t}_j, \mathbf{t}_k)^2 = \|\phi(\mathbf{t}_j) - \phi(\mathbf{t}_k)\|^2 = \phi(\mathbf{t}_j)^T \phi(\mathbf{t}_j) + \phi(\mathbf{t}_k)^T \phi(\mathbf{t}_k) - 2\phi(\mathbf{t}_j)^T \phi(\mathbf{t}_k) \tag{9}$$

Therefore K^* has to be the implicit kernel given by $K(\mathbf{t}_i, \mathbf{t}_j) = \phi(\mathbf{t}_j)^T \phi(\mathbf{t}_k)$ corresponding to $d_\phi(\mathbf{t}_j, \mathbf{t}_k)$. Here we can recognize the 'kernel trick' idea from Support Vector Machine theory: the available information is K^* and we indirectly obtain d_ϕ by using eq. 8. Now consider the matrix

$$\mathbf{Z} = \begin{pmatrix} \phi_1(\mathbf{t}_1) & \cdots & \phi_m(\mathbf{t}_1) \\ \vdots & \vdots & \vdots \\ \phi_1(\mathbf{t}_p) & \cdots & \phi_m(\mathbf{t}_p) \end{pmatrix}$$

whose rows are $\phi(\mathbf{t}_j)$, that is the transformation of $\mathbf{t}_j$ to the latent class/feature space. Then $\mathbf{K}^* = \mathbf{K} = \mathbf{Z}\mathbf{Z}^T$ is the Gram matrix for the transformed term data.

$$\mathbf{K} = \mathbf{Z}\mathbf{Z}^T = \begin{pmatrix} K(\mathbf{t}_1, \mathbf{t}_1) & \cdots & K(\mathbf{t}_1, \mathbf{t}_p) \\ \vdots & \vdots & \vdots \\ K(\mathbf{t}_p, \mathbf{t}_1) & \cdots & K(\mathbf{t}_p, \mathbf{t}_p) \end{pmatrix}$$

Following the same scheme as for LSA, we apply the SVD to the transformed term $p \times m$ matrix:

$$\mathbf{Z} = \mathbf{U}\Sigma\mathbf{V}^T \tag{10}$$

Then

$$\mathbf{K} = \mathbf{Z}\mathbf{Z}^T = \mathbf{U}\Sigma\Sigma^T\mathbf{U}^T = (\mathbf{U}\Lambda^{\frac{1}{2}})(\mathbf{U}\Lambda^{\frac{1}{2}})^T \tag{11}$$

where $\Lambda = \Sigma\Sigma^T = \Sigma^2$ is the diagonal matrix of eigenvalues of the Gram kernel matrix $\mathbf{K}$, while Σ is the diagonal matrix of singular values of $\mathbf{Z}$. Note that $\mathbf{K}$ plays the role of $\mathbf{X}^T\mathbf{X}$ in the original LSA formulation. Then the immersion of $\phi(\mathbf{t}_i)$ is given by $\phi^s(\mathbf{t}_i) = \Sigma^{-1}\mathbf{U}^T\phi(\mathbf{t}_i) = \Lambda^{-\frac{1}{2}}\mathbf{U}^T\phi(\mathbf{t}_i)$.

Note that when solving optimization problem 7 the matrix argument to be optimized has the form $\tilde{\mathbf{S}} = \mathbf{Z}\mathbf{Z}^T$, where $\mathbf{Z} = \mathbf{U}\Lambda^{\frac{1}{2}}$. The similar expression for $\mathbf{K}$ in eq. 11, indicates that the solution $\mathbf{K}^* = \mathbf{Z}\mathbf{Z}^T$ to optimization problem 7 provides straightforwardly the immersion of terms in the latent space and we take $\mathbf{K} = \mathbf{K}^*$.

The task of assigning labels to terms remains open. We assume that documents in the data base share a similar structure and length. For instance, for electronic databases such as LISA, ERIC, ISI Web of Knowledge and others, documents are described by a title, an abstract and some keywords. Then we can assume the use of Euclidean distance (or cosine similarity) for documents without incurring in the problems that arise when using these proximity measures for terms. Then we will perform a cluster analysis on the documents of the data base and take the resulting clusters of the partition as initial topic classes (for the documents). Then we assign labels to terms by voting on the classes of documents in which these terms appear. Now we are ready to apply the fusion procedure described in Section 2.

A similar approach to Kernel Latent Semantic Analysis can be found in (15). This paper focuses on the use of a specific similarity measure for documents without taking into account classification labels or combination of different similarity measures. Nevertheless it also uses the idea of kernelize the original Latent Semantic Analysis model.

3.1. Assigning probabilities of terms to semantic classes

Up to now we have an explicit vector representation for terms in the latent kernel space, given by $\phi^s(\mathbf{t}_i) = \Lambda^{-\frac{1}{2}}\mathbf{U}^T\phi(\mathbf{t}_i)$. Then the semantic classes in the latent space can be identified with clusters of transformed term data. We will apply a Gaussian mixture model-based clustering (8) to estimate the final semantic classes $c_1, \ldots, c_q$, so that we will obtain an estimation of $P(c_i|\mathbf{t}_j)$.

Each cluster will be represented by a parametric distribution, a Gaussian multivariate distribution. Each specific cluster k will be modeled by an individual Gaussian distribution $f_k(\mathbf{t}) = \varphi_k(\mathbf{t}|\mu_k, \Sigma_k)$, where μ_k and Σ_k are the mean vector and covariance matrix respectively of the k component distribution. The prior probability (weight) of component k is a_k. The mixture density is: $f(\mathbf{t}) = \sum_{k=1}^{q} a_k f_k(\mathbf{t}) = \sum_{k=1}^{q} a_k \varphi_k(\mathbf{t}|\mu_k, \Sigma_k)$.

There are several advantages in using this model: there are well-studied statistical inference techniques available, we have flexibility to choose the component distribution, we can obtain a density estimator for each cluster and a 'soft' classification is available, that is, each term may belong to more than one semantic class (via the use of conditional probabilities $P(c_i|\mathbf{t}_j)$). These advantages are shared with models such as Probabilistic Semantic Indexing (11) and Latent Dirichlet Allocation (2), but our model provides in addition explicit Euclidean representations for terms (and documents) that can be used, for instance, to produce term and/or document maps.

To estimate the components of the mixture we use the Expectation-Maximization (EM) algorithm (7). Computational details can be consulted in (8).

4.   Experimental work

To test the performance of the proposed latent class extraction method we have selected a subset of 938 documents from the ISI Web of Knowledge by querying the database for the following eight subjects: 'bioinformatics' AND 'pattern recognition', 'document classification' AND 'pattern recognition', 'multimedia database retrieval' AND 'video', 'biometric recognition' AND 'fingerprint', 'speech recognition' AND 'statistical pattern recognition', 'manifold learning' AND 'ISOMAP', 'image fusion' AND 'satellites', 'image fusion' AND 'medicine'. Hence there are two main topics in this test database: pattern recognition and image fusion. We keep the terms that occur in more than 8 documents that results in a 1836 term vocabulary, after filtering out a list of empty words such as 'the', 'while', etc.

To extract semantic classes, and following the method developed in Section 3, that will be referred to as Kernel Latent Method (KLM), we apply a hierarchical top-down cluster

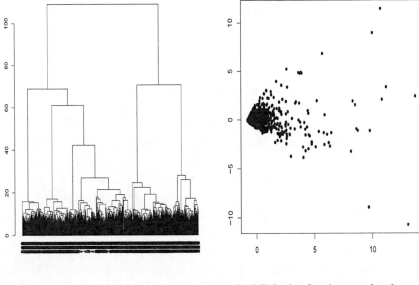

(a) Dendrogram of the document partition.

(b) MDS plot for the term by document matrix.

Figure 1. Dendrogram reveals the cluster structure of documents while this is not the case for the terms.

analysis procedure (using the Ward method and the Euclidean distance) on the document by term matrix $\mathbf{X}$. The dendrogram is shown in Figure 1(a). The dendrogram suggests a clear two-cluster partition. Indeed, the right branch of the dendrogram exactly corresponds to the documents covering the topic 'image fusion' (two classes) and the left branch to 'pattern recognition' documents. Note that Figure 1(b) does not suggest any cluster structure for terms (the same conclusion is reached using the clustering procedure), which agrees with our previous statement that Euclidean distance can be used on 'controlled-length' documents but not on terms.

If we want to refine the partition, a reasonable choice is to cut the dendrogram so that we obtain a six class partition. Both the two-class and the six-class partitions are also supported by the use k-means algorithm. In addition k-means algorithm, imposing eight clusters, retrieves the eight document topics very accurately. Thus we also consider this latter partition to check if the proposed methodology is able to recover the original topics as latent classes.

Next we assign labels to terms by the voting scheme explained in Section 3. We need these labels to obtain $\mathbf{S}^*$ in eq. 3 for each of the considered document partitions (2, 6 and 8 clusters respectively). We fix parameter τ in each case by cross validation and obtain $\mathbf{S}^*$ and then the fusion kernel $\mathbf{K}^*$ for the three partitions. Next we obtain the Euclidean coordinates corresponding to the immersions of terms in the three respective latent semantic spaces (as described in Section 3, coordinates that are given by $\mathbf{Z}$ in eq. 11.

Now we use the Gaussian mixture model-based clustering (8) to estimate the final probabilities $P(c_i|\mathbf{t}_j)$ in each one of the three previous scenarios, as proposed in Section 3.. To this aim we use the first 50 components of the term representation (that is, their scores on the 50 most relevant dimensions). We choose 2, 6 and 8 components for the mixture model, respectively. We assign terms to semantic classes using the rule

$$\text{Class of } \mathbf{t}_j = \arg\max_{c_i} P(c_i|\mathbf{t}_j) \tag{12}$$

Most of the estimated probabilities are very close to one which reveals a clear cluster structure in the (high dimensional) latent space. Alternatively, we perform hierarchical cluster analysis and MDS on the term representations in the latent class space. The results are given in Figure 2. The dendrograms suggest to retain 2, 6 and 8 clusters of terms respectively. These clusters of terms exactly coincide with the latent classes c_i extracted by the Gaussian mixture model. Note that the three MDS plots show term cluster structure because of the use of the fusion kernel $\mathbf{K}^*$. This is not the case for the MDS plot shown in Figure 1(b) where the Euclidean distance has been used.

In addition to the original LSA model for the extraction of semantic classes there are others such as Probabilistic Latent Semantic Indexing (11) and Latent Dirichlet Allocation (2). In both papers latent semantic classes are modeled by the components of a mixture of multinomial distributions. We have used the Griffiths and Steyvers' implementation LDA (10) on the original document by term matrix $\mathbf{X}$ imposing 2, 6 and 8 classes. Several tests were run for the parameter values $\alpha \in \{0.1, 1, 50/T\}$ for the Dirichlet parameter and $\beta \in \{0.1, 1/W\}$ for the multinomial parameter (see (2) for further details), where T is the number of topics (clusters or latent variables) and W is the number of unique words in the dictionary. Next we compare the semantic classes obtained of LDA with the ones found by our method.

In order to interpret and compare the extracted latent classes we show the 10 most representative words (20 in the case of two classes) for the semantic classes obtained for both methods. The results are shown in Tables 1, 3,5,6,7.

In the case of two document classes, the latent semantic classes obtained by KLM coincide with the two main database topics: 'pattern recognition' and 'image fusion'. In addition, the words shown in the two first columns of Table 1 are quite representative of these topics.

Regarding LDA, the two induced latent classes do not coincide with the two main topics of the database as is shown in Table 2. The shown representative words of cluster 1 correspond to the 'image fusion' topic while the ones shown for cluster 2 correspond to 'pattern recognition'. It seems that the most representative terms of the LDA latent classes correspond to the original document topic classes but this does not hold in general.

In the case of six classes, the correspondence between the obtained semantic classes using our KLM and the terms labeling is not perfect but very accurate: only 16 terms are wrongly assigned to the theoretical terms labeling. However the analysis of Table 3, where the 10 most representative words of each semantic are shown, reveals a clear correspondence between the obtained semantic classes and the original subjects corresponding to the eight queries used to build the data base. Cluster 2 aggregates terms related with 'Bioinformatics', 'Text Classification' and 'Speech Recognition' while the rest of the clusters can be identified with the other 6 original queries. Regarding the results obtained with LDA. Table

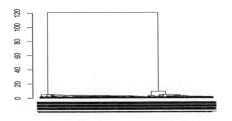

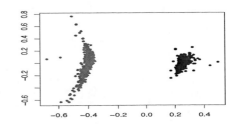

(a) Term dendrogram. Two-cluster document partition.

(b) MDS for terms. Two-cluster document partition.

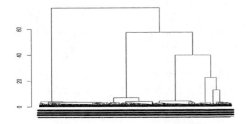

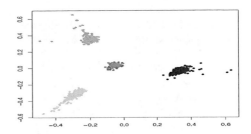

(c) The same as in Fig. 2(a), six-cluster document partition.

(d) The same as Fig. 2(b), six-cluster document partition.

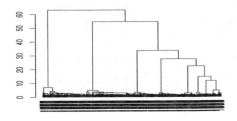

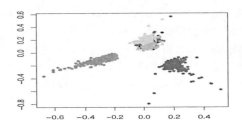

(e) The same as Fig. 2(a), eight-cluster document partition.

(f) The same as Fig. 2(b), eight-cluster document partition.

Figure 2. Structure plots for terms in latent semantic space.

Table 1. 20 closest words to the 2 centroids of the latent semantic classes estimated using the proposed method (left) and 10 most likely words a two-topic LDA analysis, with $\alpha = 50/2$, $\beta = 0.01$ and 200 iterations (right).

Kernel Latent Method		Latent Dirichlet Allocation	
Cluster 1	Cluster 2	Cluster 1	Cluster 2
GAUSSIAN	LESIONS	FUSION	RECOGNITION
DENSITY	PHYSICIANS	INFORMATION	METHOD
NEIGHBOR	SCINTIGRAPHY	IMAGES	PATTERN
SINGAPORE	UPTAKE	SYSTEM	ANALYSIS
GENERALIZED	SUSPECTED	RESULTS	APPROACH
MIXTURE	RADIOTHERAPY	METHODS	DIFFERENT
EFFECTIVELY	ABNORMAL	SYSTEMS	CLASSIFICATION
DISTRIBUTIONS	SPECTCT	TECHNIQUES	ALGORITHM
IDENTITY	FOLLOWUP	DATABASE	ELSEVIER
EXTENDED	POSITRON	SATELLITE	PERFORMANCE
PROGRAMMING	MARKERS	ACCURACY	APPLICATIONS
TEMPLATES	LESION	IMPACT	RIGHTS
MULTIDIMENSIONAL	TUMORS	HOWEVER	FEATURES
STORED	ANATOMIC	PROCESSING	RESULTS
REPRESENTATIONS	PHANTOM	APPLICATION	TECHNOL
LOCALLY	CONSECUTIVE	PRESENT	FEATURE
KERNEL	TRACER	RETRIEVAL	BIOMETRIC
POLITECN	RADIAT	SENSING	PROBLEM
HARDWARE	CARCINOMA	TECHNIQUE	ALGORITHMS
BINARY	COREGISTERED	DETECTION	APPLIED

4 shows a lack of correspondence between LDA latent classes and original document topics. Nevertheless, the words shown in Table 5 are representative for several of the original topics.

When eight classes of documents are considered the results are even more satisfactory for KLM than in the previous scenarios. As is shown in Table 6 the eight semantic classes obtained by KLM match the eight original queries, while the situation for LDA latent semantic classes is similar to the six-class case.

5.   Conclusions

In this work we have proposed the Kernel Latent Method as a technique to address the task of semantic latent classes extraction from document-by-term matrices. This method, based on transformation/combination of several similarity term matrices, has been evaluated on structured documents from scientific papers databases. The number of latent semantic classes is fixed using a hierarchical top-down cluster analysis procedure on documents.

Experimental results illustrate the performance of the method, which is able to recover the original document topics that were used to query the ISI World of Knowledge database as latent semantic term classes. The proposed Kernel Latent Method obtained coherent

Table 2. Contingency table for 2 latent semantic classes obtained using our kernel latent method (which gives a perfect terms labeling) and LDA. Rows refer to KLM and columns to LDA.

496	642
476	222

Table 3. 10 closest words to the 6 centroids of the latent semantic clusters estimated using the proposed method.

1 Medicine	2 Bioinf./ Text Clas. /Speech	3 Satellite image
LESIONS	PROGRAMMING	VEGETATION
PHYSICIANS	MICROARRAY	IKONOS
UPTAKE	ENTROPY	THEMATIC
SCINTIGRAPHY	GAUSSIAN	QUICKBIRD
SUSPECTED	GENERALIZED	REMOTELY
ABNORMAL	DENSITY	FOREST
RADIOTHERAPY	GENOMIC	SENSED
POSITRON	GENOME	CHANNELS
MARKERS	BIOLOGICAL	MAPPER
SPECTCT	TESTING	ENVIR.

4 Fingerprint	5 Video	6 Manifold Learning
IDENTITY	CONTENTBASED	ISOMAP
AUTHENTIC.	QUERIES	MANIFOLD
SECURITY	INDEXING	EMBEDDING
FINGERPRINT	VIDEOS	NONLINEAR
PERSON	MULTIMEDIA	LOWDIMENSIONAL
TEMPLATES	BROWSING	DIMENSIONALITY
LANSING	SEMANTIC	ISOMETRIC
MINUTIAE	QUERYING	MULTIDIMENSIONAL
TEMPLATE	STORAGE	HIGHDIMENSIONAL
CRYPTOGRAPHIC	SPATIOTEMP.	DISTANCES

Table 4. Contingency table for 6 latent semantic classes obtained using the true terms labels and LDA. Rows refer to the true labels and columns to LDA.

55	108	116	166	181	48
0	8	5	21	3	0
33	54	73	22	31	197
10	16	27	34	46	14
297	17	63	9	15	13
2	93	29	6	18	6

Table 5. 10 most likely words a six-topic LDA analysis, with $\alpha = 50/6$, $\beta = 0.01$ and 200 iterations

Cluster 1	Cluster 2	Cluster 3
IMPACT	DATABASE	SYSTEM
RESULTS	PROCESSING	APPLICATIONS
ACCURACY	INFORMAT	INFORMATION
FUSION	NUMBER	HOWEVER
METHODS	RETRIEVAL	METHODS
COMPARED	APPROACH	APPLICATION
PERFORMED	MULTIMEDIA	IMPORTANT
MEDICINE	PROCESS	DETECTION
ACCURATE	FEATURE	SINGLE
STUDIES	AUTOMATIC	DEVELOPMENT

Cluster 4	Cluster 5	Cluster 6
CLASSIFICATION	RECOGNITION	DIFFERENT
PERFORMANCE	PATTERN	METHOD
RESULTS	SYSTEMS	IMAGES
FEATURES	ELSEVIER	FUSION
RECOGNITION	RIGHTS	SATELLITE
BIOMETRIC	ANALYSIS	ANALYSIS
TECHNOL	PRESENT	APPLIED
ALGORITHMS	RESEARCH	SENSING
FINGERPRINT	BIOINFORMATICS	REMOTE
LEARNING	APPROPRIATE	RESOLUTION

Table 6. 10 closest words to the 8 centroids of the latent semantic clusters estimated using the proposed method.

Cluster 1	Cluster 2	Cluster 3	Cluster 4
Medicine	Satellite image	Fingerprint	Video
LESIONS	VEGETATION	IDENTITY	CONTENTBASED
PHYSICIANS	THEMATIC	AUTHENTICATION	QUERIES
UPTAKE	REMOTELY	LANSING	INDEXING
SCINTIGRAPHY	IKONOS	BIOMETR	VIDEOS
RADIOTHERAPY	SENSED	PERSON	QUERYING
SPECTCT	QUICKBIRD	TEMPLATES	BROWSING
SUSPECTED	MAPPER	MINUTIAE	STORAGE
ABNORMAL	LANDSAT	MICHIGAN	INTERNET
POSITRON	GROUND	PERSONAL	SEMANTIC
MARKERS	FOREST	SECURITY	MULTIMEDIA

Cluster 5	Cluster 6	Cluster 7	Cluster 8
Speech Recognition	Bioinformatics	Manifold Learning	Document Classification
ACOUSTIC	PROTEINS	ISOMAP	CHARACTER
MARKOV	GENOMIC	MANIFOLD	CHARACTERS
HIDDEN	PROTEOMICS	NONLINEAR	DOCUMENT
SPEECH	GENOME	LOWDIMENSIONAL	PRINTED
DISCRIMINATIVE	BIOLOGICAL	EMBEDDING	HANDWRITTEN
GAUSSIAN	MICROARRAY	DIMENSIONALITY	DOCUMENTS
MINIMUM	PROTEOMIC	HIGHDIMENSIONAL	OFFLINE
MIXTURE	MOLECULAR	ISOMETRIC	CONNECTED
GEORGIA	PROFILES	MULTIDIMENSIONAL	INVARIANT
ATLANTA	GENETIC	DISTANCES	DIVIDED

Table 7. 10 most likely words a eight-topic LDA analysis, with $\alpha = 50/8$, $\beta = 0.01$ and 200 iterations

Topic 1	Topic 2	Topic 3	Topic 4
ACCURACY	FUSION	SYSTEM	METHODS
FUSION	SATELLITE	DATABASE	IMPACT
RESULTS	IMAGES	PROCESSING	HOWEVER
PERFORMED	SENSING	SYSTEMS	PRESENT
ACCURATE	REMOTE	INFORMAT	INFORMATION
CLINICAL	RESOLUTION	IMPORTANT	APPLICATION
COMBINED	DETECTION	RETRIEVAL	COMPARED
IMPROVED	SPATIAL	MULTIMEDIA	SINGLE
IMAGES	DIFFERENT	INFORMATION	MEDICINE
TOMOGRAPHY	INFORMATION	EXPERIMENTS	APPROPRIATE

Cluster 5	Cluster 6	Cluster 7	Cluster 8
PERFORMANCE	PATTERN	ELSEVIER	METHOD
FEATURE	RECOGNITION	TECHNIQUES	RESULTS
BIOMETRIC	CLASSIFICATION	APPLICATIONS	ANALYSIS
FINGERPRINT	APPROACH	RIGHTS	DIFFERENT
LEARNING	PROBLEM	FEATURES	APPLIED
TECHNOL	STATISTICAL	NUMBER	TECHNIQUE
EXPERIMENTAL	BIOINFORMATICS	RESEARCH	IMPROVE
ALGORITHMS	ANALYSIS	IDENTIFICATION	IMAGES
RECOGNITION	STRUCTURE	AUTOMATIC	QUALITY
ALGORITHM	MODELS	DEVELOPMENT	COMPARISON

latent classes when using different partitions for clustering documents.

The proposed method can be used whenever we have different similarity matrices and labels. For instance, it can be used to combine the document by term matrix and the coci-tation matrix for document retrieval/classification/visualization purposes. This task will be addressed in future extensions of this work. To further develop the present work we are preparing a large database with controlled queries, document classes assigned by experts so that we can measure the quality of the produced latent classes for our method and others in a more systematic way.

Acknowledgments

We thank the support of the Spanish Grant Nos. MEC-2007/04438/00 and DGULM-2008/00059/00.

References

[1] Beyer K., Goldstein J., Ramakrishnan R., Shaft U. *When is "Nearest Neighbor" Meaningful? Springer.* Lecture Notes in Computer Science, vol. 1540, 1999, pp. 217-235.

[2] Blei D., Ng A., Jordan M. *Latent Dirichlet Allocation.* Journal of Machine Learning Research, vol. 3, 2003, pp. 993-1022.

[3] Charles, D. Fyfe, C. *Kernel Factor Analysis with Varimax Rotation.* ijcnn, vol. 3, pp.3381, IEEE-INNS-ENNS International Joint Conference on Neural Networks (IJCNN'00)-Volume 3, 2000

[4] Cherkassky, V. and Mulier, F. *Learning from Data: Concepts, Theory, and Methods.* Adaptive and Learning Systems for Signal Processing, Communications and Control Series. John Wiley & Sons. 1998

[5] Cucker, F. and Smale, S. (2002), *On the Mathematical Foundations of Learning.* Bulletin of the American Mathematical Society, 39(1), 1-49.

[6] Deerwester S., Dumais S., Furnas G., Landauer T., Harshman R. *Indexing by Latent Semantic Analysis.* Journal of the American Society for Information Science, vol. 41, Issues 6, 1990, pp. 391-407.

[7] Dempster A., Laird N., Rubin D. *Maximum likelihood from incomplete data via the EM algorithm.* Journal of the Royal Statistical Society, vol. 39, no. 1, pp. 1-38, 1977.

[8] C. Fraley, C. and Raftery, A. E. (2002). *Model-based clustering, discriminant analysis, and density estimation.* Journal of the American Statistical Association 97:611–631.

[9] González, J. and Muñoz, A. (2010) *Functional Data Analysis techniques to improve similarity matrices in discrimination problems.* Working Paper, Department of Statistics. University Carlos III of Madrid. Submitted.

[10] Griffiths, T.L. and Steyvers, M. (2004). *Finding scientific topics.* Proceedings of the National Academy of Sciences of the United States of America, 101, Suppl 1, 5228.

[11] Hofmann T. *Probabilistic Latent Semantic Indexing.* Proceedings of SIGIR 99, 1999, pp. 50-57.

[12] Martin de Diego I. , Muñoz A. , Martinez Moguerza J. *Methods for the combination of kernel matrices within a support vector framework.* Machine Learning, vol. 78, Issues 1-2, 2010, pp. 137-174.

[13] Martin-Merino M. , Muñoz A. *Visualizing asymmetric proximities with SOM and MDS models.* Neurocomputing, vol. 63, 2005, pp. 171-192.

[14] Muñoz A. *Compound key word generation from document databases using a hierarchical clustering ART model.* Intelligent Data Analysis, vol. 1, Issue 1, 1997, pp. 25-48.

[15] Park, L.A.F. and Ramamohanarao, K. (2009). *Kernel Latent Semantic Analysis using an Information Retrieval based Kernel.* Proceeding CIKM '09 Proceeding of the 18th ACM conference on Information and knowledge management.

[16] Moguerza, J. and Muñoz, A. (2006) *Support Vector Machines with Applications.* Statistical Science, 21(3), 322-336.

In: Support Vector Machines
Editor: Brandon H. Boyle
ISBN: 978-1-61209-342-0
© 2011 Nova Science Publishers, Inc.

Chapter 7

SVR FOR TIME SERIES PREDICTION

M. Serdar Yumlu[*]*and Fikret S. Gurgen*[±]

Department of Computer Engineering, Boğaziçi University,
34342 Bebek, Istanbul, Turkey

Abstract

This chapter makes a comparison of support vector machines and neural prediction models for the financial time series prediction problem. Support Vector Machines (SVMs) are very successful at classification and regression tasks and provide a good alternative to neural network architectures. Unlike neural networks training which requires nonlinear optimization with the danger of getting stuck at local minima, the SVM solution is always unique and globally optimal. By considering this unique and globally optimal property, we have used SVM as a regression approach to financial time series forecasting. This chapter discusses the advantages and disadvantages of each model by using a real-world data: 22 years Istanbul Stock Exchange ISE 100 index data from 1988 to 2010. Several performance metrics are used to compare these models including regression metrics, prediction trend accuracy metrics and special metrics such as Spearman's and Kendall's rank correlation coefficients Finally, it is observed that the support vector predictors becomes advantageous in capturing volatility in index return series when it is compared to global and feedback neural models.

Keywords: Support Vector Predictors (SVP), Financial Time Series Prediction (FTSP), Artificial Neural Networks (ANN), Global, feedback, smoothed piecewise neural models, Istanbul Stock Exchange (ISE), Volatility.

[*] Email: yumlu2@yahoo.com

[±] Email: gurgen@boun.edu.tr

1. INTRODUCTION

Financial markets are incredible systems. Millions of people try to make more money trading over thousands of instruments all around the world every day. National economies are strongly linked and heavily influenced of the performance of their stock markets. Moreover, recently the markets have become a more accessible investment tool, not only for strategic investors but also for ordinary investors as well. Consequently they are not only related to macroeconomic parameters, but they influence everyday life in a more direct way. Is there a relationship that can help investors to understand where the market will go? Is it possible to predict the future of the stock market? This chapter tries to answer these questions by investigating the use of machine learning techniques and approaches in time series prediction using a specific field of risk estimation of asset returns [1, 4].

In recent years, several machine learning approaches have provided an alternative tool for both forecasting researchers and practitioners. Unlike the traditional model-based methods, a novel machine learning technique is introduced. Artificial Neural Networks (ANNs) are data-driven and self-adaptive and they make very few assumptions about the models for the problems under study. ANNs learn from examples and attempt to capture the subtle functional relationship among the data. Recently, Support Vector Machines (SVM) have been proposed as another novel approach to time series prediction problems with its specific type of learning and its structural risk minimization principle based estimation approach. Both ANN and SVM models are well suited to time series prediction problems.

The financial market is a complex, evolutionary, and nonlinear dynamical system. The financial time series are inherently noisy, non-stationary, and deterministically chaotic [5]. This means that the distribution of financial time series is changing over the time. Not only is a single time series non-stationary in the sense of the mean and variance of the series, but the relationship of the time series to other related time series may also be changing such as the effect of currency rates to stock exchanges. Financial time series prediction is fitting a model to the data that is changing over time. Modeling such dynamical and non-stationary time series is expected to be a challenging task.

Support Vector Machines (SVMs) has become a popular pattern recognition technique. SVMs are very successful at classification and regression tasks and provide a good alternative to neural network architectures. Unlike neural networks training which requires nonlinear optimization with the danger of getting stuck at local minima, the SVM solution is always unique and globally optimal. By considering this unique and globally optimal property, we have used Support Vector Predictors as a prediction approach to financial time series prediction using an emergent stock market data: the Istanbul stock exchange index, ISE 100. The results have shown that the kernel selection is the most important part of SVP applications in prediction tasks. SVP is shown to be a significant predictor for financial time series by providing good predictions for the future options of the Istanbul stock exchange market.

Prediction is finding an approximate mapping function between the input and the output data space. Financial time series prediction problem aims to find underlying patterns, trends, cycles and forecast future using historical and currently observable data. Over the past few years, neural networks have been successfully used for modeling financial time series ranging from options price [6], stock index volatility prediction [2] to currency exchange [7]. Neural networks are universal function approximates that can map any nonlinear function without a priori assumption about the data. Unlike traditional statistical models, neural networks are data-driven; they use data as the primary factor for the model to be extracted [8, 9]. So neural networks are less susceptible to the model misspecification problem than most of the parametric models, and they are more powerful in describing the dynamics of financial time series than traditional statistical models [4, 10]. Cao proposed support vector machines experts for time series prediction. The SVM experts approach has two-stage neural network architecture of both a self-organizing map (SOM) for clustering and applying multiple SVMs for partitioned regions. Cao experimented significant improvement in forecasting power using Sunspot and Santa Fe data sets [11]. Tsai and Wand created a stock price forecasting model using artificial neural networks (ANNs) and decision trees and showed that ANN + DT models have significant predictive power over single ANN and DT models [12]. Kim proposed SVMs as promising methods for the prediction of financial time series comparing her model with back-propagation neural networks and case-based reasoning on Korea composite stock price index [13].

Stock prices vary with changes in volatilities of the underlying risk factor and as a consequence, accurate prediction of future stock prices requires a forecast of asset return's volatility. Volatility is the measure of the changeability in the asset returns. This variance is timedependent which is known as the heteroskedasticity. Financial time series of stock returns shows time-dependent variance and this takes us to predict the volatility.

A volatility model like the one proposed in this chapter is used to forecast the absolute magnitude of asset returns. These forecasts are used in market risk management, portfolio selection, market timing etc. and many other financial decisions. For this purpose, predictability of the volatility is important. A portfolio manager may want to sell a stock or a portfolio before the market becomes too volatile or a trader may want to know the expected volatility to give right decision while buying or selling a stock. All these financial decisions are based on market risk and risk management. A risk manager has the right to know that his portfolio may likely decline in near future. Market risk management plays a crucial role in giving the final decision. None of the players want a volatile market. Value at risk became a standard in market risk management. Value at risk estimation is based on the forecasting of the volatility of market risk factors. So, estimating the volatility of asset returns, which is a basic risk factor component of the stock market, gives valuable information for the future risk in the market and this will make the players to consider the expected high or low volatility in the market.

Conditional variances are not directly observable features, but in the literature there are numerous studies and approaches to estimate volatilities using historical asset returns. This variance is time-dependent and using past asset returns to model heteroskedastic behavior was first proposed by Engle [14] with Autoregressive Conditional Heteroskedasticity (ARCH) process. Bollerslev [15] generalized this approach offering Generalized Autoregressive Conditional Heteroskedasticity (GARCH) model which conditional variances are governed by a linear autoregressive process of past squared returns and variances. Both of these models lack in modeling a volatility fact which is known as the "leverage effect" which is known as the effect of the sign of the innovations. For this purpose, asymmetric extensions of the GARCH have been proposed. One of the most spread one, exponential GARCH (EGARCH) has been proposed by Nelson [16]. EGARCH considers modeling the sign effect besides using past squared innovations and past variance forecasts.

2. RELATED WORK

There are both traditional and machine learning methods and studies published that can be related to financial time series prediction in the literature. Murphy used technical analysis for stock market prediction previously [17]. Brooks used value at risk metrics for forecasting of exchange rates [18].

Yümlü, et al. has investigated the use of global, recurrent and smoothed neural network models in financial time series prediction [1-4]. Girosi and Poggio have shown that radial basis functions possess the property of best approximation. An approximation scheme has this property if, in the set approximating functions there is one function which has minimum approximating error for any given function to be approximated. They have also shown that this property was not shared by multilayer perceptrons [19]. Weigend used a single non-linear gate and non-linear experts, and called the model non-linear gated experts [20].

Van Gestel applied the Bayesian evidence framework to least squares support vector machine (LS-SVM) regression in order to infer nonlinear models for predicting a time series and the related volatility [21]. Cao proposed a model using the support vector machines (SVMs) experts for time series forecasting on sunspot data and SantaFe data sets in two stages. First Self-organizing feature map (SOM) is used as a clustering algorithm to partition the whole input space into several disjointed regions. A tree-structured architecture is adopted in the partition to avoid the problem of predetermining the number of partitioned regions. In the second part, multiple SVMs that best fit partitioned regions are constructed by finding the most appropriate kernel function and the optimal free parameters of SVMs [11]. Cao and Tay had dealt with the application of SVM in financial time series forecasting. They investigate the variability in performance of SVM using adaptive parameters on Chicago Mercantile Market future contracts. According to Cao and Tay SVM outperforms back-propagation neural networks in financial forecasting [23]. Tay and Cao also proposed a modified version of SVMs, called C-ascending SVM, to model non-stationary financial time series. They modified the regularized risk function in SVM where E-insensitive errors are penalized heavily than distant E-insensitive error on Chicago Mercantile Market data [22].

Kim applied SVM to stock price index prediction and compared the results with back-propagation neural networks and case-based reasoning and showed that SVMs plays a significant role of an alternative to neural networks [13]. Yang et al. applied SVR to financial prediction by varying the margins of the SVR to reflect the change in volatility of the financial data in Hang Seng Index data [24]. Wang et al. used a modularized connectionist model introducing a time variant HMM model for time series prediction. Their approach achieves significant improvement in the generalization performance over global models [25].

Chen and Shis applied SVM and neural networks on six Asian stock markets rather than US or European markets [26]. Kaynak et al. used a different model of Grey system theory-based models in time series prediction. They investigated the use of grey models using Fourier series on highly noisy data of USD/Euro parity between 2005 and 2007. Their simulations have shown that modified grey model GM (1, 1) using Fourier series in time is the best in model fitting and forecasting [27].

3. PREDICTION MODELS

This chapter focuses on the dependency between the past and the future, the dependency between the input and the output in a financial time series prediction problem using machine learning techniques. The prediction of the market is without doubt an interesting task. In the literature, there are a number of methods applied to accomplish this task. They use various approaches, ranging from highly informal ways (e.g. the study of a chart with the fluctuation of the market) to more formal ways (e.g. linear or non-linear regressions).

Technical analysis (TA) is defined as the study of market (price) actions for the purpose of forecasting future price trends [17]. Using technical data such as price, volume, and highest and lowest prices per trading period the technical analyst uses charts to predict future stock movements. Fundamental analysis (FA) studies the effect of supply and demand on price. All relevant factors that affect the price of a security are analyzed to determine the intrinsic value of the security. If the market price is below its intrinsic value then the market is viewed as undervalued and the security should be bought. If the market price is above its intrinsic value, then it should be sold. Examples of relevant factors that are analyzed are financial ratios; e.g. Price to Earnings, Debt to Equity, Industrial Production Indices, Gross National Product (GNP) and Consumer Price Index (CPI).

Several methods for inductive learning have been developed under the common label "Machine Learning". All these methods use a set of samples to generate an approximation of the underlying function that generated the data. The aim is to draw conclusions from these samples in such a way that when unseen data are presented to a model it is possible to infer the explained variable from these data.

In general for a time series prediction problem, a predictors role is to fit a model to the given times series data and find an approximate mapping function between the input and the output data space. Financial time series forecasting problem aims to find underlying patterns, trends, cycles and predict future using historical and currently observable financial data. A time series $x_t, t = 1,2,3,\ldots,N$ is taken, x_t can be a vector including several attributes of a time series. The kth predictor is obtained by

$$y_t^k = f(x_{t-1}, x_{t-2}, \ldots, x_{t-m}; w_k),$$
$$k = 1,2,3,\ldots,K.$$

The real value of x_t is predicted as y_t with a prediction error of e_t. W is the parameter vector of the model proposed. k^{th} prediction is obtained by using obtained w parameters by setting $w = w_k$. Prediction error e_t forms a sequence of independent, identically distributed (iid) random variable with zero mean and σ^2 variance.

Linear predictors (LP) can be defined as

$$y_t^k = a_0^k x_t + a_1^k x_{t-1} + a_2^k x_{t-2} + a_3^k x_{t-3} + \ldots + a_m^k x_{t-m}$$

m is known as the prediction horizon. LP has not been successful for especially time series problems as it is not relevant for the non-stationary structure of time series data sets and for this reason LP is not used for comparison in this chapter. Polynomial Predictors (PP) are polynomials of time variable t and is shown as below for an nth order polynomial predictor

$$y_t^k = a_0^k + a_1^k t + a_2^k t^2 + a_3^k t^3 + \ldots + a_n^k t^n$$

Neural Predictors (NP) are similar to linear predictors in the principle but they differ in the sense that they use a nonlinear regression implemented by various neural networks such as MLP, recurrent neural networks or mixture of experts structure to form

$$y_t^k = f(x_{t-1}, x_{t-2}, \ldots, x_{t-m}; w_k)$$

where w_k is a matrix of weights of the neural network model.

3.1 Artificial Neural Networks

Artificial neural networks (ANN) can be used to perform classification and regression tasks. More specifically it has been proved by Cybenko that any function can be approximated to an arbitrary accuracy by a neural network [8]. For Neural Predictors multi-layer perceptrons (MLP) and radial basis functions (RBF) are used for comparison purposes.

Multi-layer Perceptron (MLP) is a useful network that is able learn the non-linearity in data and is very useful in both regression and classification problems. As a subset of regression problem, function approximation in time series has been studied before and research at this area has not been come across with results that satisfy any participant in the field. The Universal Approximation Property mentions that an MLP can approximate any nonlinear function to an arbitrary degree of accuracy with a suitable number of hidden layers [28]. Most of the studies are Auto-Regressive (AR) model's simulations having assumed that the data depends on p previous elements in the time series. For this purpose, a window is defined that is including the previous p samples in the data set and having their weighted sums. This technique is known as the sliding windows technique.

The class of Radial Basis Functions (RBF) was first used to solve interpolation problems --fitting a curve exactly through a set of points. RBF methods have their origins in techniques for performing exact interpolation of a set of data points in a multi-dimensional space [29]. Consider a mapping from a d-dimensional input space x to a one-dimensional target space t. The data set consists of N input vectors x^n, together with corresponding targets t^n. The goal is to find a function $h(x)$ such that

$$h(x) = t^n, \quad n = 1, \ldots, N$$

The RBF approach introduces a set of N basis functions, one for each data point, which take the form $\phi(\|x - x^n\|)$ where $\phi(.)$ is some non-linear function. The nth function depends on the distance $\|x - x^n\|$, usually taken to be Euclidean, between x and x^n. The output of the mapping is then taken to be a linear combination of the basis functions.

3.2 Support Vector Machines

Support Vector Machine (SVM), based on Statistical Learning Theory, was first developed by Vapnik [30]. It has become a hot topic of intensive study due to its successful application in classification tasks and regression tasks [8, 9], specially on time series prediction and finance related applications.

Support vector machine is a very specific type of learning algorithms characterized by the capacity control of the decision function, the use of the kernel functions and the sparsity of the solution. Established on the unique theory of the structural risk minimization principle to estimate a function by minimizing an upper bound of the generalization error, SVM is shown to be very resistant to the over-fitting problem, eventually achieving a high generalization performance [30, 33]. Another key property of SVM is that training SVM is equivalent to solving a linearly constrained quadratic programming problem so that the solution of SVM is always unique and globally optimal, unlike neural networks training which requires nonlinear optimization with the danger of getting stuck at local minima.

In classification case [31], we try to find an optimal hyperplane that separates two classes. In order to find an optimal hyperplane, we need to minimize the norm of the vector w, which defines the separating hyperplane. This is equivalent to maximizing the margin between two classes. In the case of regression [32], the goal is to construct a hyperplane that lies close to as many of the data points as possible. Therefore, the objective is to choose a hyperplane with small norm while simultaneously minimizing the sum of the distances from the data points to the hyperplane.

Both in classification and regression, we obtain a quadratic programming (QP) problem where the number of variables is equal to the number of observations. Basically, the SVM regressor maps the inputs into a higher dimensional feature space in which a linear regressor is constructed by minimizing an appropriate cost function. Using Mercer's theorem, the regressor is obtained by solving a finite dimensional QP problem in the dual space avoiding explicit knowledge of the high dimensional mapping and using only the related kernel function.

This chapter shows the usage of SVM in regression in a financial time series prediction problem. When using SVM in regression tasks, the Support Vector Regressor must use a cost function to measure the empirical risk in order to minimize the regression error. There are many choices of the loss functions to calculate the cost, e.g., least modulus loss function, quadratic loss function, the $\varepsilon -$ intensive loss function, etc.

3.3 Support Vector Predictors (SVP)

Support vector predictor is a very specific type of learning algorithms characterized by the capacity control of the decision function, the use of the kernel functions and the sparsity of the solution. Established on the unique theory of the structural risk minimization principle to estimate a function by minimizing an upper bound of the generalization error, SVP is shown to be very resistant to the over-fitting problem, eventually achieving a high generalization performance [30, 33].

SVP usage in prediction in a financial time series prediction problem is explained in this chapter. When using SVP in prediction tasks, the Support Vector Predictor must use a cost function to measure the empirical risk in order to minimize the prediction error. There are many choices of the loss functions to calculate the cost, e.g., least modulus loss function, quadratic loss function, the ε-intensive loss function, etc.

Support Vector Prediction is the application of SVMs into prediction problems. The goal is to construct a hyper plane that lays close to as many of the data points as possible [32]. The problem is to minimize the sum of distances from the data points to the hyper plane defined. Following section briefly describes the mathematical formulation of SVP using the ε-intensive loss function that is also used as the loss function in this study.

Let us assume, $x_t, t = 1,2,3,...,N$ as our data set. Our goal is to find a function $f(x)$ that has a ε deviation from the target data points.

$$f(x) = w^T.\phi(x) + b$$

We map our data into a feature space where it hopefully can be approximated by a hyper plane. $\phi(x)$ is used for the high dimensional feature space mapping. By applying a kernel function, we take the input space into another space that we can be able to model our non-linear data.

The decision boundary defined by the hyper plane can be found by solving the problem given in equation below subject to $y_i(w^T x_i + b) \geq 1, \forall_i$.

$$\min_w \frac{1}{2} w^T.w$$

For the prediction problem, the idea is the same again, to minimize the error, but for the hyper plane which maximizes the margin, part of the error is tolerated. The error under the threshold ε (epsilon) is considered as zero.

The problem defined above then becomes

$$\begin{cases} y_i - (w^T.\phi(x) + b) \leq \varepsilon \\ (w^T.\phi(x) + b) - y_i \leq \varepsilon \end{cases}$$

x_i is the input and y_i is the output of the prediction and the ε is the margin defined. In the non-linear case, the problem is converted into a minimization problem of defined in equation below subject to $y_i(w^T x_i + b) \geq 1 - \xi_i, \xi_i \geq 0$.

The general kernel function, $K(x_i, x_j)$, is given in the equation below.

$$\min_{w} \frac{1}{2} w^T . w + C \sum_{i=1}^{n} \xi_i$$

$$K(x_i, x_j) = \phi(x_i)^T \phi(x_j)$$

Each sample is multiplied by the value of the examples trained. If we substitute this multiplication with the kernel function defined above, this enables SVP to approximate easily in the feature space. Both C and ξ_i parameters are optimized using grid search. When we use the real kernel function, $K(x_i, x_j)$, the general prediction formula for the non-linear case then will become

$$f(x) = \sum_{i=1}^{T} \theta_i \phi(x, x_i) + b$$

4. EXPERIMENTS

The time series data set is selected from an emerging market, Istanbul Stock Exchange (ISE). ISE 100 is selected as the series reflecting all the characteristics of the market because it includes the most active and volumetric 100 stocks in the market. ISE was established in 1988 and all the data up to 2010 is gathered to analyze the behaviour of SVP in time series prediction against the neural networks approach. Data set includes 9346 daily observations starting from 04 January 1988 to 16 April 2010. Data set is divided into train and test sets applying cross-validation techniques. Last six-month performance of the ISE 100 index is selected as the test set and used for testing the performance of the models generated using this unseen data.

Table 1. ISE 100 Index

ISE 100 Index daily closing data (USD based)		
Start Date	:	04-01-1988
Finish Date	:	16-04-2010
Size	:	9346 daily observations
Training Set	:	9113 daily observations
Test Set Size	:	233 (last six months)

The closing values of ISE 100 with their USD and EURO (after 1994) conversions are given in Figure 1.

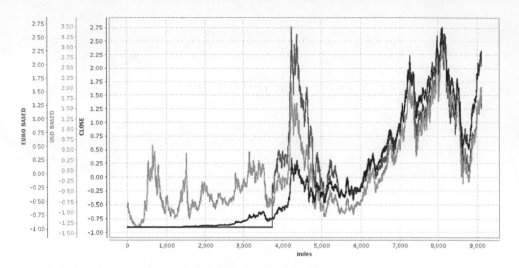

Figure 1. ISE 100 Index Series (Euro Based Close, USD Close, Close respectively).

Continuously compounding is applied to calculate the return series for modeling. Basically logarithmic difference is taken to generate this return series which is given in Figure 2.

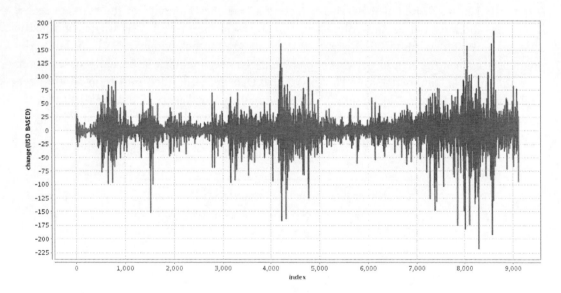

Figure 2. ISE 100 Index Return Series.

This chapter compares the usage of SV Predictors and their ability in time series prediction using financial data set of ISE 100 index against SVP including an MLP based predictor as an artificial neural network (ANN) model, a Radial Basis Function (RBF) network model. Results have shown that besides its success and powerful generalization ability, it is not easy to find the appropriate kernel and parameters like C and ξ_i for the financial time series prediction problem. nu-SVP and epsilon-SVP are used for SV prediction models. Nu-SVP uses the parameter nu to control the number of support vectors. The differences between nu-SVP and epsilon-SVP lie in that Nu-SVP introduces parameter nu to control the number of support vector. And Nu-SVP uses the parameter nu instead of parameter epsilon in Epsilon-SVP. Nu-SVP is also used with RBF kernel as well.

The results are compared using several comparison metrics including classical regression metrics, prediction trend accuracy metrics and special metrics such as Spearman's and Kendall' s rank correlation coefficients which are showing statistical dependence and associations between the predicted and real series respectively. Kendall rank coefficient is used as a statistical hypothesis test to understand whether the predicted and real time series values are statistically independent or not. Kendall's test is a non-parametric because it does not rely on any assumptions on the real and predicted time series distributions. Spearman's rank coefficient is also a non-parametric measure of statistical dependence between real and the predicted time series. These two metrics are always compared with each other for this reason we have reported both of them in the comparison table.

All models are trained using the training set defined in the data set section. Then these models are validated using cross-validation and the results are calculated on the unseen test data set which includes the last six-month performance of ISE 100 series. Prediction and real data comparison on the test data set (last six month of ISE 100 index series) are given in Figure 3.

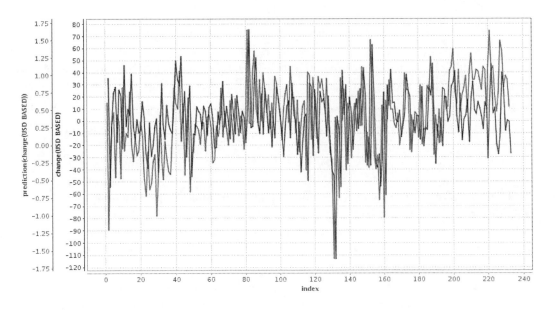

Figure 3. Predicted vs. Real Data on Test Series.

According to the results experimented, SVP model using nu-SVP type is more successful than others. Epsilon-SVP (e-SVP) type did not perform well enough among these models which have to be investigated deeply.

Table 2. Prediction Models Comparison Table

Metrics / Predictors	ANN	RBF	e-SVP(rbf)	e-SVP(sig)	nu-SVP(sig)
prediction_trend_accuracy	0,69	0,78			0.734
root_mean_squared_error	0.013	0.012	24.432	24.449	0.026
absolute_error	0.010	0.009	18.684	18.695	0.018
normalized_absolute_error	1,05	1,009	1,005	1,006	1,023
root_relative_squared_error	1,044	1,003	1	1,001	1,02
squared_correlation	0,003		0,011	0,012	0,011
spearman_rho	0,04	0,076	0,095	0,101	0.014
kendall_tau	0,024	0,056	0,065	0,069	0.011

Regression performance metrics such as root mean square error, absolute error tells that SVP and artificial neural network type predictors provide similar performance on the ISE 100 series prediction. Correlation analysis on the predicted and real values also tells that SVP models are good predictors at time series prediction on a financial stock market index time series in an emerging market. Artificial neural networks and radial basis functions are good function approximates and provides some prediction power in time series prediction but they stuck on the local minima problem and providing successful neural models are prone to several factors including data selection and parameter optimization. Epsilon-SVP did not show any significant power over other predictors both with radial basis function and sigmoid kernels. Nu-SVP with its higher prediction trend accuracy and better Spearman and Kendall correlation statistics shows satisfactory prediction power on the time series prediction problem.

5. CONCLUSION

The results have stated that SVPs are very good non-linear approximates that can easily be applied to financial time series forecasting problems as well. One of the key properties of SVP is that training the SVP is equivalent to solving a linearly constrained quadratic programming problem. Unlike neural networks training which requires nonlinear optimization with the danger of getting stuck at local minima, the solution of SVP is always unique and globally optimal. Besides its success and powerful generalization ability, it is not easy to find the appropriate kernel and parameters like C and ξ for the financial time series prediction problem. Support Vector Predictors will provide a useful alternative to neural networks in pattern recognition problems. Ensembles of support vector predictors, combinations of mixture of experts' techniques are left as future research topics.

REFERENCES

[1] Serdar Yümlü, Fikret S. Gürgen, Nesrin Okay: Global, Recurrent and Smoothed Piecewise Neural Models for Financial Time Series Prediction. *Artificial Intelligence and Applications* 2005: 134-139.

[2] Yumlu S., Gurgen F., Okay N., "A comparison of global, recurrent and smoothed piecewise neural models for Istanbul stock exchange (ISE) prediction", *Pattern Recognition Letters*, Volume 26, Issue 13, pp. 2093-2103, October 2005.

[3] Yumlu, M. S., F. S. Gurgen and N. Okay, "Turkish Stock Market Analysis Using Mixture of Experts", in *Proceedings of Engineering of Intelligent Systems (EIS)*, Madeira, March 2004.

[4] Yumlu M. S., F. S. Gurgen and N. Okay, "Financial Time Series Prediction Using Mixture of Experts", *Proceedings of the Eighteenth International Symposium on Computer and Information Sciences, ISCIS 2003*, Antalya, pp. 553-560, Springer Verlag LNCS 2869, November 2003. ISBN 3-540-20409-1 Springer Verlag, 2003 (SCIE).

[5] S.A.M. Yaser, A.F. Atiya, Introduction to financial forecasting, *Appl. Intell.* Vol. 6, pp. 205-213, 1996.

[6] J.Hutchinson, A. Lo, T. Poggio, A non-parametric approach to pricing and hedging derivative securities via learning networks, *J. Finance*, 49 Vol. 3, pp. 851-889, 1994.

[7] G.O. Zhang, Y.H. Michael, Neural network forecasting of the British Pound/US Dollar Exchange Rate, *Omega* 26 Vol. 4, pp. 495-506, 1998.

[8] C. M. Bishop, *Neural Networks for Pattern Recognition*, Oxford Univ. Press, 1995.

[9] Bishop, M. C., *Pattern Recognition and Machine Learning*, Springer, 2006.

[10] Yao J.T., Tan C.L., *Guidelines for Financial Forecasting with Neural Networks*, 2001.

[11] Cao L., Support vector machines for time series forecasting, *Neurocomputing*, Volume 51, pp. 321-339, 2003.

[12] Tsai C, et al. Stock Price Forecasting by Hybrid Machine Learning Techniques, *Proceeding of the International Multi-Conference of Engineers and Computer Scientists* 2009 Vol. I IMECS 2009, March 18-20, 2009, Hong Kong

[13] Kim K., Financial Time Series forecasting using support vector machines, *Neurocomputing*, Volume 55, pp. 307-319, 2003.

[14] Engle, R., "Autoregressive Conditional Heteroskedasticity with Estimates of the Variance of United Kingdom Inflation", *Econometrica*, Vol. 50, pp. 987-1007, 1982.

[15] Bollerslev, T., "Generalized Autoregressive Conditional Heteroskedasticity", *Journal of Econometrics*, Vol. 31, pp. 307-327, 1986.

[16] Nelson, D., "Conditional Heteroskedasticity in Asset Returns: A New Approach", *Econometrica,* Vol. 59, pp. 349-370, 1991.

[17] Murphy, J. J., *Technical Analysis of Futures Markets*, New York Institute of Finance, 1986.

[18] Brooks, C., "Linear and Non-linear (Non)-Forecastibility of High-Frequency Exchange Rates", *Journal of Forecasting*, Vol. 16, pp. 125-145, 1997.

[19] Girosi, F. and T. Poggio, "Regularization Algorithms for Learning that are Equivalent to Multilayer Networks", *Science*, Vol. 247, pp. 978-982, 1990.

[20] Weigend, A. S., B. A. Huberman and D. E. Rumelhart, "Predicting the Future: A Connectionist Approach", *International Journal of Neural Systems*, Vol. 1(3), pp. 193-209, 1990.

[21] Van Gestel, Tony, et al., 2001. Financial Time Series Prediction Using Least Squares Support Vector Machines Within the Evidence Framework, *IEEE Transactions on Neural Networks*, Volume 12, Number 4, July 2001, Pages 809-821.

[22] Tay, Francis E. H. and L. J. Cao, 2002. Modified support vector machines in financial time series forecasting, *Neurocomputing*, Volume 48, Issues 1-4, October 2002, Pages 847-861.

[23] Cao, L. J. and Francis E. H. Tay, 2003. Support Vector Machine With Adaptive Parameters in Financial Time Series Forecasting, *IEEE Transactions on Neural Networks,* Volume 14, Issue 6, November 2003, Pages 1506-1518

[24] Yang, Haiqin, Laiwan Chan and Irwin King, 2002. Support Vector Machine Regression for Volatile Stock Market Prediction. In: Intelligent *Data Engineering and Automated Learning: IDEAL 2002*, edited by Hujun Yin, et al., pages 391--396, Springer.

[25] Wang, X., Whigham, P., Deng, D., Time-line Hidden Markov Experts and its Application in Time Series Prediction, *Information Science Disccusion Papers* Univ. of Otago, ISSN 1172-6024.

[26] Chen, W-H., Shih, J-Y. And Wu, S. (2006) 'Comparison of support-vector machines and back propagation neural networks in forecasting the six major Asian stock markets', *Int. J. Electronic Finance*, Vol. 1, No. 1, pp.49–67.

[27] Kaynak, O., Kayacan, E., Ulutas, B., Grey System theory-based models in time series prediction, *Expert Systems with Applications* (37), pp. 1784-1789, 2010.

[28] Alpaydin, E., Introduction to Machine Learning, MIT Press, 2004.

[29] Powell, M. J. D., "Radial Basis Functions for Multivariable Interpolation: A Review." in J. C. Mason and M.G. Cox (Eds.), *Algorithms for Approximation,* pp. 143-167, Oxford: Clarendon Press, 1987.

[30] V.N. Vapnik, *The Nature of Statistical Learning Theory*, Springer, New York, 1995.

[31] C.J.C. Burges, A Tutorial on Support Vector Machines for Pattern Recognition, *Data Mining and Knowledge Discovery, Volume 2,* pp. 1.-43, Kluwer Academic Publishers, Boston, 1998.

[32] K.R. Muller, J.A. Smola, B. Scholkopf, Prediction time series with support vector machines, *Procs. of Intl. Conference on Artificial Neural Networks*, Switzerland, pp. 999-1004, 1997.

[33] J. Platt. Fast training of support vector machines using Sequential Minimization Optimization, *Advances in Kernel Methods, Support Vector Learning*, pp. 185-208, MIT Pres, 1999.

In: Support Vector Machines
Editor: Brandon H. Boyle

ISBN: 978-1-61209-342-0
© 2011 Nova Science Publishers, Inc.

Chapter 8

APPLICATION OF NEURAL NETWORKS AND SUPPORT VECTOR MACHINES IN CODING THEORY AND PRACTICE

Stevan M. Berber and Johnny Kao

The Department of Electrical and Computer Engineering,
The University of Auckland, New Zealand

Abstract

In this chapter a mathematical model of a K'/n rate conventional convolutional encoder/decoder system was developed to be applied for decoding based on the gradient descent algorithm. For the system a general expression for the noise energy function, which is required for the recurrent neural networks decoding, is derived. The derivative is based on the representation of the encoding procedure as a mapping of a K'-dimensional message into n-dimensional Euclidean encoded bit set vector. The universal nature of derivative is demonstrated through its application for particular cases of a general 1/n rate code, a 1/2 encoder, and a 2/3 rate encoder. In order to eliminate the local minimum problem presented in the recurrent neural network, another global optimisation technique called support vector machine is investigated. Preliminary simulation results have been carried out, showing its potential to be applied as an alternative method to decode convolutional codes.

Key words: convolutional codes, noise energy function, recurrent neural networks, support vector machines, genetic algorithms.

1. INTRODUCTION

Artificial neural networks (ANNs) have been applied in various fields of digital communications primarily due to their non-linear processing, possible parallel processing and efficient hardware implementations [1]. Recently, substantial efforts have been made to apply

ANN's in error control coding theory, initially, for block codes decoding [2], [3] and recently for convolutional [4], [5], [6], [7] and turbo codes decoding [8].

The task of a convolutional decoder is to find the message sequence that is the closest in the maximum likelihood sense to the noisy codeword observed at the receiver. The sequential decoding and the Viterbi algorithm have long been used for convolutional decoding. The Viterbi algorithm is known to be optimal in the maximum likelihood sense [9]. However, the complexity of this algorithm increases exponentially with the constraint length of the encoder.

In [5], [6] and [7], it was shown that the decoding problem could be formulated as a function minimisation problem and the gradient descent algorithm was applied to solve this problem. The theory developed was related to the $1/n$ rate codes, defined only for small values of n, with various constraint lengths of the convolutional encoder. It was shown that a fully parallel structure could be used to increase the processing speed of the decoder. Also, the results of simulation confirmed that the decoding performances achieved are very close to the performances achieved by the Viterbi algorithm. The developed recurrent ANN algorithm does not need any supervision. This algorithm was implemented in hardware using floating – gate MOSFET circuits [10].

The general encoder structure with any number of inputs K' and any number of outputs n, defined by its rate K'/n, is mathematically described and the related noise energy function is derived that is used to apply the gradient descent algorithm for decoding purposes. It has been shown that the rate $1/n$ codes, analysed in published literature for small values of n, are just special case of this general theory. The central problem in this development was to derive a differentiable function, called the noise energy function, and develop efficient methods to find its minimum. This led to the development of a new decoding algorithm of convolutional codes that is defined as the noise energy function minimisation problem.

Moreover, other global optimization techniques based on machine learning have been introduced lately in the field of digital communication systems [11], [12]. Support vector machine (SVM) for example, has caught considerable amount of attention lately because of their ability to solve large scale complex problems. The theory of SVM was first introduced by Vapnik and his co-workers in 1992 and it became immensely successful in the fields of pattern classification and data mining [13-15]. In the recent years, researchers start to recognize the feasibility and the performance of SVMs hence various types of work have been gradually developed to apply it in digital communications [12].

In 1995, Dietterich and Bakiri have proposed to solve a multi-class learning problem via error-correcting output codes (ECOC) [16]. Essentially this is using a unique binary codeword to represent one class of object. Thus classification can be realized by solving a series of simpler binary problems within each codeword. Once the codeword is estimated, the unknown object can be identified by maximum likelihood (ML) selection. This method is widely accepted as a way to achieve multi-class learning and is studied extensively in [17]. This approach leads to the idea that error control coding can be applied since the goal of decoding is to estimate the transmitted codeword and retrieve the original information.

The rest of the chapters is split to two major sections and organized as follows. In the second section, encoding and decoding based on recurrent neural network is presented. In that section, a general theoretical model of a K'/n rate encoder is presented. It also explains the procedure of deriving the noise energy function and the difficulties in finding its minimum, and finishes presenting the basic steps in the proposed decoding algorithm. The special cases are analysed. Section III explains the algorithm of a decoder based on SVM. Discussion of the advantages of using this approach and its complexity are also analyzed. The section ends by presenting some preliminary simulation results of its decoding performance. The conclusions are finally drawn in Section IV.

2. RECURRENT NEURAL NETWORK DECODING

2.1. Theoretical Model of the Encoder

A rate K'/n convolutional encoder that generates a set of encoded n bits for a set of K' message bits at input to the encoder at a time instant s is shown in Figure 1. The encoder is composed of K' convolutional sub-encoders defined by their constraint lengths $L_1, L_2, ..., L_{m'}$, ..., $L_{K'}$. The constraint lengths of the sub-encoders are, generally speaking, different, i.e., $L_1 \neq L_2 \neq ... \neq L_{m'} \neq ... \neq L_{K'}$. Therefore, the number of memory cells inside each sub-encoder is defied by its constraint length. At time instant s the bits contained in the mth sub-encoder cells are denoted by $b_{m'}(s + 1 - i_{m'})$, where $i_{m'} = 1, 2, ..., L_{m'}$. The set of bits from all sub-encoders, denoted by $B(s) = [B_1(s), B_2(s), ... , B_{m'}(s), ... , B_{K'}(s)]$ where $B_{m'}(s) = [b_{m'}(s), b_{m'}(s-1), ... , b_{m'}(s-L_{m'}+1)]$, are combined in the block denoted as the encoder block in Figure 1, forming at its output a set of coded bits denoted as $\gamma(B(s)) = [\gamma_1(B(s)), \gamma_2(B(s)), ... , \gamma_j(B(s)), ... , \gamma_n(B(s))]$. The additive white Gaussian noise (AWGN), represented by a set of noise samples at time instant s denoted as $W(s) = [W_1(s), W_2(s), ... , W_j(s), ..., W_n(s)]$, is added to the encoded set of bits generated at the same time instant s. Because the encoded set is transmitted through the channel as a series of bits, the noise samples can be represented as independent and identically distributed random variables $W_j(s), j = 1, 2, ... , n$.

The encoding process can be represented as a mapping of a K'–dimensional message vector $b(s) = [b_1(s), b_2(s), ..., b_{K'}(s)]$ into an n–dimensional code vector $\gamma(B(s)) = [\gamma_1(B(s)), \gamma_2(B(s)), ... , \gamma_j(B(s)), ... , \gamma_n(B(s))]$. Because this mapping depends on the structure of the shift-register stages inside each sub-encoder, it may be defined by a matrix of impulse responses g that contains all sub-matrices of impulse responses for each sub-encoder, i.e.,

$$\mathbf{g} = \begin{bmatrix} \mathbf{g}_{L_1}^1 & \mathbf{g}_{L_2}^2 & \cdots & \mathbf{g}_{L_{m'}}^{m'} & \cdots & \mathbf{g}_{L_{K'}}^{K'} \end{bmatrix} \tag{1}$$

where m^{th} sub-matrix, corresponding to the mth sub-encoder, is expressed as

$$\mathbf{g}_{L_{m'}}^{m'} = \begin{bmatrix} g_{11}^{m'} & g_{12}^{m'} & \cdots & g_{1L_{m'}}^{m'} \\ g_{21}^{m'} & g_{22}^{m'} & & g_{2L_{m'}}^{m'} \\ \vdots & & & \\ g_{n1}^{m'} & g_{n2}^{m'} & \cdots & g_{nL_{m'}}^{m'} \end{bmatrix} \tag{2}$$

In order to simplify mathematical expressions and procedures, the input binary message bits of the additive group $\{0, 1\}$ will be represented as bits of the multiplicative group $\{-1, 1\}$, like in [7] for block codes. Now, the encoding procedure can be formalised in the following way.

Let us consider the way of forming the jth bit in the code vector $\gamma(B(s))$. Let $b_1(s)$ denotes the incoming bit into the first sub-encoder and $b_1(s - i_1)$, $i_1 = 1, 2, ..., L_1$, denote the bits taken from all outputs of the shift-register stages forming the first sub-encoder. These bits are applied to the input of the feedback logic block as shown in Figure 1. Because these bits are elements of the multiplicative group $\{-1, 1\}$, the contribution of the first sub-encoder to the formation of the jth encoded bit (at j^{th} output of the encoder) can be represented as a product

$$\prod_{i_1=1}^{L_1} b_1(s+1-i_1)^{g^1_{j,i_1}}$$

$$(3)$$

where g^1_{j,i_1} are binary elements of the jth raw of the 1st–sub-matrix in $\mathbf{g}$, i.e., $g^1_{j,i_1} \in \{0, 1\}$. Taking into account the contributions of all sub-encoders, the jth encoded bit can be calculated according to the expression

$$\gamma_j(B(s)) = \prod_{i_1=1}^{L_1} b_1(s+1-i_1)^{g^1_{j,i_1}} \cdot \prod_{i_2=1}^{L_2} b_2(s+1-i_2)^{g^2_{j,i_2}} \cdots \prod_{i_{m'}=1}^{L_{m'}} b_{m'}(s+1-i_{m'})^{g^{m'}_{j,i_{m'}}} \cdots \prod_{i_{K'}=1}^{L_{K'}} b_{K'}(s+1-i_{K'})^{g^{K'}_{j,i_{K'}}}$$

$$= \prod_{m=1}^{K'} \left[\prod_{i_m=1}^{L_m} b_m(s+1-i_m)^{g^m_{j,i_m}} \right].$$

$$(4)$$

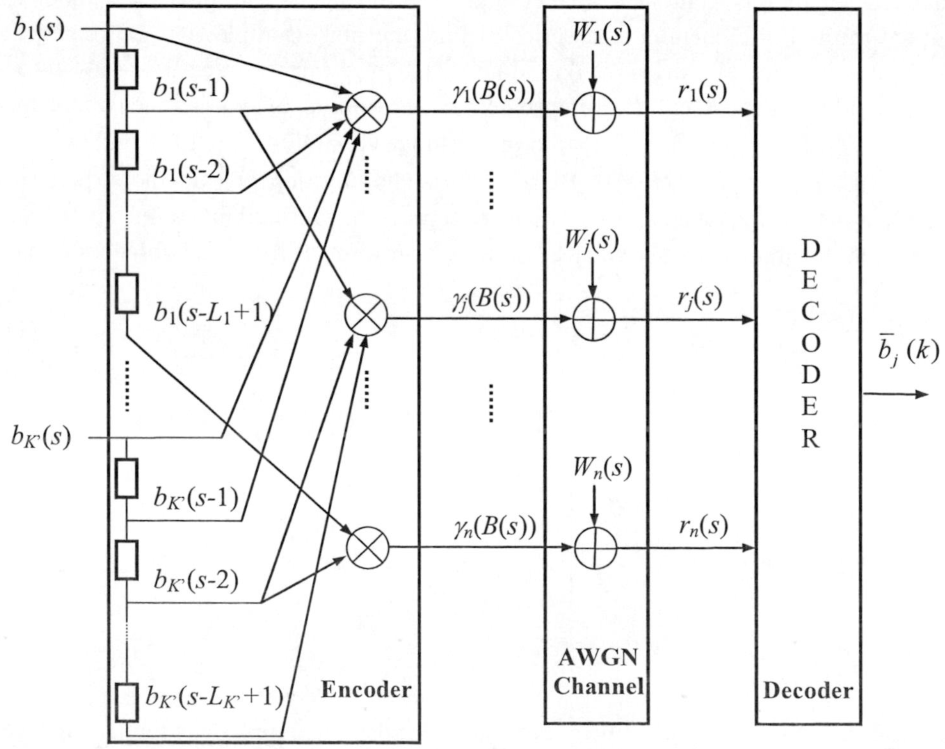

Figure 1. The structure of a K'/n encoder/decoder communication system.

Let variable k denotes the position in time of sets of K' message bits that are applied at the input of the encoder at time instants, $k = 1, 2, 3, .., k, ..., T$, before encoding. These sets can be represented as vectors in K'-dimensional Euclidean space. Any set of K' message bits is mapped into a set of n bits at the output of the encoder. The jth encoded bit at the time instant $(s+k)$ can be represented as the coordinate in n-dimensional Euclidean space, i.e.,

$$\gamma_j(k+s) = \prod_{m=1}^{K'} \left[\prod_{i_m=1}^{L_m} b_m(s+k+1-i_m)^{g_{j,i_m}^m} \right]$$

(5)

Consequently, all encoded bits at time $(s+k)$ can be represented as coordinates of a vector in n-dimensional Euclidean space. This set of n encoded bits is corrupted by AWGN noise, represented by a set of noise samples represented as a vector $W(k+s) = [W_1(k+s), W_2(k+s), ... , W_n(k+s)]$. The channel noise is added to the encoded bits and the resultant received bits are represented by the set of received coded bits $r(k+s) = [r_1(k+s), r_2(k+s), ..., r_n(k+s)]$, that can be expressed in the form

$$r(k+s) = [\gamma_1(k+s) + W_1(k+s), \gamma_2(k+s) + W_2(k+s), ..., \gamma_n(k+s) + W_n(k+s)]$$
$$= [r_1(k+s), r_2(k+s), ..., r_n(k+s)].$$

(6)

2.2. Theoretical Model of the Decoder

Because the variable k shows the position of a set of message bits in time domain, the decoding problem is to find a set of the encoded bits $\gamma(B(k+s))$ that is the closest to the set of received encoded bits $r(k+s)$ for every k. Likewise, for a sequence of T sets of K' message bits encoded at time instants k, the decoder's task is to find a sequence of message bits $B(s)$ which minimises the noise energy function $f(B) = f(B(k+s))$ defined as

$$f(B) = \sum_{s=0}^{T} \|r(k+s) - \gamma(B(k+s))\|^2 = \sum_{s=0}^{T} W^2(k+s)$$

(7)

which represents the sum of all noise vectors, $W(s+k)$, squared. The problem of optimum decoding can be defined as an optimisation problem in respect to the message sequence as follows: The optimum decoded sequence $B'(s)$ is the sequence that minimises the noise energy function $f(B)$.

The noise energy function (7) can be expressed as a function of the coordinates of vectors $\gamma(B(k+s))$ and $r(k+s)$ in n-dimensional Euclidean space, i.e.,

$$f(B) = \sum_{s=0}^{T} \left\{ [r_1(k+s) - \gamma_1(B(k+s))]^2 + \cdots + [r_n(k+s) - \gamma_n(B(k+s))]^2 \right\}$$

$$= \sum_{s=0}^{T} \sum_{j=1}^{n} \left[r_j(k+s) - \gamma_j(B(k+s)) \right]^2 \tag{8}$$

Inserting (5) into (8) we can express $f(B)$ as a function of a bit value $b_m(k)$, $m = 1, 2, \ldots,$ K', i.e.,

$$f[B(b_m(k))] = \sum_{s=1}^{T} \sum_{j=1}^{n} \left[r_j(k+s) - \prod_{m=1}^{K'} \prod_{i_m=1}^{L_m} b_m(s+k+1-i_m)^{g_{j,i_m}^{m}} \right]^2 \tag{9}$$

The gradient descent algorithm can be employed to minimise $f[B(b_m(k)]$ with respect to a single message bit $b_m(k)$ at the decoding time k. According to this algorithm, the iterative procedure of estimating a particular bit value, defined by $m = m'$, has to be applied where a new bit value $b_{m'}(k)_{new}$ is estimated taking into account an old estimated value, $b_{m'}(k)$, and the gradient of the function $f(B)$, expressed as

$$b_{m'}(k)_{new} = b_{m'}(k) - \alpha \frac{\partial f[B(b_{m'}(k))]}{\partial b_{m'}(k)} \tag{10}$$

where α is a gradient update factor to be chosen appropriately which will be explained later. The partial derivation of the function $f(B)$, in respect to the variable $b_{m'}(k)$, representing the gradient descent update factor, is obtained as follows:

$$\frac{\partial f(B)}{\partial b_{m'}(k)} = (-2) \sum_{s=1}^{T} \sum_{j=1}^{n} \left[r_j(k+s) - \prod_{m=1}^{K'} \prod_{i_m=1}^{L_m} b_m(s+k+1-i_m)^{g_{j,i_m}^{m}} \right]$$

$$\cdot \frac{\partial}{\partial b_{m'}(k)} \left[\prod_{i_1=1}^{L_1} b_1(s+k+1-i_1)^{g_{j,i_1}^{1}} \cdot \cdots \cdot \prod_{i_{m'}=1}^{L_{m'}} b_{m'}(s+k+1-i_{m'})^{g_{j,i_{m'}}^{m'}} \cdot \cdots \cdot \prod_{i_{K'}=1}^{L_{K'}} b_{K'}(s+k+1-i_{K'})^{g_{j,i_{K'}}^{K'}} \right]$$

or, deriving now the product in respect to $b_{m'}(k)$, which eliminates the term defined by $(s + k + 1 - i_{m'}) = k$, i.e., $i_{m'} = (s + 1)$, we can get

$$\frac{\partial f(B)}{\partial b_{m'}(k)} = (-2) \sum_{s=1}^{T} \sum_{j=1}^{n} \left[r_j(k+s) - \prod_{m=1}^{K'} \prod_{i_m=1}^{L_m} b_m(s+k+1-i_m)^{g_{j,i_m}^{m}} \right]$$

$$\cdot \left[g_{j,s+1}^{m'} \cdot \prod_{i_{m'}=1, i_{m'} \neq s+1}^{L_{m'}} b_{m'}(s+k+1-i_{m'})^{g_{j,i_{m'}}^{m'}} \cdot \prod_{m=1, m \neq m'}^{K'} \prod_{i_m=1}^{L_m} b_m(s+k+1-i_m)^{g_{j,i_m}^{m}} \right]$$
$$\tag{11}$$

Finally, multiplying the outer product with the bracketed difference, the first term will be a simple product of $r_j(k+s)$ and the simplified outer product, and the second term will be just the $g_{j,s+1}^{m'}{}^{th}$ exponential of the variable $b_{m'}(k)$, i.e.,

$$\frac{\partial f(B)}{\partial b_{m'}(k)} = (-2)\sum_{s=1}^{T}\sum_{j=1}^{n} g_{j,s+1}^{m'}\left[r_j(k+s)\cdot \prod_{m=1}^{K'}\prod_{\substack{i_m=1\\ i_m \neq s+1}}^{L_m} b_m(s+k+1-i_m)^{g_{j,i_m}^{m}} - b_{m'}(k)^{g_{j,s+1}^{m'}} \right]$$

(12)

In this equation the addends for which $g_{j,s+1}^{m'} = 0$ will be cancelled. The values of the message bits $b_{m'}(k)$ can be estimated by and iterative procedure based on equation (10) and implementing a recurrent neural networks structure.

The partial derivations in respect to all variables $b_m(k)$, for $m = 1, 2, ..., K'$, can be found and represented as the gradient transpose matrix $\mathbf{B'}$, i.e.,

$$\mathbf{B'} = \left[\frac{\partial f(B)}{\partial b_1(k)} \quad \frac{\partial f(B)}{\partial b_2(k)} \quad \cdots \quad \frac{\partial f(B)}{\partial b_{K'-1}(k)} \quad \frac{\partial f(B)}{\partial b_{K'}(k)} \right]^T$$

(13)

The iterative procedure of estimating all the bits applied at time instant k at the input of encoder, defined by $m = 1, 2, ... , m', ... , K'$, has to be applied. The new bit values at time instant k are represented by matrix $b(k)_{new}$, the old bit values are represented by a matrix $b(k)$ and α is a matrix of gradient update factors, i.e.,

$$\mathbf{b}(k)_{new} = \mathbf{b}(k) - \mathbf{\alpha}(k)\cdot \mathbf{B'}(k),$$

(14)

where α is to be chosen appropriately, and matrices are

$$\mathbf{b}(k)_{new} = \left[b_1(k)_{new} \quad b_2(k)_{new} \quad \cdots \quad b_{K'}(k)_{new} \right]^T,$$

(15)

$$\mathbf{b}(k) = \left[b_1(k) \quad b_2(k) \quad \cdots \quad b_{K'}(k) \right]^T, \text{ and}$$

(16)

$$\mathbf{\alpha}(k) = \begin{bmatrix} \alpha_1 & 0 & \cdots & 0 \\ 0 & \alpha_2 & \cdots & 0 \\ \vdots & \vdots & \ddots & \vdots \\ 0 & 0 & \cdots & \alpha_{K'} \end{bmatrix}.$$

(17)

The basic procedure of decoding will include the following steps, as shown in Figure 2:

1. Apply the set of all received encoded bits r to the inputs of the neural network decoder that is composed of T neural sub-networks NNp, $p = 1, 2, ..., T$.
2. Initialise randomly the values for message bits in $b(k)$ matrix.
3. For each $k = 0, 1, 2, ..., T$, update the neurons inside each NNp network of neurons for each variable $b_m(k)$ in the matrix $b(k)$, for $m = 1, 2, ..., K'$, according to the matrix expression (14). Use the estimates $\overline{b}$ (0) to $\overline{b}$ (T) to update $b(k)$ matrices for every k.

4. Repeat the number of iterations until there is no change in the matrix of estimated bits $\overline{\mathbf{b}}$, for every k, or the other stopping criterion is fulfilled.

5. Accept the last $\overline{\mathbf{b}}$ as the final estimate of the message bits.

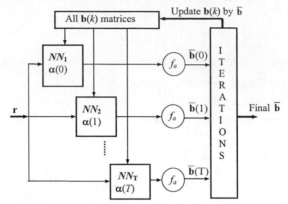

Figure 2. The Diagram of the basic decoding steps.

2.3. Application of the Theoretical Model for One and Two-Input Encoders

2.3.1. One Input Encoder

Let us analyse a simple general case when the encoder in Figur 1. has only one input, i.e., $K'=1$, and n outputs. Then we have: $m = 1$, $b_m(k) = b(k)$, $i_m = i_1 = i$, $L_m = L_1 = L$, and $\mathbf{g}$ matrix (1) contains only a single impulse response sub-matrix that specifies a single encoder as

$$\mathbf{g} = \mathbf{g}_L = \begin{bmatrix} g_{11} & g_{12} & \cdots & g_{1L} \\ g_{21} & g_{22} & & g_{2L} \\ \vdots & & & \\ g_{n1} & g_{n2} & \cdots & g_{nL} \end{bmatrix}. \tag{18}$$

Recalling (5) the output of the encoder can be expressed as

$$\gamma_j(s+k) = \prod_{i=1}^{L} b\,(s+1-i)^{g_{j,i}} \tag{19}$$

as it was obtained in [11], and the noise energy function (9) is

$$f[B(b(k))] = \sum_{s=1}^{T}\sum_{j=1}^{n}\left[r_j(k+s) - \prod_{i=1}^{L} b(s+k+1-i_m)^{g_{j,i}} \right]^2 \tag{20}$$

and its derivatives in respect to variable $b_m(k) = b(k)$ is

$$\frac{\partial f(B)}{\partial b(k)} = (-2)\sum_{s=1}^{T}\sum_{j=1}^{n} g_{j,s+1}\left[r_j(k+s)\cdot \prod_{i=1,i\neq s+1}^{L} b(s+k+1-i)^{g_{j,i}} - b(k)^{g_{j,s+1}} \right] \tag{21}$$

which confirms results obtained in [11]. Let us analyse a simple encoder, defined by the rate ½, the constraint length $L=3$ and the impulse generator matrix and structure as shown in Figure 3.

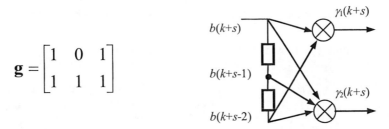

$$\mathbf{g} = \begin{bmatrix} 1 & 0 & 1 \\ 1 & 1 & 1 \end{bmatrix}$$

Figure 3. Generator matrix and 1/2-rate encoder structure.

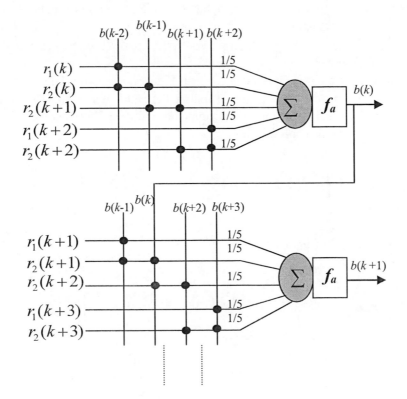

Figure 4. Neural network decoder structure. Only 2 neurons are presented.

The partial derivation $\partial f(B)/\partial b(k)$ can be found from (21) as

$$\frac{\partial f(B)}{\partial b(k)} = -2r_1(k)b(k-2) \quad -2r_2(k)b(k-1)b(k-2) \quad +4b(k)- 2r_2(k+1)b(k+1)b(k-1) +2b(k)$$
$$-2r_1(k+2)b(k+2)-2r_2(k+2)b(k+2)b(k+1)+4b(k)$$

The message bits are represented as elements of the multiplicative group $\{-1, 1\}$ which causes negation of the $b(k+s)$ terms. The procedure of updating the bit value is based on this equation

$$b(k)_{new} = b(k) - \alpha \frac{\partial f(B)}{\partial b(k)} \qquad (22)$$

where α is a gradient update factor that needs to be chosen appropriately [6]. In this case we chose it to be $\alpha = 10$. For the assumed old estimate of the message bit $b(k) = b(k)_{old}$, after solving (22) and defining the activation function f_a, we may have

$$b(k)_{new} = f_a \left\{ \begin{array}{l} \frac{1}{5}[r_1(k)b(k-2) + r_2(k)b(k-2)b(k-1)] \\ \\ +\frac{1}{5}[r_2(k+1)b(k-1)b(k+1) + r_1(k+2)b(k+2)] \\ \\ +\frac{1}{5}[r_2(k+2)b(k+1)b(k+2)] \end{array} \right\} \qquad (23)$$

The activation function can be a sigmoid, a hard-limiter or a ramp function. The structure of the neuron-network decoder is presented in Figure 4.

2.3.2. Two Input Encoder

Let us now analyse a case when the encoder in Figure 1 has two inputs, i.e., $K'=2$, and $n = 3$ outputs. Then we have $m = 1, 2$, and $\mathbf{g}$ matrix (1) contains two impulse response sub-matrices that specifies shift-register connections of both sub-encoders. Recalling (5) the output of the encoder can be expressed as

$$\gamma_j(B(s)) = \prod_{m=1}^{K'=2} \left[\prod_{i_m=1}^{L_m} b_m(s+k+1-i_m)^{g_{j,i_m}^m} \right] \qquad (24)$$

and the noise energy function (9) is

$$f[B(s)] = \sum_{s=1}^{T} \sum_{j=1}^{3} \left\{ r_j(k+s) - \prod_{m=1}^{K'=2} \left[\prod_{i_m=1}^{L_m} b_m(s+k+1-i_m)^{g_{j,i_m}^m} \right] \right\}^2 \qquad (25)$$

Let us analyse the application of the proposed theory on an example convolutional coder shown in Figure 5. The unit impulse generator matrix contains two sub-matrices that specify the first and the second encoder. We can now apply the gradient descent algorithm. According to the iterative procedure of estimation a new bit value $b_m(k)_{new}$ is estimated taking into account an old estimated value, $b_m(k)$, and the gradient of the noise energy function $f(B)$, expressed as

$$b_m(k)_{new} = b_m(k) - \alpha \frac{\partial f[B(b_m(k))]}{\partial b_m(k)}, \qquad (26)$$

where α is a gradient update factor. For this example the noise energy function defined by (25) can be developed in this form.

$$
\begin{aligned}
f(B) = \sum_{s=0}^{T} \big[& (r_1(k+s) \\
& - b_1(k+s)b_2(k+s-1)b_2(k+s-2)b_2(k+s-3))^2 \\
& + (r_2(k+s) - b_1(k+s-1)b_2(k+s)b_2(k+s-2))^2 \\
& + (r_3(k+s) - b_1(k+s-1)b_2(k+s)b_2(k+s-3))^2 \big]
\end{aligned}
\tag{27}
$$

If we expend this expression for $s = 0$ to T and then find the first partial derivations with respect to $b_1(k)$ and $b_2(k)$ we may have

$$
\begin{aligned}
\frac{\partial f(B)}{\partial b_1(k)} = & -2r_1(k)b_2(k-1)b_2(k-2)b_2(k-3) \\
& - 2r_2(k+1)b_2(k+1)b_2(k-1) \\
& - 2r_3(k+1)b_2(k+1)b_2(k-2) + 6b_1(k)
\end{aligned}
\tag{28}
$$

and

$$
\begin{aligned}
\frac{\partial f(B)}{\partial b_2(k)} = & -2r_2(k)b_1(k-1)b_2(k-2) \\
& - 2r_3(k)b_1(k-1)b_2(k-3) \\
& - 2r_1(k+1)b_1(k+1)b_2(k-1)b_2(k-2) \\
& - 2r_1(k+2)b_1(k+2)b_2(k+1)b_2(k-1) \\
& - 2r_2(k+2)b_1(k+1)b_2(k+2) \\
& - 2r_1(k+3)b_1(k+3)b_2(k+2)b_2(k+1) \\
& - 2r_3(k+3)b_1(k+2)b_2(k+3) + 14b_2(k)
\end{aligned}
\tag{29}
$$

$$
\mathbf{g} = \lfloor \mathbf{g}_{L_1} \mid \mathbf{g}_{L_2} \rfloor
= \left[\begin{array}{cccc|cccc}
1 & 0 & 0 & 0 & 0 & 1 & 1 & 1 \\
0 & 1 & 0 & 0 & 1 & 0 & 1 & 0 \\
0 & 1 & 0 & 0 & 1 & 0 & 0 & 1
\end{array} \right]
$$

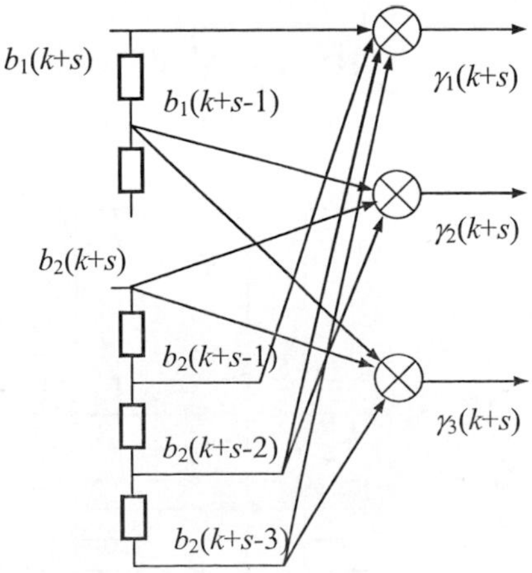

Figure 5. Generator matrix and the structure of a 2/3 encoder.

We assumed that any squared value of all b's is one, i.e., $b_i^2(s+k-1+i_m)=1$. Now, the gradient decent updating rule expressed generally by (26), for the defined values of the updating factors $\alpha_1=1/6$ and $\alpha_2=1/14$ that eliminate the influence of the previous estimated values, are

$$
\begin{aligned}
b_1(k)_{new} = 1/3[& r_1(k)b_2(k-1)b_2(k-2)b_2(k-3) \\
& + r_2(k+1)b_2(k+1)b_2(k-1) \\
& + r_3(k+1)b_2(k+1)b_2(k-2)]
\end{aligned}
\tag{30}
$$

and

$$
\begin{aligned}
b_2(k)_{new} = 1/7[& r_2(k)b_1(k-1)b_2(k-2) + r_3(k)b_1(k-1)b_2(k-3) \\
& + r_1(k+1)b_1(k+1)b_2(k-1)b_2(k-2) + r_1(k+2)b_1(k+2)b_2(k+1)b_2(k-1) \\
& + r_2(k+2)b_1(k+1)b_2(k+2) + r_1(k+3)b_1(k+3)b_2(k+2)b_2(k+1) \\
& + r_3(k+3)b_1(k+2)b_2(k+3)]
\end{aligned}
\tag{31}
$$

Based on these equations the appropriate neurons structure is presented in Figure 6, where each dotted node represents a multiplier, which makes the basis elements of the neural network of the decoder.

The developed RNN decoder presented in Figure 4. has been tested and simulated in the presence of the Additive White Gaussian Noise. The simulated communication system was structured as shown in Figure 1. and the neural network was designed according to Figure 4. The results of simulation are the bit error rate (BER) graphs that are obtained and drawn alongside with the theoretical curve for BPSK system as a function of signal to noise ratio (SNR). The SNR is expressed as the bit energy to power noise density ratio, E_b/N_0. The values of SNR are increased in steps of 1 dB and for each point the measured BER is plotted for three cases: the RNN decoder, the Viterbi decoder, and no-coding case. The BER graphs were obtained for both the soft- and hard-decision modes and for parallel and sequential decoding with and without application of the simulated annealing (SA).

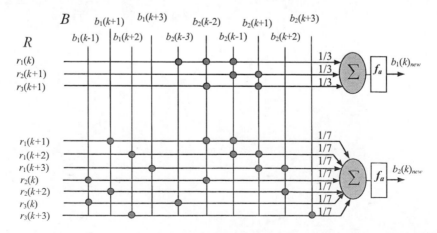

Figure 6. Structure of a doubled neuron.

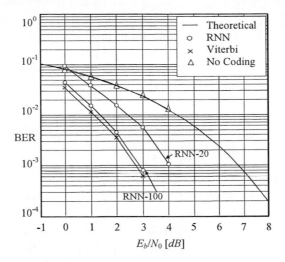

Figure 7. BER curves for variable number of network iterations.

There are two basic modes of the system operation. The first mode, when the outputs of neurons are updated in parallel yielding a new estimate of the message vector $B(s+k)$, is defined as the parallel update mode. In contrast the sequential mode is applied in the network if neurons are updated one-by-one, starting from $b(s)$ and finishing with $b(s+T)$. The estimated message bits are used as an input to the decoder in the second iteration. After a fixed number of iterations the decision can be made on one or more message bits in vector $B(s+k)$. As the decoder depth T is chosen to give sufficient confidence on the decision for the first bit $b(k)$, here we make a decision on this bit only by rounding the output values to +1 or −1, whichever is closer. Alternatively, the speed of the decoder can be improved by making decisions on a window of limited number of bits at a time. In this case we can expect degradation of the performance of the decoder. In order to avoid the problem of local minima the simulated annealing techniques can be used, which incorporates gradual addition of the noise that decreases in each subsequent iteration [18]. Figure 7. presents decoding characteristic of RNN decoder for 20 and 100 iterations. Obviously, when SA is applied like in this case, the number of iterations per decoding bit has a large effect on decoding performance. The performance increases as the number of iterations per bit increases, which is in accordance with the theory that SA algorithms will find the global optimum of the NEF with a probability approaching 1, if the rate of noise decrease is slow enough. The BER characteristics of the decoder will depend on the update mode, number of iterations, characteristics of the activation function, and on the decision procedure that can be soft or hard as it was presented in [18], [19].

3. Support Vector Machine Decoding

Conventionally SVM are formulated to classify only two types of objects, or so-called *classes*. Classification is achieved in two stages: the initial learning or training stage, and the actual decoding stage. At the first stage, some training examples are given to the machine to create certain decision functions in order to differentiate the two classes. During the second stage, the unforeseen object is then classified by those decision rules. To deal with more sophisticated problems, Kreßel introduced a pairwise support vector machine, also known as the one-against-one support vector machine to handle a multi-class problem [20]. In this algorithm, the decision is made from comparing all the combinations of class pairs. Therefore, for a N-class problem, $N(N-1)/2$ classifiers are constructed. Studies by Hsu [21] and Abe [22] have shown that this algorithm in general is well-suited for a large multi-class problem in terms of performance-complexity tradeoff. Therefore this algorithm is chosen to be applied in the decoder.

3.1.1. SVM Decoder Analysis

Before presenting the SVM decoder algorithm, some modifications and assumptions on the encoding procedure has to be made. To reduce the complexity of the explanation and be consistent throughout this paper, this section will follow the same notations from the previous section, but only consider for a $1/n$ encoder. The extension to a K'/n encoder can be followed naturally. In summary, encoding is a mapping procedure of a message vector $b(s) \in \{0, 1\}$, into an n–dimensional code vector $\gamma(B(s)) = [\gamma_1(B(s)), \gamma_2(B(s)), \dots , \gamma_n(B(s))]$, for time instant $s = 1, 2, \dots T$. If T is finite and relatively short, then every sets of message sequence can be associated with a class label y. Let the vector $\mathbf{x}_i = \{x_1, x_2, \dots, x_q\}$ to denote a received noisy sequence which has been corrupted by noise or other impairment in the channel. This vector, with $q = nT$ number of parameters or features, forms a basic object for the SVM to classify. The underlying assumption is that each set of message sequence must have a one-to-one unique correspondence of the encoded codeword.

3.1.2. The Training Stage

This is an initial stage which only needs to be performed once only, unless the channel condition has varied significantly. The inputs of the SVM decoder are l sets of corrupted sequence that is transmitted from the encoder, and its associated class label. This training set can be represented as $(\mathbf{x}_1, y_1), (\mathbf{x}_2, y_2), \dots, (\mathbf{x}_l, y_l)$, where $\mathbf{x}_i \in \Re^q$, $i = 1, \dots, l$ and $y_i \in \{1, \dots, N\}$ for N possible message sequences. The output is a reduced set of those training data. These are used as decision variables, also called the *support vector* (SV). Every SV, denoted by $\mathbf{x}_v$, is associated with a Lagrangian weight α_v ($\alpha_v > 0$) and an output $o_v \in \{+1, -1\}$ to indicate the desired decision result. As this algorithm is comparing two codewords at one time, therefore all combinations of codeword pairs are used during training. Hence this method is also known as *one-versus-one* SVM. Since this algorithm is a natural extension of a conventional two-class SVM, the two are very similar. During the initial training stage, a decision function of a non-linear SVM is constructed for each combination of codeword pair via,

$$d^{ij}(\mathbf{x}) = \sum_{v^{ij} \in S^{ij}} o_{v^{ij}} \alpha_{v^{ij}} K(\mathbf{x}_{v^{ij}}, \mathbf{x}) + b^{ij} \quad \text{for } i, j = 1, \dots, N; j \neq i \qquad (32)$$

where S^{ij} denotes the set of SVs for the codeword pair ij, $K(\mathbf{x}, \mathbf{x}_v) = \phi^T(\mathbf{x}_v)\phi(\mathbf{x})$ is a kernel function, where $\phi(\mathbf{x})$ maps the training data vector $\mathbf{x}_v$ into the high-dimensional feature space, and b^{ij} is a bias term.

Define a coefficient vector, $\mathbf{w}^{ij}$, such that

$$\mathbf{w}^{ij} = \sum_{k=1}^{l^{ij}} o_k \alpha_k \phi(\mathbf{x}_k) \tag{33}$$

where l^{ij} is the number of training data for the ith and j^{th} codeword.

To determine the appropriate parameters for $\mathbf{w}^{ij}$ and b^{ij}, the following optimization problem is solved [21],

$$\text{minimize} \frac{1}{2}(\mathbf{w}^{ij})^T \mathbf{w}^{ij} + C \sum_t \xi_t^{ij} \tag{34}$$

Subject to the following constraints,

$$(\mathbf{w}^{ij})^T \phi(\mathbf{x}_t) + b^{ij} \geq +1 - \xi_t^{ij}, \text{if } y_t = i$$
$$(\mathbf{w}^{ij})^T \phi(\mathbf{x}_t) + b^{ij} \leq -1 + \xi_t^{ij}, \text{if } y_t = j \tag{35}$$
$$\xi_t^{ij} \geq 0, C \geq 0$$

where C is the tradeoff parameter between the training error and the margin of the decision function, and ξ_t^{ij} is the slack variable to compensate for any non-linearly separable training points.

In essence, this is a classic *quadratic programming* (QP) problem with inequality constraints. There are many algorithms to solve this problem. For example, the *sequential minimal optimization* (SMO) algorithm proposed by [23] is a very popular method. Another is called *iterative single data algorithm* (ISDA) proposed by Kecman and Huang [11]. The latter is well suited for solving a problem with a large scale dataset, such as in this case, by breaking down the problem to optimize one data point at a time.

3.1.3. The Decoding Stage

At the actual decoding stage, the receiver will observe a noisy sequence, $\mathbf{z} = \{z_1, z_2,..., z_q\}$. This becomes a new test object for the SVM decoder. The problem of decoding thus becomes a multi-class pattern classification problem. The likelihood of the noisy sequence $\mathbf{z}$ is transmitted from the ith codeword can be calculated via,

$$D_i(\mathbf{z}) = \sum_{j=1, j \neq i}^{N} \text{sign}(d^{ij}(\mathbf{z})) \tag{36}$$

For each codeword pair, a *vote* is placed to the class which $\mathbf{z}$ more likely belongs to, and it carries on for $i = 1, 2,..., N$. Finally the received noisy sequence $\mathbf{z}$ is classified to the class label y_i which has the highest number of votes. This procedure is commonly referred as *voting*. This class label represents the estimate of the transmitted codeword. Once it has been identified, the task of retrieving the associated message vector b is not difficult, which is the same as in the Viterbi decoder.

3.2. Advantages of SVM Decoder

The main reason for employing SVM to apply on the decoding problem, over other conventional methods of artificial intelligence, such as a multi-layer neural network, is because there are no local minima problems. Unlike neural networks, SVM is formulated as a quadratic programming problem. Therefore the global optimum solution, instead of local ones, can be obtained. Moreover, it is more robust to any outliers. In this particular SVM algorithm the training time is reduced because there are less support vectors produced [22].

Like other artificial intelligence systems, the distinct advantage of such algorithm is the adaptability. Through the learning stage, the receiver can have a physical awareness and the ability to adapt to its communication environment, where noise and other types of undesired interferences are impairing the data.

Another benefit of an adaptable decoder is that the tradeoff between complexity and error control capability can be controlled according to the application. For traditional error control algorithms, the decoding strategies are usually fixed, regardless to the quality of the channel. Therefore the bit error rate may exceed to the user's requirement, especially when the signal-to-noise ratio (SNR) is increased. This may imply that some extra time and energy is wasted for the performance that the user does not need. In support vector machines, both the accuracy and the complexity of the decoder are governed by the number of the support vectors produced during the training stage, which are relatively under the designer's control. Therefore this algorithm has great potentials for the emerging software-defined radios where adaptability becomes the essential consideration.

3.3. Complexity of SVM Decoder

Currently the main assumption in employing such a technique is that the number of possible message sets N must be finite so the receiver can create the decision rules for all the possible outcomes. If N gets greater, more decision functions need to be constructed hence the decoding complexity is increased. This could be considered as one of possible constraints in application of this method.

The analysis of complexity of SVM is completely different for the two phases. The complexity of SVM during the training phase is related to the optimization algorithm that it is used to solve the QP problem [11]. At the testing phase, where all the support vectors have been identified, the complexity will be the same, regardless of the training algorithm. For the application of error control coding, it mainly concerns with the computational complexity at the testing stage because the training phase only constitutes a very insignificant amount of time comparing to the total decoding time.

Table 1 compares the computational complexity of SVM at the decoding stage with other conventional methods for decoding convolutional code, such as the *soft-output Viterbi Algorithm* (SOVA) and the *maximum a posteriori* (MAP) algorithm. The complexity of SVM is derived from examining the number of operators required for a complete classification, which is based on equation (36). The conventional methods are taken from the study in [24]. The comparison is made on the MAP algorithm because the current SVM decoder uses a *radial basis function* (RBF) kernel, which requires exponential operation, similar to MAP.

The pairwise SVM algorithm needs to test through $N(N-1)/2$ number of decision rules before making a classification. The RBF kernel is assumed because it is a popular kernel and it is also the kernel function implemented in the decoder design. It is interesting to observe from table 1 that the complexity of SVM decoder has a vastly different characteristic comparing to conventional methods. It is completely controlled by the number of support vectors and the length of codeword to be processed, whereas the conventional algorithms depend heavily on the structure of the encoder. Therefore, as the number of memory elements increases in the encoder, the decoding complexity for SOVA and MAP must increase exponentially as shown from table 1. This is a major drawback of those techniques for applications such as deep space communication where the order of memory can reach to 10 or more [25]. However, this would not have any effect for the SVM decoder as long as the length of each codeword remains the same. The independency of encoder structure becomes another advantage for the SVM decoder. Although the SVM decoder can only process N bits at a time, multiple decoders can be employed in parallel to increase the decoding speed.

3.4. SVM Decoder Design

A simulator of a communication system that consists of a rate 1/2 convolutional encoder, AWGN channel and a pairwise-SVM decoder are designed in order to evaluate the BER performance of SVM decoder. The convolutional encoder is the same one-input encoder described in section 2.3.1. A readily available software called LIBSVM [26], is implemented for constructing the pairwise SVM and for training and testing the data points. The radial basis function (RBF) is chosen as the main kernel function to map the input space to the higher dimensional feature space. The RBF function with a width of γ is defined as,

$$K(\mathbf{x},\mathbf{y}) = \exp(-\gamma \|\mathbf{x}-\mathbf{y}\|^2) \tag{37}$$

where the value of γ is set at the recommended value of $1/N$.

Table I. Computational complexity of SVM and other decoding algorithms

	SVM*	SOVA**	MAP**
# Multiplications	$\dfrac{N(N-1)}{2}(S(N+2))$	$T\left[2\left(2^k \cdot 2^v\right)\right]$	$T\left(5 \cdot 2^k \cdot 2^v + 6\right)$
# Subtractions	$\dfrac{N(N-1)}{2}(SX)$	-	-
# Additions	$\dfrac{N(N-1)}{2}(SX+S)$	$T\left[2\left(2 \cdot 2^k \cdot 2^v + 9\right)\right]$	$T\left(2 \cdot 2^k \cdot 2^v + 6\right)$
# Exponentials	$\dfrac{N(N-1)}{2}(S)$	-	$T\left(2 \cdot 2^k \cdot 2^v\right)$

* A RBF kernel function is assumed; X is the length of the whole codeword to classify; N is the total number of possible codewords; S is the number of support vector in each class.

** k and v is the number of input and the memory elements of the encoder respectively; T is the number of time stages required to decode the same amount of information as the SVM decoder.

According to [27], the performance of RBF kernel is much comparable to other types of kernel, such as a polynomial or linear function. Hence at this stage there is no need to consider those other kernels.

To produce the training data, all the possible codewords from a message of certain length, are corrupted by additive Gaussian noise at SNR of 0 dB and sent repeatedly to the pairwise SVM decoder to generate the decision functions. It is deliberately set at a high noise level to represent the 'worst-case' scenario. Then at the testing stage, *monte carlo* simulations were conducted of random codeword and tested in various levels of noises. The received signal is classified by the pairwise SVM decoder and hence the original message word can be estimated directly because of the one to one correspondence between the message and code word is assumed. This cycle is repeated while recording the number of errors that the decoder makes.

In all simulations, *binary phase shift keying* (BPSK) was used for modulation. In addition, a soft-decision Viterbi decoder was implemented in the simulator as a benchmark to compare the bit error rate (BER).

3.5. Simulation Results

3.5.1 Effect of Training Size on SVM Decoder

The initial simulation investigates the impact of using different number of training data on the decoding accuracy. There are a total of 16 possible codewords to classify at the decoder's side. For simulation purposes, the length of codeword to be processed at one time is 8 bits. The channel consists of additive Gaussian noise with a mean of zero and variance (i.e. noise power) of $N_0/2$. Table 2 summarizes the results of the SVM decoder. The training size specifies the total number of training examples used to construct the decision rules for all the codewords. Figure 8. shows the BER curve obtained by the SVM decoder in comparison with the traditional Viterbi decoder, which is based on maximum likelihood (ML). The results are comparable with the Viterbi decoder if adequate training data is given, suggesting that SVM does tend to converge to a global optimum solution (similar to ML decoding). The small training time, shown from table 2, is an advantage of using a pairwise algorithm. Moreover, with a higher training size hence a larger number of support vectors (decision variables), the BER results are generally better as expected. However, there is a limit that the training data can improve the decoder's performance. Beyond that, not only the decoding accuracy is saturated, also the decoding time will be extended if more support vectors are generated from the trained model. Figure 9. displays the result of such investigation, showing that the performance gain is generally saturated when the number of training data reaches over 1000.

Table 2. SVM performance under different training sizes

Training Size	Training time (sec)*	#SVs	BER (SNR 0 dB)	BER (SNR 4 dB)
160	0.0625	153	0.012	2.88×10^{-4}
480	0.0938	372	0.008	1.98×10^{-4}
1,600	0.2344	879	0.006	1.35×10^{-4}

* Simulations were conducted on an Intel Pentium 4 computer with a CPU of 2.4 GHz running Matlab®

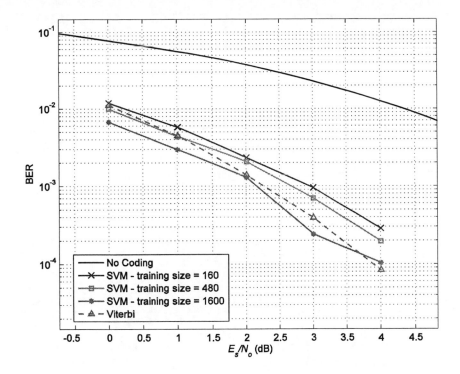

Figure 8. BER performance of SVM decoder for various training sizes.

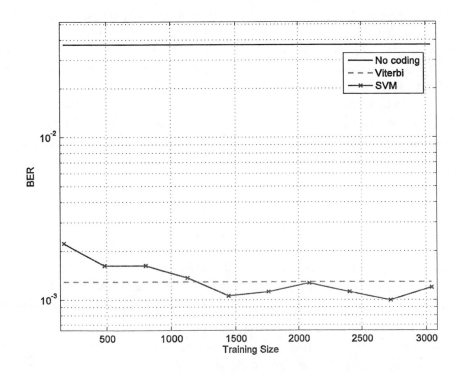

Figure 9. BER performance of SVM decoder under different training sizes; E_s/N_o fixed to 2 dB.

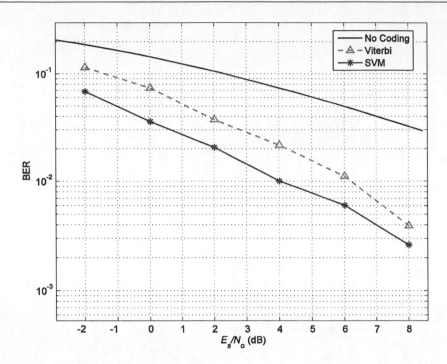

Figure 10. BER performance of SVM decoder under Rayleigh's fading; training size is 1600.

3.5.2. Effect of Rayleigh's fading

To further explore the BER characteristic and the system performance of the SVM decoder, the channel model in the simulator is extended to a Rayleigh fading channel. It is a popular model for estimating the multi-path fading characteristics in a land mobile radio channel [28]. In the simulation, no interleaver was used as a compensation for the bursting errors in the fading channel. Figure 10. demonstrates a coding gain of 2 dB from the SVM decoder over the conventional Viterbi decoder. Such improvement is due to the adaptive nature of this decoding scheme, which makes it suitable for more erratic channel conditions. In this general, the Viterbi algorithm is optimized for Gaussian, memory-less channel, therefore it is less effective for a fading channel, in which the noise and the fading signal have a memory-like behaviour.

CONCLUSIONS

A mathematical model of the encoder and decoder structure for the general convolutional K'/n rate codes is developed and analysed. A general formula for the noise energy function $f(B)$ and its derivation $\partial f(B)/\partial b_m(k)$, representing the gradient descent update factor, were derived. This formula is applied for the following specific cases defined by the code rate to convolutional encoders, $r = 1/n$, ½ and 2/3. The results of simulation are presented and compared with the results obtained by Viterbi algorithm. The convolutional decoders based on the neural network can have advantages in respect to decoders based on the Viterbi algorithm in the case when a high speed processing is needed that can be achieved by parallel processing.

In addition to decoding based on neural network, a completely new approach to decode convolutional code using support vector machines is designed. By treating each codeword as a unique class, classification can be realized by a pairwise SVM. Simulation results suggest that the BER of the SVM decoder is comparable and even better than the conventional Viterbi algorithm for the simulated cases- a coding gain of 2dB is achieved under a Rayleigh's fading channel. However, the number of codewords to identify is currently a limiting factor for the decoder, which can be compensated by parallel processing. Nevertheless, the independency of encoder structure and adaptability to channel conditions makes this decoder scheme a high potential for future communication systems.

REFERENCES

[1]   J. Viterbi, "Error bounds for convolutional codes and an asymptotically optimum decoding algorithm", *IEEE Trans. Inform. Theory*, IT-13: 260-269, Apr. 1967.

[2]   Hamalainen and J. Henriksson, "A Recurrent Neural Decoder for Convolutional Codes" In *Proceedings of 1999 IEEE International Conference on Communications,* Vancouver, Canada, June 6 – 10, 1999, pp. 1305 - 1309.

[3]   Hamalainen and J. Henriksson, "Convolutional Decoding Using Recurrent Neural Networks" In *Proceedings of International Joint Conference on Neural Networks*, vol. 5, IEEE, 1999, pp. 3323-3327.

[4]   Hamalainen and J. Henriksson, "Novel Use of Channel Information in a Neural Convolutional Decoder", In *Proceedings of the IEEE-INNS-ENNS International Joint Conference on Neural Networks, IJCNN 2000*, vol. 5, IEEE, 2000, pp. 337-342.

[5]   S. B. Wicker and X. Wang, "An Artificial Neural Net Decoder", *IEEE Trans. Communications*, vol. 44, no. 2, Feb. 1996, pp. 165-171.

[6]   M. Ibnkahla, "Applications of Neural Networks to Digital Communications – a Survey", *Signal Processing 80*, Elsevier Science B.V., 2000, pp. 1185 – 1215.

[7]   J. Bruck and M. Blaum, "Neural Networks, Error-Correcting Codes, and Polynomials over the Binary *n*-Cube", *IEEE Transaction on Information Theory*, vol. 35, no. 5, September 1989, pp. 976 – 987.

[8]   B. Ciocoiu, "Analog Decoding Using a Gradient-Type Neural Networks", *IEEE Transaction on Neural Networks*, vol. 7, no. 4, July 1996, pp. 1034 – 1038.

[9]   M. E. Buckley, and S. B. Wicker, "A Neural Network for Predicting Decoder Error in Turbo Decoders", *IEEE Communications Letters*, vol. 3, no. 3, May 1999, pp. 145 – 147.

[10]   Rantala and S. Vatunen, T. Harinen and M. Aberg, "A Silicon Efficient High Speed L = 3 Rate 1/2 Convolutional Decoder Using Recurrent Neural Networks", In *Proceedings of ESSCIR'01, 27th European Solid-State Circuits Conference,* Vilach, Austria, 2001, pp. 452 -455.

[11]   T.-M. Huang, V. Kecman, and I. Kopriva, *Kernal Based Algorithms for Mining Huge Data Sets*. Berlin: Springer, 2006.

[12]   L. Wang, *Soft Computing in Communications*. Berlin: Springer, 2004.

[13] E. Brorvikov, "An Evaluation of Support Vector Machines as a Pattern Recognition Tool," University of Maryland, College Park 1999.

[14] K. K. Chin, "Support Vector Machines applied to Speech Classification," in *Department of Computer Speech and Language Processing*. Master of Philosophy: University of Cambridge, 1999.

[15] L. Wang, *Support Vector Machines: Theory and Applications*. Berlin: Springer, 2005.

[16] T. G. Dietterich and G. Bakiri, "Solving Multiclass Learning Problem via Error-Correcting Output Codes," *Journal of Artificial Intelligence Research*, vol. 2, pp. 263-286, 1995.

[17] Passerini, M. Pontil, and P. Frasconi, "New Results on Error Correcting Output Codes of Kernel Machines," *IEEE Transactions on Neural Networks*, vol. 15, pp. 45-54, 2004.

[18] S. M. Berber, P.Secker, and Z. Salcic, "Theory and Application of Neural Networks for $1/n$ Rate Convolutional Decoders", Engineering Application of Artificial Intelligence, Elsevier, 18, 2005, pp. 931 – 949.

[19] Secker, P. J., Berber, S. M., Salcic, Z. A., 2003. A Generalised Framework for Convolutional Decoding Using a Recurrent Neural Network. *The 4th International Conference on Information, Communications and Signal Processing*, Singapore, 15 – 18 December, paper 3A7.6.

[20] U. Kreßel, *Pairwise classification and support vector machines*. Cambridge, MA: MIT Press, 1999.

[21] C.-W. Hsu and C.-J. Lin, "A comparison of methods for multiclass support vector machines," *Neural Networks, IEEE Transactions on*, vol. 13, pp. 415-425, 2002.

[22] S. Abe, *Support Vector Machines for Pattern Classification*. London: Springer, 2005.

[23] J. Platt, "Sequential Minimal Optimization: A Fast Algorithm for Training Support Vector Machines," Microsoft Research Technical Report MSR-TR-98-14, 1998.

[24] V. Branka and J. Yuan, *Turbo Codes- Principles and Applications*, 3rd ed.: Kluwer Academic, 2002.

[25] R. Wells, *Applied Coding and Information Theory for Engineers*. New Jersey: Prentice-Hall Inc., 1999.

[26] C.-C. Chang and C.-J. Lin, LIBSVM : a library for support vector machines, 2001. Software available at http://www.csie.ntu.edu.tw/~cjlin/libsvm.

[27] S. Keerrthi and C.-J. Lin, "Asymptotic behaviors of support vector machines with Gaussian kernel," *Neural Computation*, vol. 15, pp. 1667-1689, July 2003.

[28] S. Haykin, *Communication Systems*, 4th ed.: John Wiley and Sons Inc., 2000.

In: Support Vector Machines
Editor: Brandon H. Boyle

ISBN: 978-1-61209-342-0
© 2011 Nova Science Publishers, Inc.

Chapter 9

PATTERN RECOGNITION FOR MACHINE FAULT DIAGNOSIS USING SUPPORT VECTOR MACHINE

Bo-Suk Yang* and Achmad Widodo

School of Mechanical Engineering, Pukyong National University,
San 100 Yongdang-dong, Nam-gu, Busan 608-739, South Korea

ABSTRACT

Recently, pattern recognition became a famous method in the area of artificial intelligent and machine learning. Various kinds of majors using this method is for detecting and recognizing the objects such as face detection, character recognition, speech recognition, information and image retrieval, cancer detection and so on. In this chapter, the complete study of pattern recognition for machine fault diagnosis is presented. In this study, fault occurrence in the machine is considered as the object of recognition. The complete study consists of basic theory of feature representation in time and frequency domain, feature extraction method and classification process using support vector machine (SVM). The case study is also presented using data acquired from induction motor to clearly describe fault diagnosis procedure. Moreover, a new classification method using wavelet support vector machine (W-SVM) is introduced to enrich the understanding of classification method. W-SVM is used to induction motor for fault diagnosis based on vibration signal. The results show that W-SVM has potential to serve fault diagnosis routine.

1. INTRODUCTION

This chapter presents the use of pattern recognition method for machine fault diagnosis by means of support vector machine (SVM). Nowadays, the development of pattern recognition technique has been successfully applied in many areas such as face detection, verification, and recognition, object detection and recognition, handwritten character and digit

---

* E-mail address: bsyang@pknu.ac.kr

recognition, text detection and categorization, speech and speaker verification, recognition, information and image retrieval, prediction and so on. However, it is relatively rare to find a complete study that presents the methodology of machine fault diagnosis using support vector machine. Therefore, it is an encouragement to contribute a novel machine fault diagnosis technique which applicable in real system. In machine fault diagnosis problem, SVM is employed for recognizing special patterns from acquired signal, and then these patterns are classified according to the fault occurrence in the machine. After signal acquisition, a feature representation method can be performed to define the features e.g. statistical feature of signal [1] for classification purposes. These features can be considered as patterns that should be recognized using SVM. Conventional pattern recognition method and artificial neural networks (ANN) are studied that the sufficient samples are available, which is not always true in practice [2]. SVM based on statistical learning theory that is of specialties for a smaller number of samples has better generalization than ANN and guarantee the local and global optimal solution are exactly the same [3]. Meantime, SVM can solve the learning problem with a small number of samples. Due to the fact that it is hard to obtain sufficient fault samples in practice, SVM is introduced into machines fault diagnosis due to its high accuracy and good generalization for a smaller number of samples [4].

2. PRELIMINARY KNOWLEDGE

2.1. Fault Diagnosis

Fault diagnosis can be defined as detecting, isolating and identifying an impending or incipient failure condition, the effected component is still operational even though at a degrade mode [5]. The term of fault diagnosis should include the performance of detecting an abnormal condition, determining which component is failing or has failed and estimating the nature and extent of the failure (fault). A modern fault diagnosis system requires massive database that form a collection of data from multiple and diverse sensors. The information of machine condition should be extracted, in the form of features, from such data base and used to input to fault diagnosis system. Machine fault diagnosis is integrated system architecture with following modules

- A proper sensors and suitable sensing strategies to acquire and process the data of critical process variables and parameters
- An operating mode identification routine that determines the current operational status of the system and correlates fault-mode characteristics with operating conditions
- A feature extractor that can calculate and extract from raw data or condition indicators to be used by diagnosis module
- A diagnostic module that assesses through on line measurements the current state of critical machine component

Fault diagnosis systems should have ability to detect the performance of machine, degradation levels and incipient fault based on property changes trough detectable phenomena.

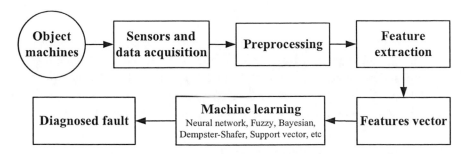

Figure 1. Intelligent fault diagnosis system.

Moreover, the systems also should be addressed to able to identify the specific subsystem or the component of system being monitored that is failing, as well as the specific failure process that has occurred. In this chapter, an intelligent fault diagnosis will be discussed due to its excellent performance that can automatically diagnose the incipient fault in machine. Intelligent fault diagnosis is concerned with the development of algorithms and techniques, including the application of artificial intelligent, that are able to determine whether the behavior of a system is normal. Furthermore, it should capable to be an expert system which is based on experience with the system. Using this experience, a mapping is built that efficiently associates the observations to the corresponding diagnoses. Usually, this method adopts machine learning techniques such as neural network, fuzzy system, support vector machine, etc. to perform learning process using data examples from machine and to make generalization and decision about machine condition.

Figure 1 depicts the diagram of the intelligent fault diagnosis system with machine learning technique. The data acquisition must be performed on objects machines using suite sensors. Vibration sensors are the most popular for doing condition monitoring and fault diagnosis. Usually, the raw data from data acquisition process need preprocessing to reduce the noise and increase the salient characteristic of signal. Wavelet transform can be performed as preprocessing tool to make raw data better and have high signal-to-noise ratio (SNR). Then, feature extraction is addressed to extract the condition indicators (feature vectors) that are used by diagnosis module. Feature vectors will be inputs of machine learning techniques for generalization and then make decision according to the faults occurrence in the machine objects.

2.2. Time Domain Analysis

Time-domain analysis is directly based on the time waveform itself. Many experts have developed the techniques for time domain analysis. Time synchronous analysis (TSA) is one of most popular technique which can handle time domain problem. The idea of TSA is to use the ensemble average of the raw signal over a number of evolutions in an attempt to remove or reduce noise and effects from other sources, so as to enhance the signal components of interest. The TSA can be defined as

$$\bar{s}(t) = \frac{1}{N} \sum_{n=0}^{N-1} s(t + nT) \qquad 0 \le t \le T \tag{1}$$

where $s(t)$ denotes the signal, T is averaging period and N is number of samples averaging. The detail of TSA will not be discussed in this chapter; interested readers are suggested to refer to [6] who have used TSA for gear fault detection.

The advanced technique for time domain analysis is applying time series models to waveform data. The main idea of time series model is to fit the time waveform data to a parametric time series model and extract features based on this parametric model. The popular models used in the literature are the autoregressive (AR) model and the autoregressive moving averaging (ARMA) model. An ARMA model of order p, q denoted by

$$x_1 = a_1 x_{t-1} + \ldots + a_p x_{t-p} + \varepsilon_t - b_1 \varepsilon_{t-1} - \ldots - b_q \varepsilon_{t-q} \tag{2}$$

where x is the waveform signal, ε is independent normally distributed with mean 0 and constant variance σ^2, and a_i, b_i are model coefficients.

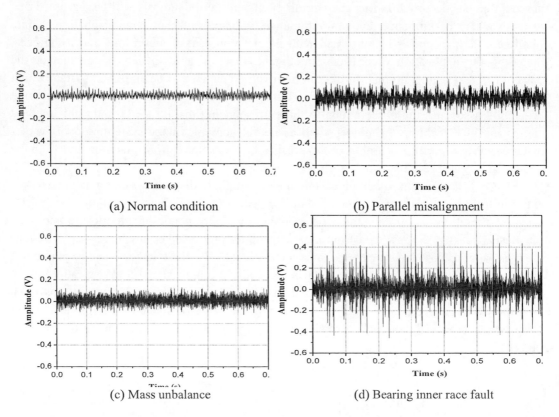

Figure 2. Time signals from the machinery fault simulator.

In this chapter, the simple of traditional time-domain analysis that calculates characteristic features from time waveform signals as descriptive statistics such as mean, RMS, shape factor, skewness, kurtosis, crest factor, entropy estimation, and entropy error are presented. Figures 2 and 3 depict the time waveform data acquired using machinery fault simulator and their statistical features [7]. Figure 2 shows that the waveform of normal condition is quite clear about period running speed. In the faulty bearing waveform, there are many impulses related to the inner race defect.

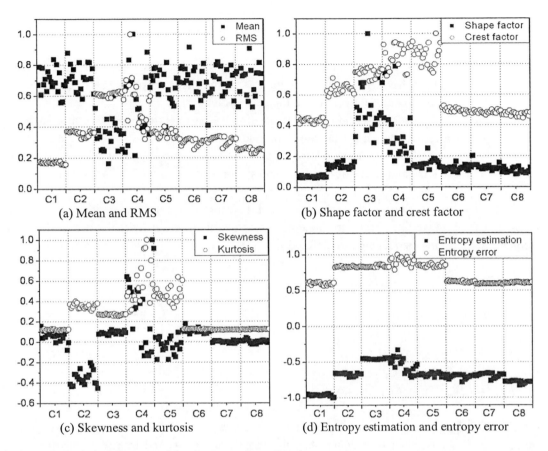

(a) Mean and RMS

(b) Shape factor and crest factor

(c) Skewness and kurtosis

(d) Entropy estimation and entropy error

Figure 3. Statistical features of the time waveform signal.

2.3. Frequency Domain Analysis

Frequency-domain analysis is based on the transformed signal in frequency domain. The advantage of frequency-domain analysis over time-domain analysis is its ability to easily identify and isolate certain frequency components of interest. The most widely used conventional analysis is the spectrum analysis by means of fast Fourier transform (FFT). The main idea of spectrum analysis is to either look at the whole spectrum or look closely at certain frequency components of interest and thus extract features from the signal. The most commonly used tool in spectrum analysis is power spectrum that defined as

$$P_{xx}(f) = E[X(f)X^*(f)] \tag{3}$$

where $X(f)$ is the Fourier transform of $x(t)$ and $X(f)^*$ denotes the complex conjugate of $X(f)$.

A spectrum can be analyzed quickly using the following steps

1. Identify operating speed and its multiples (order).
2. Identify the dominant frequencies that are multiples of operating speed. Included are blade pass in fans, vane pass in pumps, and gear mesh in gearbox.
3. Identify nonsynchronous multiplies of operating speed such as bearing frequencies.
4. Identify beat frequencies; two frequency components close to each other, their amplitudes add and subtract during the beat cycle.
5. Identify frequencies that do not depend directly on operating speed such as natural frequencies or frequency from adjacent machines.
6. Identify sidebands that are related to a low-frequency component of vibration that modulates the amplitude of high frequency vibration.

In the case of bearing, when a rolling element bearing passes over a bearing defect in the races or cages, pulse-like forces are generated that result in one or combination of bearing frequencies. Bearing frequencies are defined as

$$BPFO = (N/2)\, \Omega\, \{1 - (B/P)\cos\phi\} \tag{4}$$

$$BPFI = (N/2)\, \Omega\, \{1 + (B/P)\cos\phi\} \tag{5}$$

$$BSF = (P/2B)\, \Omega\, \{1 - (B/P)^2 \cos^2\phi\} \tag{6}$$

$$FTF = (\Omega/2)\, \{1 - (B/P)\cos\phi\} \tag{7}$$

$BPFO$ is ball pass frequency of the outer race; generated by rollers passing over defective outer race. $BPFI$ is ball pass frequency of the inner race; generated by rollers passing over defective inner race. BSF is ball spin frequency; generated by ball defects.

FTF is fundamental train frequency; generated by cage defects or improper movements. Then, N is number of rolling elements, P is pitch diameter (mm), B is ball or roller diameter (mm) and Ω is rotating speed in revolution per second.

Figure 4 depicts the BPFO and BPFI of bearing acquired from machine fault simulator.

3. FEATURE-BASED DIAGNOSIS SYSTEM

The process of traditional condition monitoring and fault diagnosis can be summarized as follows: data acquisition, data preprocessing, data analysis and decision making. Here, the data that represents the machine condition called condition-based monitoring. Nevertheless, there is problem of such a system in data transferring and storage. For instance, when monitoring of large system of rotating machinery will be performed, the installation of many sensors is needed to assure the diagnosis reliability. Such many sensors result in huge dimensionality of data.

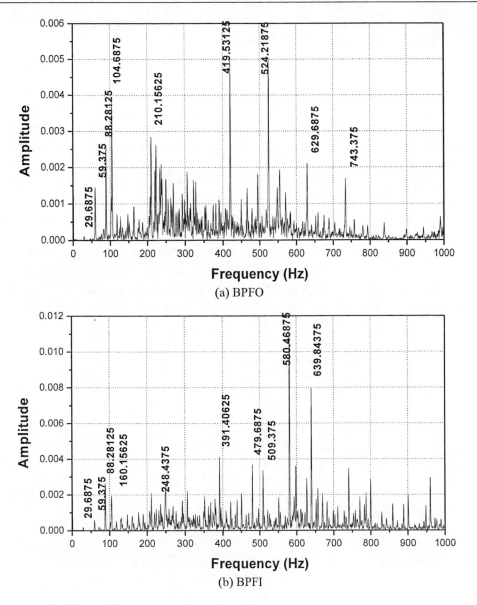

Figure 4. Bearing frequencies.

With the globalization and fast growth of the computer and information technology, on-line condition monitoring and fault diagnosis has gained much attention. Data transfer and storage problem become serious. If direct transferring a plenty of raw data will be performed, so time delays due to heavy traffic may be experienced which results in the lost of monitoring and diagnosis.

Therefore, representing data as features is a best solution for this problem that is expected able greatly reduces the requirement of transfer number and save storage space. The represented data as feature is similar to compress the data from many domains with keeping the information as high as possible. Thus, a relative technique has developed such as feature representation, feature extraction and feature selection.

The typical feature-based condition monitoring and diagnosis framework is illustrated in Figure 5 which can be summarized as follows:

- The data are on-line acquired from machine as a raw data that need preprocessing to condition the data as good as possible for emerging the salient condition of machine. These data can be vibration signals, current and volt signals, sound signals, flux signals, etc. Corresponding to object, the different preprocessing procedure can be used such as filtering (high, low and band-pass), wavelet transform, averaging, smoothing and so on.
- The features are calculated from various domains: time, frequency, cepstrum or wavelet domain. In this way, the information of raw data is kept as good as possible to address the analysis method in the next. Furthermore, the transfer and storage problem of data can be solved.
- Many calculations of feature parameters in many domains result high dimensionality of data features. Not all of them are useful for condition analysis; sometimes some of them even can increase the difficulty of analysis and degrade the accuracy. So reducing the dimension of data features is necessary which can remove the irrelative and garbage features.
- According to monitoring object, the features which can significantly represent machine performance should be selected.
- The selected features are then sent to condition monitoring and fault diagnosis system to define the machine condition.

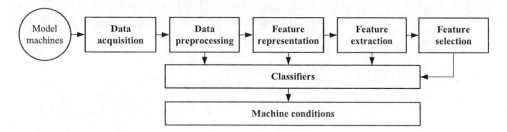

Figure 5. Feature-based condition monitoring and fault diagnosis system.

3.1. Data Preprocessing

Data preprocessing describes any kinds of preprocessing on a raw data to enhance the reliability and thereby to improve the accuracy for signal analysis purpose. Data preprocessing may be performed on the data for understanding the nature of the data and extracting more meaningful knowledge from a given set of data. After data acquisition process, the problems with data often cannot be avoided. Several data problems can exist such as corrupt and noisy, irrelevant, missing attributes and so on. Therefore, data preprocessing is needed to enhance the quality of data for specific purposes i.e. pattern recognition and classification.

Data preprocessing transforms the data into a format that will be more easily and effectively to be processed appropriate with desire of user. As general, data preprocessing technique can be classified as follows [8]:

- Transformation such as data filtering, data ordering, data editing, noise modeling, etc
- Information gathering using data visualization, data elimination, data selection, sampling and so on
- Generation of new information including adding new features, data fusion, data simulation, dimensional analysis, etc

In the following section, data preprocessing is applied for obtaining the meaningful knowledge from raw data using wavelet transform, averaging, enveloping and cepstrum.

3.1.1. Wavelet Transform

The wavelet transform decomposes a concerned signal into a linear combination of time scale unit. It analyzes original signals and organizes them into several signal components according to the translation of the mother wavelet or wavelet basis function which changes the scale and show the transition of each frequency component [9].

Continuous wavelet transform (CWT): The continuous wavelet transform is an integration with respect to the total time of the product of the target signal $f(t)$ and the mother wavelet $\psi_{a, b}$. Using mathematical expression, the continuous wavelet transform of the time function $f(t)$ ca be written as

$$CWT(a,b) = \int_{-\infty}^{\infty} f(t)\psi_{a,b}dt \tag{8}$$

$$\psi_{a,b} = \frac{1}{\sqrt{a}}\psi\left(\frac{t-b}{a}\right) \tag{9}$$

where a, b and $\psi_{a, b}$ are the scale, translation parameters and mother wavelet, respectively.

The transform result represents the correlation between the signal and the transform of the mother wavelet being scaled and translated. If the signal and the mother wavelet are similar, the transform result will have a large value. This means that lead and delay are translation, while the scale is an expansion and compression. As the low scale is a compressing wavelet, it becomes a rapid changing signal, that is, it improves the sensitivity in the time domain for high frequency signals and improves the sensitivity in frequency domain for low frequency signals. This makes it possible to perform a multi-resolution analysis.

Discrete wavelet transform (DWT): The orthogonal basis functions used in wavelet analysis are families of scaling function, $\phi(t)$ and associated wavelet $\psi(t)$. The scaling function can be represented by following mathematical expression

$$\phi_{j,k}(t) = \sum_{k} H_k \, \phi(2^j t - k) \tag{10}$$

where H_k represents coefficient of scaling function, k, j represent translation and scale, respectively.

Similarly, the associated wavelet can be generated using the same coefficient as the scaling function

$$\psi_{j,k}(t) = \sum_k (-1)^k \sqrt{2} h_{1-k} \; \phi(2^j t - k) \tag{11}$$

The scaling function is orthogonal to each other as well as with the wavelet function as shown in Eqs. (10) and (11). This fact is crucial and forms part of the framework for multi-resolution analysis.

$$\int_{-\infty}^{\infty} \phi(2k-t)\,\phi(2k-1)\,dt = 0 \tag{12}$$

$$\int_{-\infty}^{\infty} \psi(t)\,\phi(t)\,dt = 0 \tag{13}$$

Using an iterative method, the scaling function and associated wavelet can be computed if the coefficients are known. Figure 6 shows the Daubechies 2 and 5 scaling function and wavelet.

A signal can be decomposed into approximate coefficients $a_{j,k}$ through the inner product of the original signal at scale j and the scaling function.

$$a_{j,k} = \int_{-\infty}^{\infty} f_j(t)\phi_{j,k}(t)dt \tag{14}$$

$$\phi_{j,k}(t) = 2^{j/2}\phi(2^j t - k) \tag{15}$$

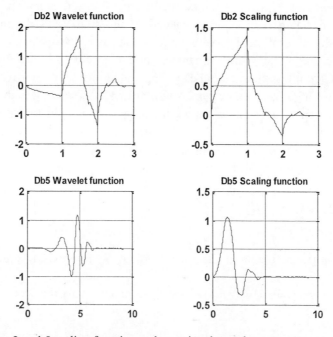

Figure 6. Daubechies 2 and 5 scaling function and associated wavelet.

Similarly the detail coefficients $d_{j,k}$ can be obtained through the inner product of the signal and the complex conjugate of the wavelet function.

$$d_{j,k} = \int_{-\infty}^{\infty} f_j(t)\,\psi_{j,k}(t)\,dt \tag{16}$$

$$\psi_{j,k}(t) = 2^{j/2}\psi(2^j t - k) \tag{17}$$

The original signal can therefore be decomposed at different scales as follows:

$$f(t) = \sum_{j=-\infty}^{\infty} a_{j_0,k}\,\phi_{j_0,k} + \sum_{j=-\infty}^{j_0}\sum_{k=-\infty}^{\infty} d_{j,k}\,\psi_{j,k}(t) \tag{18}$$

$$f[n] = \sum_{k=0}^{N-1} a_{j,k}\,\phi_{j,k}(t) = \sum_{k=0}^{N-1} a_{(j+1),k}\,\phi_{(j+1),k}(t) + \sum_{k=0}^{N-1} d_{(j+1),k}\,\psi_{(j+1),k}(t) \tag{19}$$

The coefficient of the next decomposition level ($j+1$) can be expressed as

$$a_{(j+1),k} = \sum_{k=0}^{N} a_{j,k}\int \phi_{j,k(t)}\,\phi_{(j+1),k}(t)\,dt \tag{20}$$

$$d_{(j+1),k} = \sum_{k=0}^{N} a_{j,k}\int \phi_{j,k(t)}\,\psi_{(j+1),k}(t)\,dt \tag{21}$$

$$a_{(j+1),k} = \sum_{k} a_{j,k}\,g[k] \quad \text{and} \quad d_{(j+1),k} = \sum_{k} a_{j,k}\,h[k] \tag{22}$$

The decomposition coefficients can therefore be determined through convolution and implemented by using a filter. The filter $g[k]$ is a low-pass filter and $h[k]$ is a high-pass filter.

$$y[n] = \sum_{k=1}^{N} h[k]\,x[n-k] \tag{23}$$

3.1.2. Averaging

Averaging can be divided into two types: one is synchronous averaging and the other is spectrum averaging. Synchronous averaging is very useful in reducing the random noise component in the measurement or in reducing the effect of the other interfering signals such as components from another nearby machine which requires a tachometer to synchronize each snapshot of the signal to the running speed of machine. Unlike synchronous averaging, spectrum averaging does not reduce the noise. Instead, it finds the average magnitude at each frequency where a series of individual spectra are added together and the sum is divided by the number of spectra.

3.1.3. Enveloping

The purpose of enveloping is to enhance small signals. The method first separates higher frequency bearing signals from low frequency machine vibrations by band pass filtering. The measurement problem at this point, is to detect small amplitudes. A defect signal in the time domain is very narrow, resulting in an energy component spread over a wide frequency range; consequently the harmonic amplitudes of the defect frequency are very nearly buried in noise.

3.1.4. Cepstrum

Cepstrum is the name given to a range of techniques all involving functions which can be considered as a *spectrum of a logarithmic spectrum*. The application of the power cepstrum to machine fault detection is based on the ability to detect the periodicity in the spectrum i.e. family of the uniformly spaced harmonics and side bands while being insensitive to the transmission path of the signal from an internal source to an external measurement point. The value of the main cepstrum peak was shown to be an excellent trend parameters; as it represents the average over a large number of individual harmonics, fluctuations in latter (for example as a result of load variations) were largely averaged out in the cepstrum value which gave a smooth trend curve with time.

3.2. Statistical Feature Representation

Usually, in the application of pattern classification and recognition, the data are represented by features which can be characteristic values, colors and so on. In machine condition monitoring and fault diagnosis, the statistical features are selected as patterns which can indicate the machine condition. Furthermore, statistical features are simple and useful for exploring and indicating the incipient faults when faults occurred in machines.

This section focuses on feature representation of statistical features for machine condition monitoring and fault diagnosis. Transformation of data to features plays a very important role which directly affects the performance of whole system. In other words, the better the features can reflect the performance of task the better the result will be. In order to keep data information at the highest level, features are calculated from the time domain, frequency domain and auto-regression estimation.

3.2.1. Features in Time Domain

Cumulants: The features described here are called statistical features because they are based on only the distribution of signal samples with the time series treated as a random variable. These features were also known as moments or cumulants. In most cases, the probability density function (pdf) can be decomposed into its constituent moments. If a change in condition causes a change in the probability density function of the signal then the moments may also change. Therefore, monitoring this phenomenon can provide diagnostic information.

The moment coefficients of time waveform data can be calculated using following equations

$$m_n = E\{x^n\} = \frac{1}{N}\sum_{i=1}^{N} x_i^n \tag{24}$$

where $E\{\cdot\}$ represents the expected value of the function, x_i is the ith time historical data and N is the number of data points.

The first four cumulants: mean (c_1), standard deviation (c_2), skewness (c_3) and kurtosis (c_4), can be calculated from the first four moments using the following relationships

$$c_1 = m_1 \tag{25}$$

$$c_2 = m_2 - m_1^2 \tag{26}$$

$$c_3 = m_3 - 3m_2 m_1 + 2m_1^3 \tag{27}$$

$$c_4 = m_4 - 3m_2^3 - 4m_3 m_1 + 12m_2 m_1^2 - 6m_1^4 \tag{28}$$

In addition, non-dimensional feature parameters in time domain are more popular such as shape factor and crest factor.

$$SF = x_{rms} / x_{abs} \tag{29}$$

$$CF = x_p / x_{rms} \tag{30}$$

where x_{RMS}, x_{abs} and x_p are root mean square value, absolute value and peak value, respectively.

Figure 7 describes the bearing signals and its histogram with different condition (normal and faults). From this figure, the cumulants are highlighted according to bearing condition and its values are summarized in Table 1. From Table 1, kurtosis has clear information for describing the condition of bearing. Normal bearing has kurtosis 3.0 while the fault condition has kurtosis more than 3.0. Therefore, kurtosis can indicate the incipient fault at bearing during its operation.

Table 1. Cumulants for bearing signal with different condition

Cumulants	Conditions			
	Normal	Mass unbalance	Inner race fault	Misalignment
Mean	0.0122	0.085	0.0038	0.0507
STD	0.0188	0.0314	0.0821	0.1833
Skewness	0.0802	0.0184	0.1234	0.1597
Kurtosis	3.0332	3.282	7.083	3.4315

Histogram: Upper and Lower Bound: Histograms which can be thought as a discrete probability density function (pdf) are calculated in the following way. Let d be the number of divisions that need to divide range into, let h_i with $0 \leq i \leq d$ be the columns of the histogram, then

$$h_i = \sum_{j=0}^{n} \frac{1}{n} r_i(x_i), \forall i, 0 \leq i \leq d \tag{31}$$

$$r_i(x) = \begin{cases} 1, & \text{if } \dfrac{i(\max(x_i) - \min(x_i))}{d} \leq x < \dfrac{(i+1)(\max(x_i) - \min(x_i))}{d} \\ 0, & otherwise \end{cases} \tag{32}$$

The upper bound and lower bound of histogram are defined as

$$h_L = \max(x_i) - \Delta / 2 \tag{33}$$

$$h_U = \max(x_i) + \Delta / 2 \tag{34}$$

where $\Delta = \max(x_i) - \min(x_i)/(n-1)$.

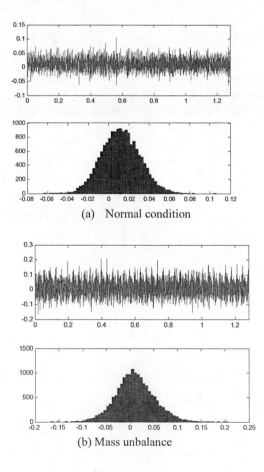

(a)   Normal condition

(b) Mass unbalance

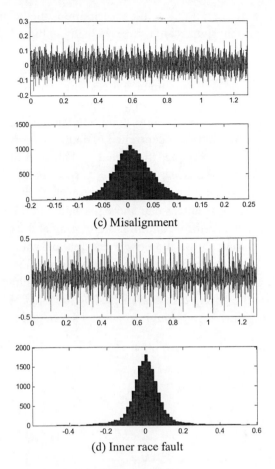

(c) Misalignment

(d) Inner race fault

Figure 7. Histogram for bearing signal with different condition.

Effectively, it is normalized by two things: the length of the sequence and the column divisions. Since the term above includes a *1/n* term and every x_i must fall into exactly one h_i column, the next effect is that $h_i = 1$ ($i = 0, ..., d$-1). The column divisions are relative to the bounding box and thus most of h_i will not be zero. This is a desirable, since it essentially removes the issue of size of a sign, and low resolution on small signs with lots of empty columns. The alternative would be to have absolute locations which would be nowhere near as closely correlated with the information in the sign itself. The examples of histogram of bearing signal with different condition can be seen in Figure 7.

Entropy Estimation and Error: In information theory, uncertainty can be measured by entropy. The entropy of distribution is the amount of a randomness of the distribution. Entropy estimation is two stage processes; first, a histogram is estimated and thereafter the entropy is calculated. The entropy estimation $E_s(x_i)$ and standard error $E_e(x_i)$ are defined as

$$E_s(x_i) = -\sum P(x_i)\ln(Px_i) \tag{35}$$

$$E_e(x_i) = \sum P(x_i)\ln P(x_i)^2 \tag{36}$$

where x_i is discrete time signals, $P(x_i)$ is the distribution on the whole signal. Here, the entropy of vibration and current signals are estimated using unbiased estimated approach.

3.2.2. Features on Frequency Domain

Through the frequency domain parameter indices, the primary diagnosis is available. In other words, the features can indicate the faults. Because these calculation indices are simple and fast so they can be used in the on-line condition monitoring. When there are some changes on the parameters, it indicates occurrence of faults. Finally, the precision diagnosis can deal with the problem. For example, the signal of ball bearing are composed of many stochastic elements, different faults have different spectrum I the frequency domain. However, in some cases the faults cannot be distinguished by power spectrum. Above mentioned, frequency parameters indices can show the faults in the beginning of the failure. So these indices can be used to perform condition monitoring and fault diagnosis.

The signal power spectrum shows the power distribution with the frequency. When the frequency elements and their power changed so the position of the main spectrum changed. On the other hand, when the frequency elements increased the power spectrum distribution become discrete whereas the power distribution is shown change. The characteristics of the frequency domain can be shown well through frequency parameter indices as follows:

Frequency center (FC)

$$FC = \frac{\int_0^{+\infty} fs(f)df}{\int_0^{+\infty} s(f)} \tag{37}$$

Mean square frequency (MSF)

$$MSF = \frac{\int_0^{+\infty} f^2 s(f)df}{\int_0^{+\infty} s(f)} \tag{38}$$

Root mean square frequency (RMSF)

$$RMSF = \sqrt{MSF} \tag{39}$$

Variance frequency (VF)

$$VF = \frac{\int_0^{+\infty} (f - FC)^2 s(f)df}{\int_0^{+\infty} s(f)df} \tag{40}$$

Root variance frequency (RVF)

$$RVF = \sqrt{VF} \tag{41}$$

where $s(f)$ is the signal power spectrum. The FC, MSF and $RMSF$ show the change position of main frequencies; VF and RVF describe the convergence of the spectrum power.

From the view of physics, the power spectrum is considered as the mass density function of a stick in the ordinate axis. Accordingly, FC is the mass center in the abscissa. When larger the density is near the origin, the distance between FC and the origin is closer. $RMSF$ is rotating radial circling the stick. The relation of the distance and density is same with aforementioned FC. Due to real calculation, the frequency spectrum needs to be discrete

$$FC = \frac{\sum_{i=2}^{N} \dot{x}_i x_i}{2\pi \sum_{i=1}^{N} x_i^2} \tag{42}$$

$$MSF = \frac{\sum_{i=2}^{N} \dot{x}_i^2}{4\pi^2 \sum_{i=1}^{N} x_i^2} \tag{43}$$

$$VF = MSF - (FC)^2 \tag{44}$$

where $\dot{x}_i = x_i - \dfrac{x_{i-1}}{\Delta}$

3.2.3. Auto-regression Coefficient

Since the different faults display different characteristics in the time series, auto-regression model is used to establish a model. The autoregressive coefficients are extracted as feature of fault condition. The first eight order coefficient of AR models are selected through Burg's lattice-based method using harmonic mean of forward and backward squared prediction errors. The definition that will be used here is as follows

$$y_t = \sum_{i=1}^{N} a_i y_{t-i} + \varepsilon_t \tag{45}$$

where a_i is the AR coefficients, y_t is the series under investigation, and N is the number of the model. The noise term or residual ε_t is almost assumed to be Gaussian white noise.

3.3. Dimensionality Reduction Using Feature Extraction

Dimensionality reduction is one of the important preprocessing steps in high-dimensional data analysis. The goal of dimensionality reduction is to embed high-dimensional data samples in a low-dimensional space while most of intrinsic information contained in the data is preserved. Once dimensionality reduction is carried out appropriately, we can utilize the compact representation of the data for various succeeding tasks such as visualization, classification, etc.

Usually, someone who works in pattern recognition area will face the high dimensionality of data, namely curse of dimensionality. It means that the processing of the data will be slow and requires a lot of memory and time. The other problem with high dimensionality of data is the classification using some algorithms will overfit to the data training. Thus, it leads to poor generalization to the training samples. Feature extraction is a general term for methods for constructing combinations of the variables which get around above problems but still describe the data sufficiently accurately. Here, several methods of feature extraction technique will be discussed to give the understanding of its process.

3.3.1. Principal Component Analysis (PCA)

PCA is a useful statistical technique that has found application in many fields, such as face recognition and image compression. It is a way of identifying patterns in data and expressing the data in such a way as to highlight their similarities and differences. Since patterns in data can be hard to find in data of high dimension, where the luxury of graphical representation is not available, PCA is a powerful tool for analyzing the data. The other main advantage of PCA is that there is no much loss information when the data are compressed. Principal components (PC) are uncorrelated and ordered such that the kth PC has the kth largest variance among all PC. The kth of PC can be interpreted as the direction that maximizes the variation of the projection of the data points such that it is orthogonal to the first k-1 PC.

Given p dimensionality data set $\mathbf{x}_i$, the m principal axis $T_1, T_2, \ldots, T_m$ where $1 \leq m \leq p$ are orthogonal axis onto which the retained variance is maximum in the projected space. Generally, $T_1, T_2, \ldots, T_m$ can be given by the m leading eigenvectors of covariance matrix

$$\mathbf{S} = \frac{1}{N} \sum_{i=1}^{N} (x_i - \mu)^T (x_i - \mu) \tag{46}$$

where $x_i \in \mathbf{x}_i$, N is the number of samples, so that

$$\mathbf{S}T_i = \lambda_i T_i \qquad i = 1, \ldots, m \tag{47}$$

where λ_i is the ith largest eigenvalue of $\mathbf{S}$. The m principal components of a given observation vector $\mathbf{x} \in \mathbf{x}_i$ are given by

$$\mathbf{y} = [y_1, \ldots, y_m] = [T_1^T x, \ldots, T_m^T x] = \mathbf{T}^T \mathbf{x} \tag{48}$$

The m principal components of $\mathbf{x}$ are the uncorrelated in the projected space. In multi-class problem, the variations of data are determined on a global basis that is the principal axis are derived from a global covariance matrix

$$\hat{\mathbf{S}} = \frac{1}{N} \sum_{j=1}^{K} \sum_{i=1}^{N} (x_i - \hat{\mu})^T (x_i - \hat{\mu}) \qquad (49)$$

where $\hat{\mu}$ is the global mean of all samples, K is the number of class, N is the number of samples in class j.

The principle axis $T_1, T_2, \ldots, T_m$ are therefore the m leading eigenvectors of $\hat{\mathbf{S}}$

$$\hat{\mathbf{S}} T_i = \hat{\lambda}_i T_i \qquad i = 1, \ldots, m \qquad (50)$$

where $\hat{\lambda}_i$ is the ith eigenvalue of $\hat{\mathbf{S}}$.

An assumption made for dimensionality reduction by PCA is that most information of the observation vectors is contained in the subspace spanned by the first m principal axis. Therefore, each original data vector can be represented by its principal component vector

$$\mathbf{y} = \mathbf{T}^T \mathbf{x} \qquad (51)$$

where $\mathbf{T} = [T_1, T_2, \ldots, T_m]$

The principal components of PCA are uncorrelated and they have sequentially maximum variances. The significant property is that the mean squared approximation error in the representation of the original inputs by the first several principal components is minimal [10].

3.3.2. Independent Component Analysis (ICA)

ICA is a technique that transform multivariate random signal into a signal having components that are mutually independent in complete statistical sense. Recently this technique has been demonstrated to be able to extract independent components from the mixed signals. Here independence means the information carried by one component can not inferred from the others. Statistically this means that joint probability of independent quantities is obtained as the product of the probability of each of them. A generic ICA model can be written as

$$\mathbf{x} = \mathbf{A}\mathbf{s} \qquad (52)$$

where $\mathbf{A}$ is an unknown full-rank matrix, called the mixing matrix, and $\mathbf{s}$ is the independent component (IC) data matrix, and $\mathbf{x}$ is the measured variable data matrix. The basic problem of ICA is to estimate the independent component matrix $\mathbf{s}$ or to estimate the mixing matrix $\mathbf{A}$ from the measured data matrix $\mathbf{x}$ without any knowledge of $\mathbf{s}$ or $\mathbf{A}$.

The ICA algorithm normally finds the independent components of a data set by minimizing or maximizing some measure of independence. Cardoso [11] gave a review of the solution to the ICA problem using various information theoretic criteria, such as mutual information, negentropy, and maximum entropy, as well as maximum likelihood approach. The fixed-point algorithm used due to its suitability for handling raw time domain data and good convergence properties. This algorithm will now be described briefly.

The first step is to pre-whiten the measured data vector $\mathbf{x}$ by a linear transformation, to produce a vector $\widetilde{\mathbf{x}}$ whose elements are mutually uncorrelated and all have unit variance. Singular value decomposition (SVD) of the covariance matrix $\mathbf{C} = E[\mathbf{xx}^T]$ yields

$$\mathbf{C} = \mathbf{\Psi\Sigma\Psi}^T \tag{53}$$

where $\mathbf{\Sigma} = \mathrm{diag}(\sigma_1, \sigma_2, ..., \sigma_n)$ is a diagonal matrix of singular values and $\mathbf{\psi}$ is the associated singular vector matrix. Then, the vector $\widetilde{\mathbf{x}}$ can be expressed as

$$\widetilde{\mathbf{x}} = \mathbf{\Psi\Sigma}^{-1/2}\mathbf{\Psi}^T\mathbf{x} = \mathbf{QAs} = \mathbf{Bs} \tag{54}$$

where $\mathbf{B}$ is an orthogonal matrix as verified by the following relation:

$$E[\widetilde{\mathbf{x}} \cdot \widetilde{\mathbf{x}}T] = \mathbf{B}E[\mathbf{s} \cdot \mathbf{s}^T]\mathbf{B}^T = \mathbf{BB}^T = \mathbf{I} \tag{55}$$

An advantage of using an SVD-based technique is the possibility of noise reduction by discarding singular values smaller than a given threshold. We have therefore reduced the problem of finding an arbitrary full-rank matrix $\mathbf{A}$ to the simpler problem of finding an orthogonal matrix $\mathbf{B}$ since $\mathbf{B}$ has fewer parameters to estimate as a result of the orthogonality constraint.

The second step is to employ the fixed point algorithm. Define a separating matrix $\mathbf{W}$ that transform the measured data vector $\mathbf{x}$ to a vector $\mathbf{y}$, such that all elements $\mathbf{y}_i$ are both mutually correlated and have unit variance. The fixed-point algorithm then determines $\mathbf{W}$ by maximizing the absolute value of kurtosis of $\mathbf{y}$. The vector $\mathbf{y}$ has the properties required for the independent components, thus

$$\widetilde{\mathbf{s}} = \mathbf{y} = \mathbf{Wx} \tag{56}$$

From Eq. (54), we can estimate $\mathbf{s}$ as follows

$$\widetilde{\mathbf{s}} = \mathbf{B}^T\widetilde{\mathbf{x}} = \mathbf{B}^T\mathbf{Qx} \tag{57}$$

From Eqs. (56) and (57) the relation of $\mathbf{W}$ and $\mathbf{B}$ can be expressed as
$$\mathbf{W} = \mathbf{B}^T\mathbf{Q} \tag{58}$$

To calculate $\mathbf{B}$, each column vector $\mathbf{b}_i$ is initialized and then updated so that ith independent component $\mathbf{s}_i = (\mathbf{b}_i)^T\widetilde{\mathbf{x}}$ may have great non-Gaussianity. Hyvarinen and Oja [12] showed that non-Gaussian represents independence using the central limit theorem.

There are two common measures of non-Gaussianity: kurtosis and negentropy. Kurtosis is sensitive to outliers. On the other hand, negentropy is based on the information theoretic quantity of (differential) entropy. Entropy is a measure of the average uncertainty in a random variable and the differential entropy H of random variable y with density $f(y)$ is defined as

$$H(y) = -\int f(y) \log f(y) dy \tag{59}$$

A Gaussian variable has maximum entropy among all random variables with equal variance [12]. In order to obtain a measure of non-Gaussianity that is zero for a Gaussian variable, the negentropy J is defined as follows:

$$J(y) = H(y_{gauss}) - H(y) \tag{60}$$

where y_{gauss} is a Gaussian random variable with the same variance as y. Negentropy is nonnegative and measures the departure of y from Gaussianity. However, estimating negentropy using Eq. (60) would require an estimate of the probability density function. To estimate negentropy efficiently, simpler approximations of negentropy suggested as follows:

$$J(y) \approx [E\{G(y)\} - E\{(v)\}]^2 \tag{61}$$

where y is assumed to be of zero mean and unit variance, v is a Gaussian variable of zero mean and unit variance, and G is any non-quadratic function. By choosing G wisely, one obtains good approximations of negentropy. A number of functions for G are:

$$G_1(v) = \frac{1}{a_1} \log \cosh(a_1 v) \tag{62}$$

$$G_2(v) = \exp(-a_2 v^2 / 2) \tag{63}$$

$$G_3(v) = v^4 \tag{64}$$

where $1 \leq a_1 \leq 2$ and $a_2 \approx 1$. Among these three functions, G_1 is a good general-purpose contrast function and was therefore selected for use in the present study.

Based on approximate form for the negentropy, Hyvarinen [13] introduced a very simple and highly efficient fixed-point algorithm for ICA, calculated over sphered zero-mean vector $\widetilde{\mathbf{x}}$. This algorithm calculates one column of the matrix $\mathbf{B}$ and allows the identification of one independent component; the corresponding independent component can then be found using Eq. (57). The algorithm is repeated to calculate each independent component.

3.3.3. Kernel PCA

Kernel PCA is one approach of generalizing linear PCA into nonlinear case using the kernel method. The idea of kernel PCA is to firstly map the original input vectors $\mathbf{x}_i$ into a high-dimensional feature space $\phi(\mathbf{x}_i)$ and than calculate the linear PCA in $\phi(\mathbf{x}_i)$. By mapping $\mathbf{x}_i$ into $\phi(\mathbf{x}_i)$ whose dimension is assumed to larger than the number of training samples m, kernel PCA solves the eigenvalue problem of Eq. (47)

$$\hat{\mathbf{S}}T_i = \hat{\lambda}_i T_i \qquad i = 1,...,m \tag{65}$$

where $\hat{\mathbf{S}}$ is the sample covariance matrix of $\phi(\mathbf{x}_i)$, $\hat{\lambda}_i$ is one of the non-zero eigenvalues of $\hat{\mathbf{S}}$ and T_i is the corresponding eigenvectors. The $\hat{\mathbf{S}}$ on the feature space can be constructed by

$$\hat{\mathbf{S}} = \frac{1}{m}\sum_{i=1}^{m}\phi(\mathbf{x}_i)\phi(\mathbf{x}_i)^T \tag{66}$$

From Eq. (66), we can obtain the non-zero eigenvalues that are positive. Let us define matrix $\mathbf{Q}$ as

$$\mathbf{Q} = [\phi(\mathbf{x}_1),...,\phi(\mathbf{x}_m)] \tag{67}$$

Then Eq. (66) can be expressed by

$$\hat{\mathbf{S}} = \frac{1}{m}\mathbf{Q}\mathbf{Q}^T \tag{68}$$

Moreover, we can construct a Gram matrix using Eq. (67) which is their element can be determined by kernel

$$\mathbf{R} = \mathbf{Q}^T\mathbf{Q} \tag{69}$$

$$\mathbf{R}_{ij} = \phi(\mathbf{x}_i)^T\phi(\mathbf{x}_i) = (\phi(\mathbf{x}_i)\cdot\phi(\mathbf{x}_j)) = K(\mathbf{x}_i,\mathbf{x}_j) \tag{70}$$

Denote $\mathbf{V} = (\gamma_1, \gamma_2, ..., \gamma_m)$ and $\mathbf{\Lambda} = \mathrm{diag}(\lambda_1, \lambda_2, ..., \lambda_m)$ are eigenvectors and eigenvalues of $\mathbf{R}$ respectively, we can calculate the orthonormal eigenvectors β_j as

$$\beta_j = \frac{1}{\sqrt{\lambda_m}}\mathbf{Q}\gamma \qquad j = 1,...,l \tag{71}$$

Then we define matrix $\mathbf{B}$ as

$$\mathbf{B} = (\beta_1,\beta_2,...,\beta_l) = \mathbf{Q}\mathbf{V}\mathbf{\Lambda}^{-1/2} \tag{72}$$

The whitening matrix $\mathbf{P}$ can be derived from Eq. (72) and expressed by

$$\mathbf{P} = \mathbf{B}\left(\frac{1}{m}\mathbf{\Lambda}\right)^{-1/2} = \sqrt{m}\mathbf{Q}\mathbf{V}\mathbf{\Lambda}^{-1} \tag{73}$$

The mapped data in feature space can be whitened by the following transformation

$$\mathbf{r} = \mathbf{P}^T\phi(\mathbf{x}_i) = \sqrt{m}\mathbf{\Lambda}^{-1}\mathbf{V}^T\mathbf{Q}^T\phi(\mathbf{x}) = \sqrt{m}\mathbf{\Lambda}^{-1}\mathbf{V}^T[K(\mathbf{x}_1,\mathbf{x}), K(\mathbf{x}_2,\mathbf{x}),..., K(\mathbf{x}_m,\mathbf{x})]$$
$$= \sqrt{m}\mathbf{\Lambda}^{-1}\mathbf{V}^T\mathbf{R} \tag{74}$$

3.3.4. Kernel ICA

Practically speaking, the kernel ICA is the combination of centering and whitening process using kernel PCA as previously explanation and iterative section using ICA. The following task is to find the mixing matrix $\mathbf{W}$ in the kernel PCA-transformed space to recover independent components $\tilde{s}$ from $\mathbf{r}$, recall Eq. (56)

$$\tilde{\mathbf{s}} = \mathbf{W}\mathbf{x} = \mathbf{W}\mathbf{r} \tag{75}$$

There are many algorithms to perform ICA. In this chapter, we employ the second order of ICA, proposed by Belouchrani et al. [14] which is adopted in ICALAB toolbox [15]. In summary, the nonlinear feature extraction using kernel ICA in this paper performs two phases: whitened process using kernel PCA and ICA transformation in the kernel PCA whitened space.

4. Support Vector Machine (SVM)

Support vector machine (SVM) is a relatively new computational learning method based on the statistical learning theory. Introduced by Vapnik and his co-workers [16-18], SVM becomes famous and popular in machine learning community due to the excellence of generalization ability than the traditional method such as neural network.

Therefore, SVM have been successfully applied to a number of applications ranging from face detection, verification, and recognition, object detection and recognition, handwritten character and digit recognition, text detection and categorization, speech and speaker verification, recognition, information and image retrieval, prediction and so on.

4.1. Basic Theory: Binary Classification by SVM

Given data input $\mathbf{x}_i$ (i = 1, 2, ..., M), M is the number of samples. The samples are assumed have two classes namely positive class and negative class. Each of classes associate with labels be $y_i = 1$ for positive class and $y_i = -1$ for negative class, respectively. In the case of linearly data, it is possible to determine the hyperplane $f(\mathbf{x}) = 0$ that separates the given data

$$f(\mathbf{x}) = \mathbf{w}^T \mathbf{x} + b = \sum_{j=1}^{M} w_j x_j + b = 0 \tag{76}$$

where $\mathbf{w}$ is M–dimensional vector and b is a scalar. The vector $\mathbf{w}$ and scalar b are used to define the position of separating hyperplane. The decision function is made using sign $f(x)$ to create separating hyperpline that classify input data in either positive class and negative class.

A distinctly separating hyperplane should be satisfy the constraints

$$\begin{aligned} f(x_i) &= 1 \quad \text{if } y_i = 1 \\ f(x_i) &= -1 \quad \text{if } y_i = -1 \end{aligned} \tag{77}$$

or it can be presented in complete equation

$$y_i f(\mathbf{x}_i) = y_i(\mathbf{w}^T \mathbf{x}_i + b) \geq 1 \quad \text{for } i = 1,2,...,M \tag{78}$$

The separating hyperplane that creates the maximum distance between the plane and the nearest data, i.e., the maximum margin, is called the optimal separating hyperplane. An example of the optimal hyperplane of two data sets is presented in Figure 8.

In Figure 8, series data points for two different classes of data are shown, black squares for negative class and white circles for positive class. The SVMs try to place a linear boundary between the two different classes, and orientate it in such way that the margin represented by the dotted line is maximized. Furthermore, SVMs attempts to orientate the boundary to ensure that the distance between the boundary and the nearest data point in each class is maximal. Then, the boundary is placed in the middle of this margin between two points. The nearest data points that used to define the margin are called support vectors, represented by the grey circles and squares. When the support vectors have been selected the rest of the feature set is not required, as the support vectors can contain all the information based need to define the classifier.

From the geometry the geometrical margin is found to be $\|\mathbf{w}\|^{-2}$.

Taking into account the noise with slack variables ξ_i and the error penalty C, the optimal hyperplane separating the data can be obtained as a solution to the following optimization problem

Minimize $\dfrac{1}{2}\|\mathbf{w}\|^2 + C\sum_{i=1}^{M}\xi_i$ \hfill (79)

subject to $\begin{cases} y_i(\mathbf{w}^T \mathbf{x}_i + b) \geq 1 - \xi_i, & i = 1,...,M \\ \xi_i \geq 0 & i = 1,...,M \end{cases}$ \hfill (80)

where ξ_i is measuring the distance between the margin and the examples $\mathbf{x}_i$ that lying on the wrong side of the margin. The calculation can be simplified by converting the problem with Kuhn-Tucker condition into the equivalent Lagrangian dual problem, which will be

$$\text{Minimize } L(\mathbf{w},b,\boldsymbol{\alpha}) = \frac{1}{2}\|\mathbf{w}\|^2 - \sum_{i=1}^{M}\alpha_i y_i(\mathbf{w}\mathbf{x}_i + b) + \sum_{i=1}^{M}\alpha_i \tag{81}$$

The task is minimizing Eq. (81) with respect to $\mathbf{w}$ and b, while requiring the derivatives of L to α to vanish. At optimal point, we have the following saddle point equations

$$\frac{\partial L}{\partial \mathbf{w}} = 0, \quad \frac{\partial L}{\partial b} = 0 \tag{82}$$

which replace into form

$$\mathbf{w} = \sum_{i=1}^{M}\alpha_i y_i \mathbf{x}_i, \qquad \sum_{i=1}^{M}\alpha_i y_i = 0 \tag{83}$$

From Eq. (83), we find that $\mathbf{w}$ is contained in the subspace spanned by the $\mathbf{x}_i$. Using substitution Eq. (83) into Eq. (82), we get the dual quadratic optimization problem

$$\text{Maximize } L(\alpha) = \sum_{i=1}^{M}\alpha_i - \frac{1}{2}\sum_{i,j=0}^{M}\alpha_i\alpha_j y_i y_j \mathbf{x}_i \mathbf{x}_j \tag{84}$$

subject to $\qquad\qquad\qquad \alpha_i \geq 0,\, i = 1, \dots, M.$

$$\sum_{i=1}^{M}\alpha_i y_i = 0 \tag{85}$$

Thus, by solving the dual optimization problem, one obtains the coefficients α_i which is required to express the $\mathbf{w}$ to solve Eq. (79). This leads to non-linear decision function.

$$f(\mathbf{x}) = sign\left(\sum_{i,j=1}^{M}\alpha_i y_i(\mathbf{x}_i\mathbf{x}_j) + b\right) \tag{86}$$

SVMs can also be used in non-linear classification tasks with application of kernel functions. The data to be classified is mapped onto a high-dimensional feature space, where the linear classification is possible. Using the non-linear vector function $\Phi(\mathbf{x}) = (\phi_1(\mathbf{x}), \dots, \phi_l(\mathbf{x}))$ to map the n-dimensional input vector $\mathbf{x}$ onto l-dimensional feature space, the linear decision function in dual form is given by

$$f(\mathbf{x}) = sign\left(\sum_{i,j=1}^{M}\alpha_i y_i(\Phi^T(\mathbf{x}_i)\Phi(\mathbf{x}_j)) + b\right) \tag{87}$$

Working in the high-dimensional feature space enables the expression of complex functions, but it also generates the problem. Computational problem occur due to the large vectors and the overfitting also exists due to the high-dimensionality. The latter problem can be solved by using the kernel function. Kernel is a function that returns a dot product of the feature space mappings of the original data points, stated as $K(\mathbf{x}_i, \mathbf{x}_j) = (\mathbf{\Phi}^T(\mathbf{x}_i)\mathbf{\Phi}_j(\mathbf{x}_j))$. When applying a kernel function, the learning in the feature space does not require explicit evaluation of $\mathbf{\Phi}$ and the decision function will be

$$f(\mathbf{x}) = sign\left(\sum_{i,j=1}^{M} \alpha_i y_i K(\mathbf{x}_i, \mathbf{x}_j) + b\right) \tag{88}$$

Any function that satisfies Mercer's theorem [16, 19] can be used as a kernel function to compute a dot product in feature space. There are different kernel functions used in SVMs, such as linear, polynomial and Gaussian RBF. The selection of the appropriate kernel function is very important, since the kernel defines the feature space in which the training set examples will be classified. The definition of legitimate kernel function is given by Mercer's theorem. The function must be continuous and positive definite. In this work, linear, polynomial and Gaussian RBF functions were evaluated and formulated in Table 2.

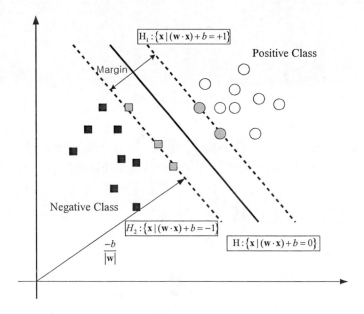

Figure 8. Classification of two classes using SVM.

Table 2. Formulation of kernel functions

Kernel	$K(\mathrm{x}, \mathrm{x}_j)$
Linear	$\mathrm{x}^T \cdot \mathrm{x}_j$
Polynomial	$(\gamma\, \mathrm{x}^T \cdot \mathrm{x}_j + r)^d$, $\gamma > 0$
Gaussian RBF	$\exp(-\|\mathrm{x} - \mathrm{x}_j\|^2 / 2\gamma^2)$

4.2. SVM Solver

4.2.1. Quadratic Programming (QP)

Vapnik [20] described a method which used the projected conjugate gradient algorithm to solve the SVM-QP problem, which has been known as *chunking*. The chunking algorithm uses the fact that the value of the quadratic form is the same if you remove the rows and columns of the matrix that corresponds to zero Lagrange multipliers. Therefore, chunking seriously reduces the size of the matrix from the number of training examples squared to approximately the number of non-zero Lagrange multipliers squared. However, chunking still cannot handle large-scale training problems, since even this reduced matrix cannot fit into memory. Osuna, Freund and Girosi [21] proved a theorem which suggests a whole new set of QP algorithms for SVMs. The theorem proves that the large QP problem can be broken down into a series of smaller QP sub-problems.

4.2.2. Sequential Minimum Optimization (SMO)

Sequential minimal optimization (SMO) proposed by Platt [22] is a simple algorithm that can be used to solve the SVM-QP problem without any additional matrix storage and without using the numerical QP optimization steps. This method decomposes the overall QP problem into QP sub-problems using the Osuna's theorem to ensure convergence. In this paper the SMO is used as a solver and detail descriptions can be found in Platt [22].

In order to solve the two Lagrange multipliers α_1, α_2, SMO first computes the constraints on these multipliers and then solves for the constrained minimum. For convenience, all quantities that refer to the first multiplier will have a subscript 1, while all quantities that refer to the second multiplier will have a subscript 2. The new values of these multipliers must lie on a line in (α_1, α_2) space, and in the box defined by $0 \leq \alpha_1, \alpha_2 \leq C$.

$$\alpha_1 y_1 + \alpha_2 y_2 = \alpha_1^{old} y_1 + \alpha_2^{old} y_2 = \text{constant} \tag{89}$$

Without loss of generality, the algorithm first computes the second Lagrange multipliers α_2^{new} and successively uses it to obtain α_1^{new}. The box constraint $0 \leq \alpha_1, \alpha_2 \leq C$, together with the linear equality constraint $\Sigma \alpha_i y_i = 0$, provides a more restrictive constraint on the feasible values for α_2^{new}. The boundary of feasible region for α_2 can be applied as follows

$$\text{If } y_1 \neq y_2; \quad L = \max(0, \alpha_2^{old} - \alpha_1^{old}), H = \min(C, C + \alpha_2^{old} - \alpha_1^{old}), \tag{90}$$

$$\text{If } y_1 = y_2; \quad L = \max(0, \alpha_1^{old} + \alpha_2^{old} - C), H = \min(C, C + \alpha_1^{old} + \alpha_2^{old}) \tag{91}$$

The second derivative of the objective function along the diagonal line can be expressed as:

$$\eta = K(\mathbf{x}_1, \mathbf{x}_1) + K(\mathbf{x}_2, \mathbf{x}_2) - 2K(\mathbf{x}_1, \mathbf{x}_2). \tag{92}$$

Under normal circumstances, the objective function will be positive definite, there will be a minimum along the direction of the linear equality constraint, and η will be greater than zero. In this case, SMO computes the minimum along the direction of the constraint:

$$\alpha_2^{new} = \alpha_2^{old} + \frac{y_2\left(E_1^{old} - E_2^{old}\right)}{\eta} \tag{93}$$

where E_i is the prediction error on the ith training example. As a next step, the constrained minimum is found by clipping the unconstrained minimum to the ends of the line segment:

$$\alpha_2^{new,clipped} = \begin{cases} H & \text{if } \alpha_2^{new} \geq H; \\ \alpha_2^{new} & \text{if } L < \alpha_2^{new} < H; \\ L & \text{if } \alpha_2^{new} \leq L; \end{cases} \tag{94}$$

Now, let $s = y_1 y_2$. The value of α_1^{new} is computed from the new α_2^{new}:

$$\alpha_1^{new} = \alpha_1^{old} + s(\alpha_2^{old} - \alpha_2^{new}) \tag{95}$$

Solving Eq. (84) for the Lagrange multipliers does not determine the threshold b of the SVM, so b must be computed separately. The following threshold b_1, b_2 are valid when the new α_1, α_2 are not at the each bounds, because it forces the output of the SVM to be y_1, y_2 when the input is $\mathbf{x}_1$, $\mathbf{x}_2$ respectively

$$b_1 = E_1 + y_1\,(\alpha_1^{new} - \alpha_1^{old})\,K(\mathbf{x}_1, \mathbf{x}_1) + y_2\,(\alpha_2^{new,clipped} - \alpha_2^{old})\,K(\mathbf{x}_1, \mathbf{x}_2) + b^{old} \tag{86}$$

$$b_2 = E_2 + y_1\,(\alpha_1^{new} - \alpha_1^{old})\,K(\mathbf{x}_1, \mathbf{x}_2) + y_2\,(\alpha_2^{new,clipped} - \alpha_2^{old})\,K(\mathbf{x}_2, \mathbf{x}_2) + b^{old} \tag{97}$$

When both b_1 and b_2 are valid, they are equal. When both new Lagrange multipliers are at bound and if L is not equal to H, then the interval between b_1 and b_2 are all thresholds that are consistent with the Karush-Kuhn-Tucker conditions which are necessary and sufficient conditions for an optimal point of a positive definite QP problem. In this case, SMO chooses the threshold to be halfway between b_1 and b_2 [22].

4.3. Multi-class Classification

The discussion above deals with binary classification where the class labels can take only two values: 1 and −1. In the real world problem, however, we find more than two classes for examples: in fault diagnosis of rotating machineries there are several fault classes such as mechanical unbalance, misalignment and bearing faults. Therefore, in this section the multi-class classification strategy will be discussed.

4.3.1. One-Against-All (OAA)

The earliest used implementation for SVM multi-class classification is one-against-all methods. It constructs k SVM models where k is the number of classes. The ith SVM is trained with all of examples in the ith class with positive labels, and all the other examples with negative labels. Thus given l training data (x_1, y_1), ..., (x_l, y_l), where $x_i \in R^n$, $i = 1, ..., l$. and $y_i \in \{1, ..., k\}$ is the class of x_i, the ith SVM solve the following problem

Minimize: $\dfrac{1}{2} \| \mathbf{w}^i \|^2 + C\sum_{i=1}^{l} \xi_j^i (\mathbf{w}^i)^T$ (98)

subject to: $(\mathbf{w}^i)^T \phi(\mathbf{x}_j) + b^i \geq 1 - \xi_j^i, \;\; \text{if } y = i$ (99)

$(\mathbf{w}^i)^T \phi(\mathbf{x}_j) + b^i \leq -1 + \xi_j^i, \;\; \text{if } y \neq i$ (100)

$\xi_j^i \geq 0, \quad j = 1, ..., l$ (101)

where the training data $\mathbf{x}_i$ is mapped to a higher dimensional space by function ϕ and C is the penalty parameter.

Minimizing Eq. (98) means we would like to maximize $2/\|\mathbf{w}_i\|$, the margin between two groups of data. When data is not separable, there is a penalty term $C\sum_{i=1}^{l} \xi_{i,i}$ which can reduce the number of training errors.

4.3.2. One-Against-One (OAO)

Another major method is called one-against-one method. This method constructs $k(k-1)/2$ classifiers where each one is trained on data from two classes. For training data from the ith and the jth classes, we solve the following binary classification problem.

Minimize: $\dfrac{1}{2} \| \mathbf{w}^{ij} \|^2 + C\sum_{t} \xi_t^{ij} (\mathbf{w}^{ij})^T$ (102)

subject to: $(\mathbf{w}^{ij})^T \phi(\mathbf{x}_t) + b^{ij} \geq 1 - \xi_t^{ij}, \;\; \text{if } y_t = i$ (103)

$(\mathbf{w}^{ij})^T \phi(\mathbf{x}_t) + b^{ij} \leq -1 + \xi_t^{ij}, \;\; \text{if } y_t = j$ (104)

$\xi_t^{ij} \geq 0, \quad j = 1, ..., l$ (105)

There are different methods for doing the future testing after all $k(k-1)/2$ classifiers are constructed. After some tests, the decision is made using the following strategy: if sign $((\mathbf{w}^{ij})^T \phi(\mathbf{x}) + b^{ij})$ says $\mathbf{x}$ is in the ith class, then the vote for the ith class is added by one. Otherwise, the jth is increased by one. Then $\mathbf{x}$ is predicted in the class using the largest vote. The voting approach described above is also called as Max Win strategy.

4.3.3. Direct Acyclic Graph (DAG)

In this method, the training process is similar to OAO strategy by solving $k(k-1)/2$ binary SVM. However, in the testing process, it uses a rooted binary directed acyclic graph which has $k(k-1)/2$ internal nodes and k leaves. Each node is binary SVM of ith and jth classes. Given a test samples $\mathbf{x}$, starting at the root node, the binary decision function is evaluated.

Then it moves to either left or right depending on the output value. The detail explanation of this method is suggested to see reference [23].

4.4. Wavelet-Support Vector Machine (W-SVM)

The idea of wavelet analysis is to approach a function or signal using a family of functions which are produced by translation and dilatation of the mother wavelet function $\psi_{a,b}(x)$

$$\psi_{a,b}(x) = |a|^{-1/2}\psi\left(\frac{x-b}{a}\right) \tag{106}$$

where x, a, $b \in R$, a is the dilatation factor and b is the translation factor. The wavelet transform of any function $f(x)$ can be expressed as

$$W_{a,b}(f) = \langle f(x), \psi_{a,b}(x)\rangle, \quad f(x) \in L_2(R) \tag{107}$$

where the notation $\langle\,,\rangle$ refers to inner product in $L_2(R)$.

Eq. (107) means that any function $f(x)$ can be decomposed on wavelet basis $\psi_{a,b}(x)$ if it satisfies the condition [24,25]

$$C_\psi = \int_0^\infty \frac{|H(\omega)|^2}{|\omega|}\,d\omega < \infty \tag{108}$$

where $H(\omega)$ is Fourier transform of $\psi_{a,b}(x)$.

Following [24], the function $f(x)$ can be reconstructed as follows

$$f(x) = \frac{1}{C_\psi}\int_{-\infty}^\infty \int_0^\infty W_{a,b}(f)\,\psi_{a,b}(x)\,\frac{da}{a^2}\,db \tag{109}$$

To approximate Eq. (109), then the finite can be written as

$$\hat{f}(x) = \sum_{i=1}^l W_i\psi_{a_i,b_i}(x) \tag{110}$$

Using Eq. (110), $f(x)$ can eventually be approximated by $\hat{f}(x)$.

For a common multidimensional wavelet function, the mother wavelet can be given as the product of one-dimensional (1-D) wavelet function [25]

$$\psi(x) = \prod_{i=1}^N \psi(x_i) \tag{111}$$

where $\mathbf{x} = (x_1, ..., x_N) \in R^N$. So, every 1-D wavelet mother $\psi(x)$ must satisfy Eq. (108).

Recalling the decision function for SVM in Eq. (88), the dot product can be replaced using kernel function as it was done by [16], so that $K(\mathbf{x}, \mathbf{x}') = K(\langle \mathbf{x} \cdot \mathbf{x}' \rangle)$. In SVM theory, any function which satisfies the Mercer's condition can serve as kernel function [16, 19].

Suppose K is a continuous symmetric function on R^N, such that integral operator T_K: $L_2(R^N) \rightarrow L_2(R^N)$,

$$(T_K)f(\cdot) = \int_{R^d} K(\cdot, \mathbf{x}) f(\mathbf{x}) \, d\mathbf{x} \tag{112}$$

is positive. Let $\phi_i \in L_2(R^N)$ be the eigenfunction of T_k associated with the eigenvalue $\lambda_i \geq 0$ and be normalized in such a way that $\| \phi_i \|_{L_2} = 1$, then the kernel function $K(\mathbf{x}, \mathbf{x}')$ can be expanded as

$$K(\mathbf{x}, \mathbf{x}') = \sum_{i=1}^{\infty} \lambda_i \, \phi_i(\mathbf{x}) \, \phi_i(\mathbf{x}') \tag{113}$$

and must satisfy the positivity condition of the following integral [19]

$$\int \int_{L_2 \otimes L_2} K(\mathbf{x}, \mathbf{x}') f(\mathbf{x}) f(\mathbf{x}') \, d\mathbf{x} \, d\mathbf{x}' \geq 0 \ , \forall f \in L_2(R^N) \tag{114}$$

For building a new kernel using wavelet, it may be helpful to refer to the frame theory, introduced by Duffin and Schaeffer [26], which is an extension of the normalized orthogonal basis. In the frame theory, one can reconstruct perfectly a function f in a Hilbert space H from its inner product $\langle , \rangle$ with family vectors $\{\psi_k\}$ if they satisfy

$$A \| f \|^2 \leq \sum_k |\langle f, \overline{\psi}_k \rangle|^2 \leq B \| f \|^2 \tag{115}$$

where the constants A and B satisfy the condition $0 < A \leq B < \infty$.

Any function in Hilbert space can be decomposed as follows

$$f = \sum_k \langle f, \overline{\psi}_k \rangle \psi_k = \sum_k \langle f, \psi_k \rangle \overline{\psi}_k \tag{116}$$

where $\overline{\psi}_k = (T * T)^{-1} \psi_k$ is the dual frame of ψ_k and T is the frame operator [24].

In $L_2(R^N)$, if $f = \{\psi_i\}$ is a frame and $\{\lambda_i\}$ is a positive increasing sequence, a function $K(\mathbf{x}, \mathbf{x}')$ can be given by

$$K(\mathbf{x},\mathbf{x}') = \sum_{i=1}^{\infty} \lambda_i \, \psi_i(\mathbf{x}) \, \psi_i(\mathbf{x}') \tag{117}$$

Eq. (113) is similar to Eq. (117) since both of them satisfy the condition for kernel function. Moreover, a mother wavelet $\psi_{a,b}(x)$ is called a frame wavelet if $\psi \in L_2(R^N)$, $a > 1$, $b > 0$ and the family function

$$\{\psi_{mn}\} = \{D_{am} T_{nb} \psi\} \tag{118}$$

where D and T are unitary dilatation operator and unitary translation operator, respectively, while a is scale parameter and b is translation parameter.

A wavelet kernel function can be constructed by any mother wavelet which can generate frame wavelet while satisfying the Mercer's condition in Eq. (114). In addition to the inner product, there exists a kernel called translation-invariant kernel [27, 28] such that

$$K(\mathbf{x},\mathbf{x}') = K(\langle \mathbf{x} - \mathbf{x}' \rangle) \tag{119}$$

If the translation-invariant kernel is admissible in SVM kernel function, then the necessary and sufficient condition of Mercer's theorem must be satisfied. The other theorem stated that a translation-invariant kernel is an admissible support vector (SV) kernel if only if the following Fourier transforms [27]

$$F[K](\omega) = (2\pi)^{-N/2} \int_{R^N} \exp(-j(\omega \cdot \mathbf{x})) \, K(\mathbf{x}) \, d\mathbf{x} \tag{120}$$

is non-negative. Based on the mother wavelet, the wavelet kernel which satisfies the translation-invariant theorem can be given as

$$K(\mathbf{x},\mathbf{x}') = K(\mathbf{x} - \mathbf{x}') = \prod_{i==1}^{N} \psi\left(\frac{x_i - x_i'}{a_i}\right) \tag{121}$$

The construction of wavelet kernel function using Haar, Daubechies and Symlet can be shown in Figure 9.

5. Application for Fault Diagnosis of Induction Motor

The utility of induction motor in industry is unavoidable and it becomes important parts to drive their process for producing the products. The issue of robustness and reliability is very important to guarantee the good operational condition. Therefore, faults detection and classification of induction motors has received considerable attention in recent years. Early fault detection and diagnosis can reduce the consequential damage, breakdown maintenance and reduce the spare parts of inventories. Moreover it can increase the prolong machine life, performance, and availability of machine.

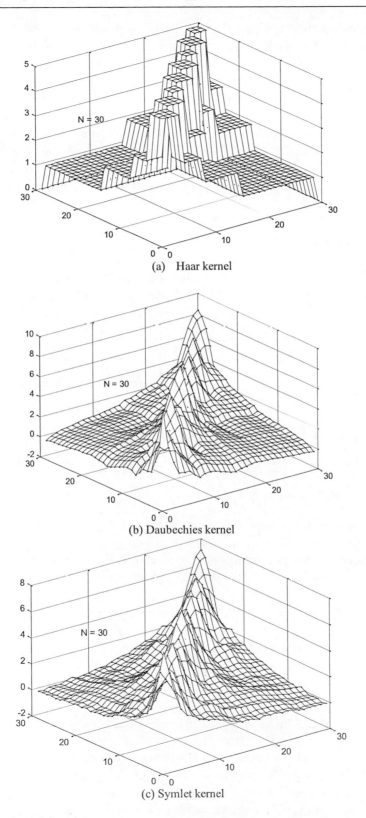

(a)   Haar kernel

(b) Daubechies kernel

(c) Symlet kernel

Figure 9. Wavelet kernel function.

Therefore, establishing intelligent system for faults detection of induction motor is very useful and important. To face this issue, the research area in pattern recognition and machine learning has been applied to perform condition monitoring, faults detection and classification. The kernel trick is one of the crucial tricks for machine learning. Its basic idea is to project the input data into a high-dimensional implicit feature space with a nonlinear mapping, and then the data is analyzed so that nonlinear relations of the input data can be described. The researchers who contribute the theoretical development of wavelet kernel are reported in [29-31]. However, the application is still rare in faults detection and classification of induction motor. Hence, a new intelligent faults detection and classification method called W-SVM is established. This method is used to induction motor for faults detection based on vibration signal.

5.1. Fault Diagnosis Method

A novel faults diagnosis method for the induction motor is proposed in Figure 10, which is based on component analysis and SVM multi-class classification.

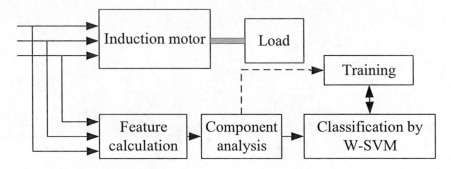

Figure 10. The proposed system using W-SVM.

The procedure of the proposed system can be summarized as follows:

Step 1: the data acquisition is carried out through self-designed test rig.
Step 2: features calculation using statistical features parameter from time and frequency domains.
Step 3: reducing the feature dimension and extracting the component analysis which is useful in the classification process.
Step 4: the classification process for diagnosing the faults is carried out using W–SVM based on one-against-all multi-class classification.

5.2. Experiment and Data Acquisition

Data acquisition was conducted on induction motor of 160 kW, 440 volt, 2 poles as shown in Figure 11. Six accelerometers were used to pickup vibration signal at drive-end and non drive-end on vertical, horizontal and axial direction, respectively. The maximum frequency of the used signals and the number of sampled data were 60 Hz and 16384, respectively. The condition of induction motor is briefly summarized in Table 3. Each condition was labeled as class from 1 to 7. Feature representation for training and classification was presented in Table 4. There are totally 126 features calculated from 6 signals, 21 features and 98 data calculated from 7 condition 14 measurements.

Figure 11. Data acquisition of induction motor.

Table 3. Condition of induction motor

Class No.	Condition	Description	Others
1	Bent rotor	Maximum shaft deflection	1.45mm
2	Eccentricity	Static eccentricity (30%)	Air-gap: 0.25 mm
3	MCDE	Magnetic center moved (DE)	6 mm
4	MCNDE	Magnetic center moved (NDE)	6 mm
5	Normal	No faults	-
6	Unbalance	Unbalance mass on the rotor	10 gr
7	Weak-end shield	Stiffness of the end-cover	-

Table 4. Feature representation

Signals	Position DE and NDE	Feature parameters		
		Time domain	Frequency domain	Reg. Coeff.
Vibration	Vertical	Mean	RMS freq.	a_1- a_8
	Horizontal	RMS	Freq. Center	
	Axial	Shape factor	RVF	
		Skewness		
		Kurtosis		
		Crest factor		
		Entropy error		
		Entropy estimation		
		Histogram lower		
		Histogram upper		

5.3. Feature Extraction and Reduction

Basically feature extraction is mapping process of data from higher dimension into low dimension space. This step is intended to avoid the curse dimensionality phenomenon. Structure of three first original features, those are mean, RMS and shape factor are plotted in Figure 12. This figure shows the performance of original features those are containing overlap in some conditions. Then, applying component analysis is suggested to make original features well clustered.

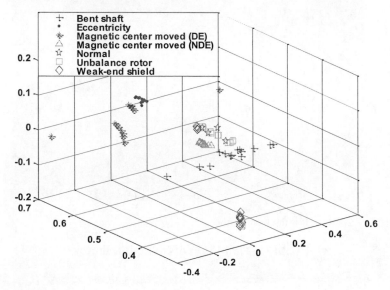

Figure 12. Original features.

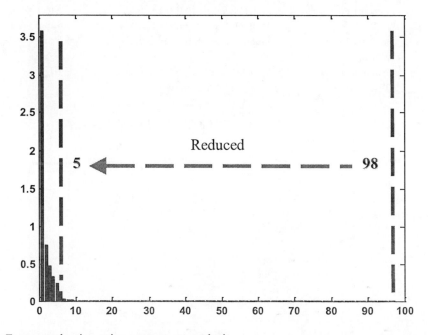

Figure 13. Feature reduction using component analysis.

Component analysis via ICA, PCA and their kernel are then used to extract and reduce the feature dimensionality based on eigenvalue of covariance matrix as described in Figure 13. After performing component analysis the feature have been changed into independent and principal components, respectively. The first three independent and principal components from PCA, ICA and their kernel are plotted in Figure 14.

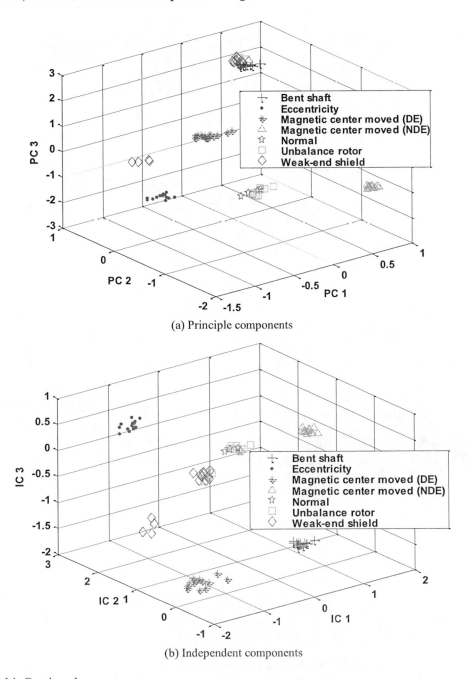

(a) Principle components

(b) Independent components

Figure 14. Continued on next page.

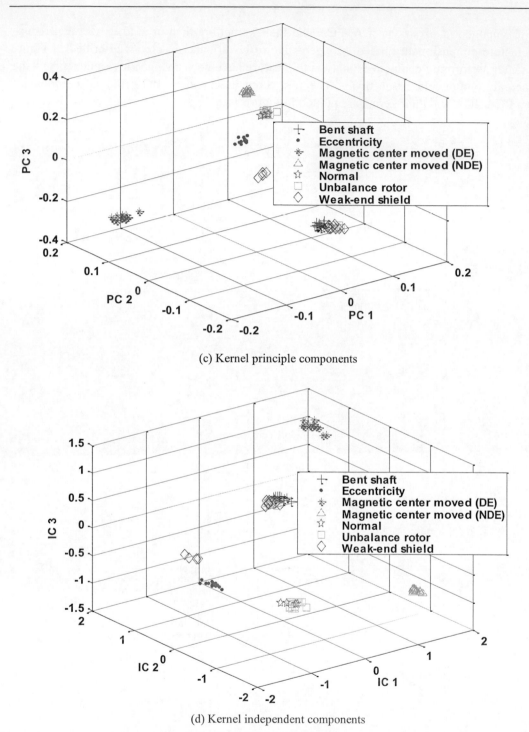

(c) Kernel principle components

(d) Kernel independent components

Figure 14. The first three principal and independent components.

It can be observed that the clusters for seven conditions are separated well. It indicates that component analysis can perform feature extraction and all at once do clustering each condition of induction motors. According to the eigenvalue of covariance matrix, the features were changed into component analysis and reduced only 5 component analysis needed for classification process. The other features are discarded due to small of eigenvalue of covariance matrix. The selected component analysis is then used by W-SVM classifier as input vectors for fault diagnosis using classification routine.

5.4. Classification

The SVM based multi-class classification is applied to perform the classification process using one-against-all methods. The tutorial of this method has been clearly explained in [23]. To solve the SVM problem, Vapnik [20] describe a method which used the projected conjugate gradient algorithm to solve the SVM-QP problem. In this study, SVM-QP was performed to solve the classification problem of SVM. The parameter C (bound of the Lagrange multiplier) and (condition parameter for OP method) were 1 and 10^{-7}, respectively. Wavelet kernel function using Daubechies series was performed in this study. The parameter δ in wavelet kernel refers to number of vanishing moment and is set 4. In the training process, the data set was also trained using RBF kernel function as comparison. The parameter γ for bandwidth RBF kernel was user defined equal to 0.5.

5.5. Results and Discussion

The complex separation boundaries are presented in Figure 15 from which the separation of W-SVM can be shown. In these figures, the circle refers to the support vector that states the correct recognition in W-SVM. Each condition of induction motor is well recognized using Daubechies wavelet kernel. In the classification process using W-SVM, each condition of induction motors can be clustered well. The good separation among conditions shows the performance of W-SVM doing recognition of component analysis from vibration signal features. The performance of classification process is summarized in Table 5. All data set come from component analysis are accurately classified using Daubechies wavelet kernel and SVM and reached accuracy 100% in training and testing, respectively. SVM using RBF kernel function with kernel width $\gamma = 0.5$ is also performed in classification for comparison with Daubechies wavelet kernel. The results show that the performance of W-SVM is similar to SVM using RBF kernel function, those are 100% in accuracy of training and testing, respectively. In the case of number support vectors, SVM with RBF kernel function needs lower than W-SVM except kernel PCA.

Table 5. Results of classification

Kernel	Accuracy (Train/Test), %				Number of SVs			
	IC	PC	Kernel IC	Kernel PC	IC	PC	Kernel IC	Kernel PC
Wavelet Daubechies	100/100	100/100	100/100	100/100	35	39	39	17
RBF-Gaussian ($\gamma = 0.5$)	100/100	100/100	100/100	100/100	22	22	25	33

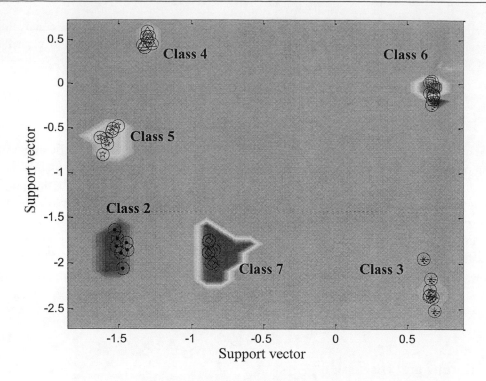

(a) Daubechies kernel with PC data

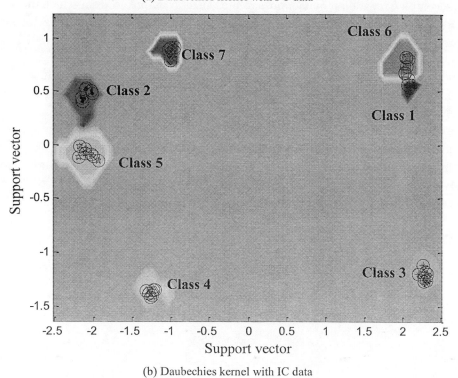

(b) Daubechies kernel with IC data

Figure 15. Continued on next page.

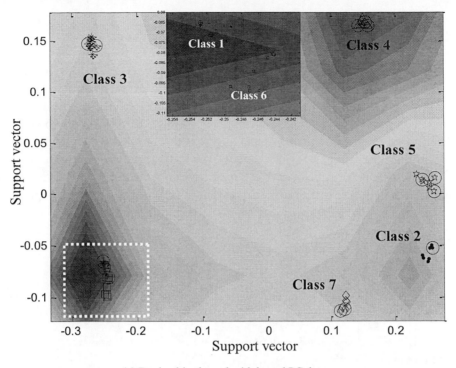

(c) Daubechies kernel with kernel PC data

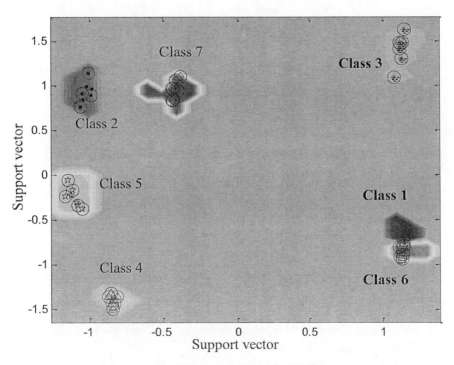

(d) Daubechies kernel with kernel IC data

Figure 15. Separation boundaries of W-SVM.

CONCLUSION

In this chapter, a complete study of pattern recognition for machine fault diagnosis using support vector machine have been deeply studied. Some basic theories including signal analysis in time and frequency domains, which are used for feature representation are reviewed to give preliminary understanding in fault diagnosis procedure. Feature extractions using linear and nonlinear technique via component analysis are presented to obtain optimal feature for good fault classification. Support vector machine which is known as new technique in machine learning is highlighted to understand the classification procedure for fault diagnosis system. Moreover, wavelet support vector machine (W-SVM) is introduced to contribute a relatively new technique in classification method used to fault diagnosis routine. Finally, W-SVM is validated and applied to induction motor fault detection and classification based on vibration signal. The results show that W-SVM is well performed and reached high accuracy in training and testing process based on experimental work.

REFERENCES

[1]   E.G. Milewski, *The Essentials of Statistics*, vol. 1, Research and Education Association, Piscataway, NJ, 1996.

[2]   M. Zacksenhouse, S. Braun, M. Feldman. (2000). Toward helicopter gearbox diagnostics from a small umber f examples. *Mechanical Systems and Signal Processing*, 14(4), 523-543.

[3]   O. Barzilay, V.L. Brailovsky. (1999). On domain knowledge and feature selection using a support vector machine. *Pattern Recognition Letters*, 20(5), 475-484.

[4]   A. Widodo, B.S. Yang. (2007). Support vector machine in machine condition monitoring and fault diagnosis: a review, *Mechanical Systems and Signal Processing*, 21(6), 2560-2574.

[5]   G. Vachtsevanos, F. Lewis, M. Roemer, A. Hess, B. Wu. Intelligent Fault Diagnosis and Prognosis for engineering Systems. 1st Editon. New Jersey: John Wiley and Sons; 2006.

[6]   G. Dalpiaz, A. Rivola, R. Rubini. (2000). Effectiveness and sensitivity of vibration processing techniques for local fault detection in gears. *Mechanical Systems and Signal Processing*, 14, 387–412.

[7]   B.S. Yang, T. Han, W.W. Hwang. (2005). Application of multi-class support vector machines for fault diagnosis of rotating machinery. *Trans. KSME Journal of Mechanical Science and Technology*, 19(3), 845-858.

[8]   A. Famili, W.M Shen, R. Weber, E. Simoudis. (1997). Data preprocessing and intelligent data analysis. *Inteligent Data Analysis, 1*, 3-23.

[9]   C.S. Burrus, R.A. Gopinath, H.Guo. Introduction to Wavelets and Wavelet Transforms. New Jeresy: Prentice-Hall; 1998.

[10] I.J. Jolliffe. *Principal Component Analysis*. New York: Springer; 1986.

[11] J.F. Cardoso. (1998). Blind signal separation: statistical principles. *Proceeding of the IEEE* 86 (10), 2009-2020.

[12] A. Hyvärinen, E. Oja. (2000). Independent component analysis: algorithms and applications. *Neural Networks*, 13 (4-5), 411-430.

[13] A. Hyvärinen. (1999). Fast and robust fixed-point algorithms for independent component analysis. *IEEE Trans. Neural Networks*, 10, 626-634.

[14] A. Belouchrani, K. Abed-Meraim, J.F. Cardoso and E. Moulines. (1993). Second-order blind separation of temporally correlated sources. *Proceedings of International Conference on Digital Signal Processing*, Cyprus, 346-351.

[15] A. Cichocki, S. Amari, K. Siwek and T. Tanaka, ICALAB for signal processing; Toolbox for ICA, BSS and BSE, http://www.bsp.brain.riken.jp/ICALAB/ICALABSignalProc/.

[16] V.N. Vapnik. The Nature of Statistical Learning Theory. New York: Springer; 1995.

[17] B. Boser, I. Guyon, V.N. Vapnik. (1992). A training algorithm for optimal margin classifiers. *Proceedings of Fifth Annual Workshop on Computational Learning Theory*, New York.

[18] C. Cortes, V. Vapnik. (1995). Support-vector networks. *Machine Learning*, 20(3), 273-297.

[19] N. Cristianini N.J. Shawe-Taylor. An Introduction to Support Vector Machines. Cambridge: Cambridge University Press; 2000.

[20] V.N. Vapnik. *Estimation Dependences Based on Empirical Data*, Berlin: Springer Verlag; (1982).

[21] E. Osuna, R.R. Freund and F.F. Girosi. (1997). Improved training algorithm for support vector machines. *Proceeding of IEEE Neural Networks for Signal Processing*, 276-285.

[22] J. Platt. (1999). Fast training of support vector machines using sequential minimal optimization. in: B. Scholkopf, et al. (Eds.), *Advances in Kernel Methods–Support Vector Learning*. Cambridge:MIT Press, 185-208.

[23] C.W. Hsu, C.J. Lin. (2002). A comparison of methods for multi-class support vector machines. *IEEE Trans. Neural Networks*, 13, 415-425.

[24] I. Daubechies. (1990). The wavelet transform, time-frequency localization and signal analysis. *IEEE Transaction on Information Theory*, 36, 961-1005.

[25] Q.H. Zhang, A. Benveniste. (1992). Wavelet networks. *IEEE Transaction on Neural Networks*, 3, 889-898.

[26] R.J. Duffin, A. Schaeffer. (1952). A class of nonharmonic Fourier series. *Transaction of American Mathematics Society*, 72, 341-366.

[27] A. Smola, B. Scholköpf, K.R. Müller. (1998). The connection between regularization operators and support vector kernels. *Neural Network*, 11, 637-649.

[28] L. Zhang, W. Zhou, L. Jiao. (2004). Wavelet support vector machine. *IEEE Transaction on System, Man, and Cybernetics-Part B: Cybernetics*, 34 (1), 34-39.

[29] A. Rakotomamonjy, S. Canu. (2005). Frame, reproducing kernel, regularization. *Journal of Machine Learning Research*, 6, 1485-1515.

[30] J. Gao, F. Chen, D. Shi. (2004). On the construction of support wavelet network. *IEEE International Conference on System, Man, and Cybernetics*, 3204-3207.

[31] Z. Yu, Y. Cai. (2005). Least squares wavelet support vector machines for nonlinear system identification. *LNCS* 3497, 436-441.

INDEX

A

accelerometers, 186
acid, 30, 31
actual output, 69
adaptability, 146, 151
aerosols, 32
agencies, 28
air pollutants, 27
air quality, 27, 28, 38, 39, 40, 45, 46, 47, 48
air quality model, 46
algorithm, 3, 6, 17, 23, 25, 41, 49, 52, 59, 62, 64, 76,
    78, 79, 120, 131, 132, 136, 140, 144, 145, 146,
    147, 148, 150, 151, 171, 172, 173, 179, 191,
    195
ambient air, 32
amplitude, 158
annealing, 142, 143
Argentina, 9
artificial intelligence, 146
Artificial Neural Networks, 79, 117, 118, 122
asthma, 30, 40
atherosclerosis, 6
atmosphere, 27, 30, 31, 38, 46, 47
Austria, 151

B

bacteria, 31
Bangladesh, 79
Belgium, 48
benign, 6, 9, 10, 12, 18, 19
bias, 8, 9, 12, 15, 17, 144
binary decision, 181
biopsy, 10
blood plasma, 10
blood vessels, 6, 10

bloodstream, 31
bone marrow, 6
bounds, 151, 180
brain, 4, 20, 21, 195
brain structure, 4
breast cancer, 1, 2, 3, 4, 6, 7, 17, 18, 20, 24
bronchitis, 40

C

CAD, 8, 17, 22
cancer, viii, ix, 3, 5, 6, 7, 9, 22, 153
carbon, 31, 32, 36, 38, 39, 47
carbon monoxide, 32, 36, 38, 39, 47
cardiovascular disease, 31
case studies, 73
case study, x, 2, 4, 6, 7, 18, 153
categorization, 154, 175
chemical, 30
chemical reactions, 30
chemicals, 30
Chicago, 120
China, 51, 64
chronic diseases, 40
chunking, 179
classes, 8, 9, 17, 143, 175, 176, 178, 180, 181
classification, 1, 3, 4, 5, 6, 7, 8, 9, 10, 11, 12, 16, 17,
    18, 19, 20, 21, 22, 24, 28, 32, 35, 41, 51, 78,
    117, 118, 122, 132, 145, 146, 147, 151, 152,
    153, 154, 160, 164, 170, 177, 180, 181, 184,
    186, 187, 191, 194
Clean Air Act, 32, 40
climate, 29
clustering, 22, 119, 120, 190
clusters, 190
coal, 29, 30, 47
coding, 132, 142, 146, 150, 151
coherence, 5, 23

combustion, 30, 31, 38
communication, 51, 52, 134, 142, 146, 147, 151
communication systems, 151
community, 2, 175
compensation, 53, 150
complexity, 28, 41, 46, 53, 72, 76, 132, 133, 144, 146, 147
compliance, 40, 46
compounds, 30, 31
compression, 161, 170
computed tomography, 5
computing, 79
condensation, 47
conference, 9, 13, 24
conjugate gradient method, 41
constant rate, 74
construction, 64, 184, 195
consumption, 38
controversial, 40
convergence, 45, 47, 68, 169, 172, 179
correlation, 43, 44, 45, 51, 59, 74, 117, 161
correlation coefficient, ix, 43, 44, 45, 117
CPU, 45, 46, 148
cross-validation, 12, 42, 46, 49
currency, 118
cycles, 118
Cyprus, 195

D

danger, 28, 117, 118, 128
data analysis, 158, 170, 194
data distribution, 9, 12
data mining, ix, 49, 132
data set, 9, 12, 23, 35, 36, 42, 53, 73, 75, 119, 120, 170, 171, 176, 191
data transfer, 158
database, 68, 154
deaths, 40, 47
decision trees, 119
decoding, 131, 132, 135, 136, 137, 138, 142, 143, 145, 146, 147, 148, 150, 151
decomposition, 163, 172
defects, 158
degradation, 143, 155
deposits, 30
depth, 143
derivatives, 34, 138, 177
detectable, 155
detection, 3, 4, 5, 6, 7, 9, 19, 20, 23, 24, 51, 153, 175, 184, 186
deviation, 53, 69
diffusion, 22

digital communication, 131, 132
dimensionality, 35, 69, 72, 158, 160, 170, 171, 178, 188, 189
discriminant analysis, 3, 5
discrimination, 3
diseases, 5, 21, 23
distribution, 17, 118, 164, 167, 168

E

economic downturn, 47
electricity, 41
electron, 30
emergency, 30
emission, 38, 39, 40, 46
encoding, 131, 132, 133, 135, 144
encouragement, 154
energy, ix, 29, 131, 132, 135, 138, 140, 142, 146, 150, 164
engineering, 46, 68, 76, 78, 79, 194
England, 78
entropy, 156, 157, 167, 168, 172, 173
environment, 30, 146
Environmental Protection Agency, 32, 41
EPA, 49
equality, 179
estimation process, 54
Euclidean space, 135
European market, 120
everyday life, 118
evidence, 31, 40, 120
evolution, 47
exchange rate, 120
exertion, 31
exposure, 31, 49
extraction, ix, x, 153, 155, 159, 170, 175, 188, 190

F

false positive, 5
fault detection, 156, 164, 184, 194
fault diagnosis, x, 153, 154, 155, 158, 159, 160, 164, 168, 180, 191, 194
feature selection, 21, 159, 194
FFT, 157
fiber, 6
fibrosis, 5, 22
filters, 58
financial, ix, 117, 118, 119, 120, 128
financial data, 120
flatness, 70
flexibility, 8, 44

fluctuations, 164
fluorescence, 5
forecasting, ix, 48, 79, 117, 118, 119, 120, 128
formation, 31, 134
formula, 74, 78, 150
fractal analysis, 3, 20
friction, 79
functional MRI, 4, 21
funding, 19
fusion, 23, 161

G

garbage, 160
geometry, 73, 176
glaucoma, 6
glioma, 21
globalization, 159
graph, 45, 181
grids, 46
growth, 19, 159

H

harmful effects, 28
health, 27, 28, 30, 40, 46, 47
health effects, 30
health problems, 28, 40
heart attack, 40
height, 39
heteroskedasticity, 119
high risk patients, 10
Hilbert space, 183
histogram, 165, 166, 167
historical data, 165
human, 4, 6, 27, 28, 30, 44
human brain, 44
human health, 27, 28, 30

I

identification, 4, 46, 154, 173, 195
idiopathic, 6, 23
image, 4, 6, 19, 23, 51, 52, 53, 54, 55, 56, 57, 58, 59, 63, 64, 153, 154, 170, 175
image analysis, 23
images, 3, 4, 5, 6, 7, 10, 11, 20, 21, 22, 51, 52, 53, 56, 57, 58, 59, 62, 63, 64
imaging modalities, 1
improvements, 3, 18, 27
impulses, 157

in vivo, 5, 22
independence, 171, 172
India, 67
individuals, 31
induction, viii, x, 67, 69, 153, 184, 186, 187, 190, 191, 194
information processing, 80
information technology, 159
integration, 22, 161
intervention, 46
investment, 118
investors, 118
iteration, 143

J

Java, 46

K

Korea, 119

L

Lagrange multipliers, 33, 71, 179, 180
lead, 16, 32, 161
learning, 1, 2, 3, 7, 8, 9, 10, 18, 19, 27, 28, 32, 41, 42, 52, 53, 67, 69, 76, 79, 80, 118, 132, 143, 146, 154, 155, 175, 178, 186
learning process, 155
learning task, 41
Least squares, 195
lesions, 4, 5, 7, 9, 10, 11, 12, 14, 18, 20, 22, 24
linear function, 69, 148
liver, 5
localization, 195
lung disease, 30
lung function, 30, 40

M

machine learning, ix, 6, 21, 24, 46, 118, 120, 132, 153, 155, 175, 186, 194
machinery, 156, 158, 194
magnet, 10
magnetic resonance imaging, 1, 2, 4, 6, 7, 9, 10, 17, 18, 22, 24, 25
magnitude, 119, 163
malignancy, 4, 5, 6, 21, 22, 23
mammogram, 3
mammography, 6, 7, 24, 25

management, 119
mapping, ix, 4, 20, 22, 35, 36, 44, 53, 72, 118, 131,
    133, 144, 155, 174, 186, 188
Maryland, 152
mass, 20, 68, 169, 187
matrix, ix, 35, 42, 133, 134, 137, 138, 139, 140, 141,
    170, 171, 172, 173, 174, 175, 179, 189, 190
matter, 28, 30, 36, 39, 43, 46
measurements, 3, 6, 8, 9, 10, 11, 12, 28, 48, 78, 154,
    163, 164, 187
medical, viii, 1, 3, 6, 19, 21, 22, 23, 51, 52
memory, 46, 133, 147, 150, 170, 179
methodology, 47, 154
microscope, 30
Microsoft, 152
mixing, 171, 175
modelling, 27, 29, 46, 47, 48, 68
models, viii, ix, 28, 43, 44, 45, 46, 47, 48, 51, 68, 74,
    76, 78, 117, 118, 119, 120, 156, 169, 180
modifications, 144
modules, 154
momentum, 76
Moon, 20
mortality, 27, 49
motivation, 11, 16
MRI, 1, 2, 4, 5, 6, 7, 8, 10, 12, 13, 14, 16, 18, 19, 22,
    24
MSF, 168, 169
multidimensional, 10, 182
multimedia, 51, 52
multiples, 158
multiplier, 142, 179, 191
mutation, 24

N

nasopharyngeal carcinoma, 5
National Ambient Air Quality Standards, 27, 40
Netherlands, 78
neural network, viii, ix, 3, 4, 5, 19, 20, 28, 44, 48, 51,
    52, 56, 57, 67, 68, 78, 79, 117, 118, 120, 122,
    128, 131, 132, 137, 142, 146, 150, 151, 154,
    155, 175
neurons, 44, 137, 139, 142, 143
New England, 24, 49
nitric oxide, 31, 38, 39
nitrogen, 31, 32, 36, 38, 39
nitrogen dioxide, 31, 38, 39
nodes, 41, 44, 76, 181
nodules, 5

O

oil, 30
one dimension, 69
operations, 30
optimization, viii, ix, 17, 25, 28, 41, 67, 69, 71, 72,
    76, 78, 117, 118, 128, 132, 145, 146, 176, 177,
    179, 195
organs, 31, 161
orthogonality, 172
ovarian tumor, 22
oxygen, 31
ozone, 31, 32, 36, 39, 40, 43, 46, 48, 49

P

parallel, 131, 132, 142, 143, 147, 151
parallel processing, 131, 151
parity, 120
partition, 120
pathology, 18
pattern recognition, 1, 3, 6, 68, 118, 128, 153, 160,
    170, 186, 194
PCA, 23, 170, 171, 173, 175, 189, 191
penalties, 33, 70
periodicity, 164
permeability, 10
petroleum, 30, 79
physical properties, 47
physics, 169
pitch, 158
plants, 31
pollen, 49
pollutants, 27, 28, 30, 31, 32, 36, 38, 40, 41, 42, 43,
    44, 45, 46, 47
pollution, 27, 28, 30, 37, 40, 41, 46, 47, 48
polyp, 6, 23
Portugal, 48
power generation, 30
power plants, 30, 47
precipitation, 30, 40, 41
predictability, 119
prediction models, ix, 76, 117
premature death, 30, 40
price index, 119
probability, 143, 164, 166, 171, 173
probability density function, 164, 166, 173
propagation, 119, 120
prostate cancer, 5, 22
public health, 40
pulp, 30
pumps, 158

Q

quadratic programming, 76, 128, 145, 146
quality standards, 32, 38

R

radar, 52
radio, 59, 62, 150
radius, 7, 17
rainfall, 49
ramp, 140
reactions, 31, 40
real time, 64
reasoning, 119, 120
recognition, ix, 1, 153, 164, 170, 175, 191
reduced lung function, 31
reflexes, 31
regression, viii, ix, 7, 8, 11, 12, 17, 18, 27, 28, 32, 33, 35, 36, 41, 42, 45, 49, 51, 53, 64, 67, 68, 69, 70, 72, 73, 78, 79, 80, 117, 118, 120, 122, 164, 169
regression analysis, 41
regression model, 45, 49, 169
relevance, 3, 6
reliability, 158, 160, 184
resistance, 69
resolution, 46, 161, 162, 167
response, 59, 138, 140
risk, viii, 6, 7, 23, 46, 67, 68, 69, 76, 118, 119, 120
risk factors, 119
risk management, 119
root, viii, 32, 43, 44, 67, 75, 165, 181
root-mean-square, viii, 67, 75
rules, 143, 146, 147, 148

S

safety, 32
scaling, 9, 44, 161, 162
schizophrenia, 4
scoliosis, 6, 23
sea level, 29
sensing, 59, 154
sensitivity, viii, 11, 17, 18, 67, 68, 74, 77, 78, 161, 194
sensors, 58, 154, 155, 158
shape, 11, 21, 44, 46, 156, 165, 188
shear, 69
shortness of breath, 31
showing, ix, 29, 131, 148

signals, 6, 41, 156, 160, 161, 163, 164, 165, 168, 171, 186
signal-to-noise ratio, 146, 155
signs, 167
simulation, ix, 131, 132, 133, 142, 148, 150, 161
simulations, 120, 148
Singapore, 152
skewness, 156, 165
skin, viii, 4
smog, 30, 31
smoothing, 160
snaps, 29
software, 46, 49, 146, 147
solution, viii, ix, 6, 41, 46, 58, 67, 71, 76, 117, 118, 128, 146, 148, 154, 159, 171, 176
South Korea, 153
Spain, 27, 28, 46, 49
spatial information, 4, 21
speech, ix, 153, 154, 175
spelling, 47
spin, 158
standard deviation, 165
standard error, 167
states, 4, 21, 59, 154, 191
statistics, 156
steel, 68
stock exchange, 118
stock markets, 118, 120
stock price, 119, 120
storage, 158, 159, 160, 179
stoves, 30
stress, 78
structure, 41, 44, 68, 132, 133, 134, 137, 139, 140, 141, 142, 147, 150, 151
sulphur, 30, 32, 36, 38
survival, 7
susceptibility, 76
symmetry, 59
symptoms, 30, 31
synchronize, 163

T

techniques, 1, 2, 3, 5, 6, 7, 12, 13, 14, 16, 17, 18, 68, 118, 128, 132, 143, 147, 155, 164, 194
technologies, 1, 3
technology, 1, 3
temperature, 31, 40, 41
testing, 11, 12, 17, 18, 29, 42, 44, 73, 74, 75, 76, 146, 147, 148, 181, 191, 194
texture, 1, 3, 20, 22
thyroid, 6, 23
thyroid cancer, 6

time series, ix, 68, 79, 117, 118, 119, 120, 128, 156, 164, 169
tissue, 3, 10
trade-off, 70
training, viii, ix, 2, 3, 8, 9, 12, 17, 18, 28, 32, 41, 46, 51, 53, 54, 55, 60, 61, 67, 68, 72, 73, 74, 75, 76, 77, 78, 79, 117, 118, 128, 143, 144, 145, 146, 147, 148, 149, 150, 170, 174, 178, 179, 180, 181, 187, 191, 194, 195
transformation, 2, 9, 21, 172, 175
translation, 161, 182, 184
transmission, 164
transportation, 31
trial, 12, 36, 74, 76
tumours, 3, 4, 5, 20
Turkey, 47, 117

variables, 33, 35, 41, 53, 70, 133, 137, 144, 148, 154, 170, 173, 176
variations, viii, 12, 14, 51, 164, 171
vasculature, 10
vector, 1, 2, 3, 4, 5, 6, 7, 8, 9, 11, 12, 13, 15, 16, 17, 18, 19, 20, 21, 22, 23, 24, 27, 28, 32, 41, 42, 49, 51, 53, 69, 70, 72, 74, 78, 79, 117, 119, 120, 128, 131, 132, 133, 134, 135, 143, 144, 145, 146, 147, 151, 152, 153, 155, 170, 171, 172, 173, 175, 176, 177, 184, 191, 194, 195
vehicles, 30, 31
vibration, x, 153, 158, 160, 168, 186, 191, 194
vision, viii
visualization, 5, 13, 22, 23, 161, 170
volatile organic compounds, 31
volatility, ix, 117, 118, 119, 120

U

ultrasound, 5, 6, 7, 20, 22, 23, 24, 52
United States, 27, 32, 40
urban, 27, 48
UV, 40

V

validation, 12, 13, 16, 18, 42, 49
valve, 6, 23

W

Washington, 79
water, 28, 30, 31
wavelet, x, 153, 160, 161, 162, 163, 182, 183, 184, 186, 191, 194, 195
wavelet analysis, 161, 182
welfare, 28
wheezing, 31
white blood cells, 6
World Health Organization, 40